WITHDRAWN

D1179645

NUTRITION IN BRITAIN

STUDIES IN THE SOCIAL HISTORY OF MEDICINE
Series Editors: Jonathan Barry and Bernard Harris

In recent years, the social history of medicine has become recognised as a major field of historical enquiry. Aspects of health, disease, and medical care now attract the attention not only of social historians but also of researchers in a broad spectrum of historical and social science disciplines. The Society for the Social History of Medicine, founded in 1969, is an interdisciplinary body, based in Great Britain but international in membership. It exists to forward a wide-ranging view of the history of medicine, concerned equally with biological aspects of normal life, experience of and attitudes of illness, medical thought and treatment, and systems of medical care. Although frequently bearing on current issues, this interpretation of the subject makes primary reference to historical context and contemporary priorities. The intention is not to promote a sub-specialism but to conduct research according to the standards and intelligibility required of history in general. The Society publishes a journal, *Social History of Medicine*, and holds at least three conferences a year. Its series, Studies in the Social History of Medicine, does not represent publication of its proceedings, but comprises volumes on selected themes, often arising out of conferences but subsequently developed by the editors.

Life, Death and the Elderly
Edited by Margaret Pelling and Richard M. Smith

Medicine and Charity Before the Welfare State
Edited by Jonathan Barry and Colin Jones

In the Name of the Child
Edited by Roger Cooter

Reassessing Foucault
Power, Medicine and the Body
Edited by Colin Jones and Roy Porter

From Idiocy to Mental Deficiency
Edited by David Wright and Anne Digby

NUTRITION IN BRITAIN

Science, scientists and politics in the twentieth century

Edited by David F. Smith

London and New York

First published 1997
by Routledge
11 New Fetter Lane, London EC4P 4EE

29 West 35th Street, New York, NY 10001

Typeset in Baskerville by
Ponting–Green Publishing Services, Chesham, Buckinghamshire
Printed and bound in Great Britain by
TJ Press (Padstow) Ltd, Padstow, Cornwall

British Library Cataloguing in Publication Data
A catalogue record for this book is available from
the British Library

Library of Congress Cataloging in Publication Data
The history of nutrition in Britain in the twentieth century:
science, scientists, and politics / edited by David F. Smith.
p.   cm. – (Studies in the social history of medicine)
Includes bibliographical references and index.
1. Nutrition–Research–Great Britain–History–20th century.
2. Nutrition policy–Great Britain–History–20th century.
3. Diet–Great Britain–History–20th century.
I. Smith, David F.   II. Series.
TX367.H57   1996   96–18247
613.2'0941'0904–dc20   CIP

ISBN 0–415–11214–1

CONTENTS

ILLUSTRATIONS

TABLES

NOTES ON
CONTRIBUTORS

L. Margaret Barnett received a doctorate in Modern West European History from Columbia University, New York, in 1982 and now teaches history at the University of Southern Mississippi, Hattiesburg. The author of *British Food Policy during the First World War* (1985), she is working on a biography of Horace Fletcher.

Nancy L. Blakestad received a doctorate in Modern British History from Oxford University in 1994, for her research into the history of women's higher education. She is working as project co-ordinator at the Institut für die Wissenschaften vom Menschen, Vienna, on a project supporting higher education reform in east central Europe.

Timothy Boon works at the Science Museum, London, where he was co-curator of the major gallery on twentieth-century medicine, 'Health Matters', opened in 1994. His publications include a paper on a 1937 smoke abatement film, and he is completing a Ph.D. thesis on documentary films and public health.

George Davey Smith is Professor of Clinical Epidemiology at Bristol University. His main research interests are in life-course influences on disease in adulthood, epidemiology and the prevention of sexually transmitted diseases, and epidemiological methodology, including meta-analysis. He has worked on smoking, lung cancer and healthism in Nazi Germany.

Sally M. Horrocks is Lecturer in Economic and Social History at Leicester University. Her Ph.D. research at Manchester University looked at science, technology, and food in Britain, 1870–1939, focusing on the food industry. She is currently researching science and technology in British manufacturing industry since 1945.

Diana Kuh is a senior research scientist working on a large prospective study of men and women followed up since their birth in 1946 – the Medical Research Council's National Survey of Health and Development, at the University College London Medical School. Previously she was a research fellow at Exeter University.

Tim Lang is Professor of Food Policy at Thames Valley University, London. He was Director of the London Food Commission 1984–90. He is co-author of *The New Protectionism* (1993) and *The Unmanageable Consumer* (1995), and author of numerous articles and reports on food policy.

Francis McKee works at the Wellcome Unit for the History of Medicine at Glasgow University. His research into food and nutrition focuses on aspects of the cultural history of the field. Most recently he has been studying the early history of coffee, tea and chocolate in Britain.

David F. Smith is Wellcome Lecturer in the History of Medicine at the Department of History and Economic History of Aberdeen University. He formerly held a Wellcome Fellowship in the History of Medicine at Glasgow University. His current project is entitled 'Nutritional Science and Nutritional Politics 1918–50'.

Mark W. Weatherall studied medical sciences before commencing research at the Wellcome Unit for the History of Medicine at Cambridge University. In 1994 he completed his Ph.D. thesis, 'Scientific Medicine and the Medical Sciences in Cambridge, 1851–1939'. He recently intermitted a Wellcome Fellowship to complete his clinical studies.

Charles Webster is a Senior Research Fellow at All Souls College, Oxford, and was formerly Director of the Wellcome Unit for the History of Medicine at Oxford University. His publications include *Problems of Health Care* (1988) and (as editor) *Caring for Health, History and Diversity* (1993).

A. Susan Williams is a researcher at the Social Science Research Unit, University of London Institute of Education. Her publications include *The Rich Man and the Diseased Poor* (1987), *The Politics of the Welfare State* (with Anne Oakley, 1994), and *Women and Childbirth* (1996).

INTRODUCTION

NUTRITION IN BRITAIN
Science, scientists and politics in the
twentieth century

Like history, nutrition is a multi-faceted field, so exploring the
'history of nutrition' can lead in many directions. 'Nutrition'
covers a very wide subject area, from sociology to molecular
biology, and similarly, 'nutrition scientist' can embrace a remarkably wide range of people. The membership of the Nutrition
Society (founded 1941), has included, for example, chemists,
biochemists, physiologists, medical and veterinary practitioners,
agricultural scientists, food scientists, dietitians, sociologists, psychologists and administrators, as well as 'nutritionists'. Nutrition
is also an area in which many wider interests intersect: the
implications of nutritional research potentially impinge, not only
upon the practices of doctors, dietitians and veterinary practitioners, but also upon the policies of central and local government, the agricultural, food and pharmaceutical industries, and
the domestic habits of the population. In addition, there are few
members of the general public who are not prepared to express
an opinion on matters of nutrition. 'Nutrition experts' abound,
and nutrition scientists face more acute problems than many other
scientists in establishing their expertise. During the course of the
twentieth century, those engaged in the production of scientific
nutritional knowledge have adopted various strategies either to
maximise the impact of their activities upon society, or to distance
themselves from policy matters. Nutrition has been at the core of
single-issue pressure groups and such concerns have been taken
up by a variety of movements with wide-ranging ideological commitments. 'Nutrition' has frequently been a matter for political
and public debate.

Nutrition scientists have long shown a special interest in the
history of nutrition, in the sense of the history of food. One of the

pioneers of vitamin research, Jack Drummond, co-authored *The Englishman's Food. A History of Five Centuries of English Diet*, first published in 1939.[1] In the 1960s the late Professor John Yudkin established a seminar series for historians and nutritionists at Queen Elizabeth College which has led to the publication of three collections of papers, and which is still meeting.[2] The present volume, however, is concerned not so much with the history of food as with the history of nutrition science, nutrition scientists and nutrition politics. Above all, it is about the processes by which scientists doctors, activists and politicians have sought to generate, modify and apply nutritional knowledge, policies and practices – processes which have involved the construction, modification and breaking of alliances between individuals, groups and institutions. These processes are explored in eleven chapters which consider a range of specific episodes that have taken place in Britain during the twentieth century. Some of the episodes concern interactions almost exclusively between scientists, while some involve other important actors, for example, the medical profession, dietitians, politicians, government officials, non-governmental organisations and industry.

In Chapter 1 Margaret Barnett shows that, during the first and second decades of the century, the retired American businessman Horace Fletcher enrolled the support of doctors and scientists for his view that chewing food thoroughly increases its nutritional value. One of the scientists whom Fletcher approached was the Cambridge biochemist Frederick Gowland Hopkins, who later shared a Nobel prize for the discovery of vitamins. Hopkins, and vitamins, appear in several of the other chapters. Mark Weatherall, in Chapter 2, provides an account of the early development of the Dunn Nutritional Laboratory of the Medical Research Council (MRC), which was established specifically for the study of vitamins. Weatherall shows how Walter Fletcher, the Secretary of the MRC, attempted to steer the programme of the laboratory towards fundamental biochemical research, while protecting its director from his rivals elsewhere. In Chapter 3 Sally Horrocks discusses how knowledge of vitamins was deployed by food and pharmaceutical industry scientists who sought to create new vitamin-rich foods and dietary supplements. In collaboration with their employers' advertising departments, these scientists also attempted to educate the public about vitamins, and to stimulate demand for the new products.

The 'newer knowledge of nutrition',[3] as the vitamin concept became known, was also a component of the body of knowledge which formed the basis of a new paramedical profession – dietetics. Nancy Blakestad, in Chapter 4, provides an account of the part played by King's College of Household and Social Science in the process of the professionalisation of dietetics during the 1930s. During this period, nutritional knowledge was also deployed by charitable, educational and campaigning organisations. One such organisation, the National Birthday Trust Fund (NBTF), became involved in nutrition research, as related by Susan Williams in Chapter 5. The NBTF's experiments employed Marmite and other vitamin-rich preparations as supplements for impoverished pregnant women. This research proved highly problematic and was conducted at a time when links between nutrition and poverty were the subject of considerable controversy in political, medical and scientific circles. However, one matter about which there was a degree of consensus was the desirability of increasing the consumption of milk, and Francis McKee, in Chapter 6, emphasises the importance of scientific opinion in his exploration of the popularisation of milk during the 1930s.

David Smith, in Chapter 7, discusses the role of scientists in food policy-making during the two world wars. During the First World War, a small group of senior scientists united behind a few fundamental scientific messages, but during the second the community of nutrition scientists was much larger and more fragmented. Some senior scientists successfully furthered their ambitions to formulate and oversee a scientific food policy, while an attempt at self-organisation by a larger group of more junior scientists led to the foundation of the Nutrition Society. In Chapter 8 Timothy Boon discusses a film, *World of Plenty*, which was made during the Second World War. It featured John Boyd Orr, Director of the Rowett Research Institute in Aberdeen, and expressed Orr's vision of a post-war system of food production and distribution that would meet nutritional needs.

One feature of the wartime food system was the expansion of school meals and school milk, and the establishment of welfare food schemes. Charles Webster discusses the fate of these schemes in the post-war period in Chapter 9. Within the highest echelons of government, the policy debate about these forms of nutritional welfare appears to have proceeded largely in relation to economic and political objectives, without any reference to scientific advice.

During the post-war period there has been increasing interest in the origins of the 'diseases of civilisation', particularly coronary heart disease. Most emphasis has been placed upon adult life style, including dietary habits, but more recently there has been a challenge to this position as a team of researchers at the MRC Environmental Epidemiology Unit in Southampton has advanced the view that pre-natal and early childhood nutrition is of greater importance. In Chapter 10 George Davey Smith and Diana Kuh provide an account of the development of this new research programme, but show that the dependence of adult health on childhood and intra-uterine nutrition was widely taken for granted before the Second World War.

Just as the newer knowledge of nutrition was taken up by campaigners during the 1930s, more recent knowledge of connections between diet and health has been taken up by a range of new pressure groups. In Chapter 11 Tim Lang gives an account of the activities of non-governmental organisations in the United Kingdom on a wide range of food issues from the 1970s to 1990s.

All the chapters in this volume are based upon the papers given at a joint conference of the Society for the Social History of Medicine (SSHM) and the Glasgow Nutrition Group, held in Glasgow in April 1993. This followed an earlier SSHM conference on 'Nutrition in History' in 1986, and it is hoped that on-going research in this area will be reported to further conferences during the next few years. Thanks are due not only to the authors represented here, but also to many others who gave papers or contributed as discussants, chairpeople, or in some other capacity. These include Mel Bartley, Robert Bud, Michael Clark, Catherine Geissler, Johanna Geyer-Kordesch, Bob Grimble, John Hawthorne, Harmke Kamminga, Michael Lean, Evelyn Mundell, Anne Murcott, Malcolm Nicolson, Derek Oddy, Reginald Passmore, Philip Payne, Mike Rayner, Jean Ritchie, Tim Russell, Julia Twigg, Keith Vernon, Roger Whitehead, Elsie Widdowson and Mick Worboys. Special thanks are due to the Scottish Dairy Council for their generous funding of the conference. Thanks are also due to Jonathan Barry and Bernard Harris, series editors, and two anonymous referees.

NOTES

1 J. C. Drummond and A. Wilbraham, *The Englishman's Food. A History of Five Centuries of English Diet*, London, 1939.
2 D. J. Oddy and D. S. Miller, *The Making of the Modern British Diet*, London, 1976; D. J. Oddy and D. S. Miller, *Diet and Health in Modern*

Britain, Beckenham, 1985; C. Geissler and D. J. Oddy, *Food, Diet and Economic Change Past and Present*, Leicester, 1993.
3 This phrase comes from E. V. McCollum, *The Newer Knowledge of Nutrition*, New York, 1918.

1

FLETCHERISM

The chew-chew fad of the Edwardian era

L. Margaret Barnett

In January 1904, the editors of *The Lancet* took the unusual step of endorsing a dietetic fad. 'Popular crazes in matters of medicine . . . are more often than not things to be deplored,' they wrote. 'If they are not actually harmful they are generally ridiculous, and if they are of no benefit to the general public assuredly they are, as a rule, of equally little advantage to the medical profession.'[1] This craze, however, was an exception. In the editors' view 'a more generally beneficial doctrine could hardly be chosen for the popular medical idol of the moment'.

The fad in question was Fletcherism, the brainchild of Horace Fletcher, a retired American businessman. People jokingly called it the 'chew-chew cult' because it involved chewing food excessively. Unlike a thirty-two-chew system Gladstone practised (one for every tooth), Fletcherism did not specify how many times to chew, just to masticate each mouthful until it was mixed thoroughly with saliva. Only then, said Fletcher, was food 'chemically transformed from its crude condition into the . . . form that makes it possible of digestion and absorption . . .'.[2] Let doubters make a simple test, he urged. Insalivation turned starches into a type of sugar the body could readily use: chew bread into a cream and taste it become sweeter. Thus, 'taste shows that a chemical process is going on'.[3] Ignorance of this basic fact invited auto-intoxication, the much-feared Edwardian malady, since unmasticated 'starchy foods – breads, for instance . . . pass unchanged into the intestinal tube; and simply decay there, creating noxious and poisonous products'.[4] Milk and other liquid foods also needed careful treatment in the mouth. They were to be sipped, then 'masticated' by swishing them around until all taste was gone. 'To swallow anything but pure water without tasting it into absorption produces a shock,' Fletcher warned.[5]

Starting the digestive process in the mouth gave the body more time to absorb nutrients. Someone who wolfed a meal down in only seven or eight minutes would waste two-thirds of its value, but the Fletcherite could extract a full day's nourishment from just thirty mouthfuls of bread.[6] Most people could get by on one-third fewer calories. Unappreciative of growing knowledge about vitamins and minerals, Fletcher maintained that the quality of the diet depended more on how completely food was digested than on what one ate. His system ensured perfect nutritional equilibrium and was therefore ideal for both over- and under-eaters. The one remained well nourished while automatically reducing calories, the other derived more nourishment from a narrow diet.[7]

As to how much and how often to eat, let Nature decide: eat only when truly hungry, select what the body craves, and stop when saliva no longer flows freely. The body needs more food only when previous meals are digested, so fixed mealtimes should become a thing of the past. Many should find two meals sufficient. It was sometimes reported that Fletcher ate only once a day. In fact, he constantly nibbled on candy and fruit, took at least six lumps of sugar in his coffee, and enjoyed late-night suppers. There are many stories of him flouting gastronomic convention by satisfying his cravings. Once, at the plush Waldorf-Astoria in New York, five luncheon companions let him order for all. His selection: six pints of milk, a quart of cream, oysters, fried potatoes, and bread and butter. The waiter was described as stunned.[8]

The challenge for novice chewers was not heeding the appetite but keeping the food in the mouth long enough for chemical reaction to occur. Fletcher advised eating face-down so that the tongue hung perpendicularly. Then, let Nature take charge. Special taste buds in the mouth would test the food, and only when the mix was right would the 'food gate' open to allow automatic ingestion. Only the liquid was to be swallowed. Fibrous residues that resisted insalivation were 'dangerous' and should be spat out. The food gate, or 'Nature's Food Filter', was Fletcher's great discovery: before him, Fletcher claimed, physiologists did not know it blocked off the back of the throat while food was in the mouth.[9] As one might imagine, Fletcherites at table were not an attractive sight. One contemporary wrote that they had 'added a new horror to dining out' and that 'the best that can be expected from them is the tense and awful silence which always accompanies their ex-cruciating tortures of mastication'.[10] Franz Kafka's father hid behind a newspaper at dinnertime to avoid watching the writer Fletcherise.[11] Even Horace Fletcher was seen eating 'with glum and grim determination' at Cambridge early in his dietetic career, although he later mastered the art of chewing cheerfully, thereby outwardly fulfilling a key dictum: 'Do not eat when you are mad or sad; only when you are glad'.[12]

Despite the physical contortions and the inevitable check on conversation, the fad first appeared as 'muncheons' (munching luncheons) or 'munching parties'. These affairs were co-ordinated by a master of ceremonies who, stopwatch in hand, timed the chewing of the first mouthful of food at each course and gave the signal to swallow – by ringing a bell, for example. This opener usually lasted an incredible five minutes and was intended to set a leisurely pace for the rest of the meal.[13] Fletcher claimed that even Edward VII took part. Sir Thomas Barlow, the king's physician, began recommending super-mastication to his patients after exam-ining Fletcher during tests at Cambridge University.[14] Muncheons swept upper-class circles in London in 1903 and spread to the social elites of America's big cities the following year. They were still being held in Britain in 1906, as a cartoon in *Punch* reveals. 'This is not a feast of "funeral baked meats",' the caption read. The miserable-looking diners were 'working out their own salivation'.[15]

Dietetics became a conversation piece in the early years of the century as news spread about laboratory discoveries in physiology and nutritional chemistry that were overturning time-honoured maxims. Fletcherism was only one of the faddist systems that surfaced during this period, and it was not even the only crank system concerned with reducing the amount of food eaten, as it shared some characteristics with the 'fasting' and 'no breakfast' fads. By the time Fletcherism came on the scene, 'food reform' was well entrenched in Britain, at least among the educated and well-off. The subject's widespread appeal gave J. M. Barrie a smash hit when his comedy *Little Mary* opened in London in September 1903. In this play aristocratic dyspeptics are cured when told to cut down on food – the authority being Little Mary, at first thought to be a spirit medium, but revealed at the end of the play to be the stomach.[16]

By mid-1909, Fletcherism was reportedly the dietetic system most favoured by Britain's shapers of opinion: 'professors, lawyers, physicians, clergymen, editors, newspaper and magazine writers, philosophers, financiers, men of brains and energy, leaders in the various spheres of human activity'.[17] However, although it won a respectable following in western Europe, notably in Italy, Denmark, Germany and Britain, and was known in Russia and the Austro-Hungarian Empire, Fletcherism never achieved the level of support it enjoyed in the United States. There the expression 'to Fletcherise' became a figure of speech applied to other activities besides eating, and in the inter-war period it was still used for 'chew well'. American dictionaries began listing the term in 1913.[18] In most places, the fad's popularity had peaked by 1910. It still had followers when war broke out, but with Fletcher's death in 1919, and more widespread knowledge of new nutritional principles after the war, only a few diehards such as Kafka remained faithful in the 1920s.

FLETCHERISM, SCIENCE AND MEDICINE

Various factors contributed to the vitality of Fletcherism, only a few of which can be considered here. In Britain, defence in time of war played a part, and concern about national degeneration was also important. However, support by the scientific and medical communities was the essential element in Fletcherism's success, the avenue by which it spread beyond Fletcher's immediate circle, and the reason it first took root in Britain. Fletcher appreciated the potential of scientific and medical support from the start. If he were ever to be taken seriously, he later joked, he knew he must either become a physician himself or 'go out and capture a doctor, cure him, and make him [his] megaphone'.[19] Fletcher's first attempt to find a spokesman in the United States failed.

Fletcher 'discovered' super-mastication while on business in Chicago in June 1898. Killing time by lingering over a hotel meal, he found that eating very slowly left him satisfied on less. Six months later, he had shed 50 lb and felt rejuvenated. It nevertheless proved impossible to persuade others that the achievement was medically or socially significant. During this period, Fletcher was engaged in promoting 'social quarantine', a movement which aimed to nurture the natural goodness of children and to prevent them being led into immoral ways of living. Towards the end of 1898, Fletcher published his first book on super-mastication, *What Sense? or, Economic Nutrition*, and began to advocate chewing as part of this programme of social reform.[20] During a lecture tour in November, he tried, without success, to explain the connection between chewing and child welfare to doctors in Burlington, Vermont. The next month, he approached W. O. Atwater, chief nutrition investigator for the US Department of Agriculture, who was based at Wesleyan University in Connecticut. Atwater had worked on dietary studies at Hull House, one of Chicago's famous settlement houses, the staff of which was backing social quarantine.[21] In 1895, Atwater had confirmed the nutritional standards set by Emil Voit, the German physiologist. Fletcher tried to persuade Atwater that he and Voit had grossly over-estimated the calories necessary for subsistence, but Atwater would have none of it. Rebuffed by both medical authority and bemused colleagues in the reform movement, Fletcher left the United States and in 1900 took up residence in Venice.

In Venice, Fletcher immediately found his megaphone – his future son-in-law, Ernest Van Someren, an English physician earning his living as a hotel doctor. During the autumn and winter of 1900–1, Van Someren tested Fletcher's theories on himself, and on Fletcher, Dr Pietro Leonardi (Professor of Physiological Chemistry at the University of Pavia) and members of the Venetian nobility. Crediting chewing with easing his own diabetic symptoms, Van Someren presented his findings at the annual meeting of the British Medical Association in July 1901. He fully endorsed Fletcher's claims and even described in suitably scientific language the 'secondary reflex of deglutition' that had been suppressed by non-use – the food filter.[22] At the invitation of Sir Michael Foster, the outgoing president of the International Congress of Physiology, Van Someren read his paper again at that society's annual meeting in Turin in September. Delegates from sixteen countries were present. In just three months, Fletcherism had gone from obscurity to consideration by leading physiologists. The most critical comment recorded in the discussion period was that more exact experiments by others might cast doubt on Van Someren's conclusions.[23] Four invitations to conduct such tests were immediately proffered. Fletcher, also attending the congress, accepted Foster's invitation, and December found him and Van Someren in the Physiological Laboratory of Cambridge University.

Foster was no longer active in research and it was therefore Frederick Gowland Hopkins who interrupted work on amino acids to run the trial of Fletcherism. Besides Fletcher and Van Someren, members of the laboratory team acted as test subjects. As far as Fletcher was concerned, things could hardly have gone better. He was treated with respect and invited to the annual banquet of the Royal Society. The Cambridge men all declared themselves healthier for chewing and some took it up seriously. Better still, although reportedly only 'somewhat impressed' by the test results, Hopkins admitted Fletcher's theories had substance. Indeed, the consensus was that thorough insalivation did reduce intake not only of calories but also of protein.[24] Colleagues at the University of London laughed when they heard this, saying that Fletcher must have hypnotised Hopkins's team.[25] Foster nevertheless provided a written endorsement.[26]

Foster approved only of short-term Fletcherism, however. Lengthy observations were needed before more could be said, but neither Cambridge nor the Royal Society had the equipment or funds.[27] At Foster's suggestion, Fletcher looked to America and in 1903 converted the Yale physiologist Russell Chittenden. After testing Fletcher, Chittenden concluded that people needed only two-thirds of the calories and half the protein Atwater and Voit recommended: 2,100 kcal a day for an adult male doing moderately active work, and 0.85 g of protein per kilo of body weight.[28] Credit for the vehement international dispute that then erupted over optimum levels of calories and protein in the diet thus went to Chittenden rather than to Foster or Hopkins.[29] This may have been a fortunate turn of events for medical science, since Hopkins resumed research connected with vitamins, which later earned him a Nobel prize.

Meanwhile, a flood of articles and books were published about low-calorie and low-protein experiments, how much food the body needed and 'physical efficiency'. Fletcher benefited immensely from the publicity as the experts battled it out and was soon much in demand as a speaker and writer on dietetic issues. His status became blurred: was he researcher or subject, expert or layman? Was he even a faddist? In 1908, Fletcher was invited to join the American Association for the Advancement of Science and in 1909 received an honorary M.A. from Dartmouth College, his *alma mater.* Some felt he had just rediscovered a saner, traditional life style destroyed by modernity. A Scottish doctor pointed out that the dietary standards Fletcher and Chittenden were recommending were a common experience in the Highlands. Could a hardier race be found anywhere?[30]

Most of the physiologists and biochemists now eager to meet Fletcher were intrigued by the purported level of his diet.[31] What

11

happened to the body when it received less energy than it expended was still unclear and formed an area of growing interest within the wider study of metabolism. Relatively few experiments were on record – only eight of any significance between 1888 and 1901.[32] All had used professional fasters, paid to risk their health for a few weeks, but Fletcher claimed to have improved his stamina and to have gone about his normal business on a restricted diet lasting years. He was still receiving invitations to take part in tests until the outbreak of war, but whether any further trials were conducted in Britain is uncertain. However, after visiting England in July 1913, Fletcher told friends he had had 'a perfectly splendid interview with Hopkins' and had found 'the most eminent scientists interested in the earlier experiments' repeating their old conclusions.[33] What this entailed, however, is not known.

For a while, it looked as if Hopkins's connection with Fletcher would become closer. The two evidently got on well during the Cambridge trials, for the following spring they took a madcap train journey together through central Europe, which Fletcher serialised for the San Francisco *Argonaut*.[34] Fletcher possessed a tremendous capacity for fun: travelling with him was an experience. This trip found the pair trounced at billiards by a Japanese, unmasked as the Western-educated Professor Matsusima of Tokyo, whom they had smugly challenged in a Budapest coffee house; travelling as the only men in an overnight compartment packed with the female members of an Italian opera troupe and their pets; and boozily crying over gypsy music at two in the morning. 'It was a delight to see the staid professor unbend and unfold,' Fletcher mischievously noted.

In fact, Fletcher hoped to detach Hopkins from Cambridge altogether. In 1901, in Turin, Fletcher discussed with Foster his ideas for an international institute of dietetic research, housed in Venice, which would study connections between nutrition and disease.[35] Ten illustrious figures in nutritional science, including Pavlov, signed the prospectus as potential 'scientific assessors'.[36] Foster was enthusiastic. Philanthropic support of science by a layman was no longer unusual. During the nineteenth century, American businessmen in particular had become an important source of cash for university science departments, and were sponsoring both the purchase of buildings and equipment and specific experiments.[37] After first mistaking Fletcher himself for a millionaire – a rumour Fletcher cultivated in order to gain access to influential people – Foster expected the institute to be funded by

Fletcher's older brother Isaac, a genuine member of New York's plutocratic elite.[38] This dream soon faded. Isaac tended to use strong language about his brother's dietetic foibles and had no intention of parting with a penny.

The creation of the Carnegie Institution with its half-million-dollar-a-year endowment was announced while Fletcher was still at Cambridge, reviving hope for the scheme. Their application, however, was among those rejected by the first review board in October 1902. News that the Carnegie Institution was interested in funding a centre for nutritional research in the United States offered some consolation. Henry P. Bowditch of the Harvard Medical School was one of the prospectus's signatories: the diet institute could operate in Cambridge, Massachusetts. In 1902 the Carnegie board turned to Bowditch for advice on scientific questions, and engaged another of Fletcher's supporters, the English physiologist Arthur Gamgee, to report on the status of nutritional research in the States. A former Dean of the Faculty of Medicine at the Victoria University of Manchester, and the original co-editor with Foster of the *Journal of Physiology*, Gamgee had been in private practice for some twenty years, although he was still involved in research. Foster described him as 'very hot' on Fletcher's idea of a diet institute.[39] Fletcher picked Gamgee to be director of the diet institute when a European site was ruled out, but in 1904 he and Bowditch reconsidered Foster. The latter had abandoned university life for politics and by October 1904 was 'on his beam ends' and presumably not opposed to a post abroad. Fletcher also persuaded Bowditch that it would be advantageous to bring Hopkins into the physiology department at Harvard. 'We will then have a great chemist who is our ardent friend and who believes in us stationed at the most influential seat of authority', he wrote confidently to an acquaintance. 'We will have a full battery of megaphones at our disposal pretty soon'.[40] Fletcher was to be bitterly disappointed. In 1906, the Carnegie Institution named Atwater's assistant, Francis G. Benedict, head of a new facility to be built in Boston. This was a double blow. Benedict's examination of Fletcher in the Wesleyan calorimeter in 1903 was an experience the latter preferred to gloss over.[41]

FLETCHERISM AND DEGENERATION

Fletcher's adoption of super-mastication in 1898 not only rid him of surplus weight but also banished chronic health problems. An 'experiment' involving tramps, whom he paid to Fletcherise free meals at a Chicago restaurant, was similarly rewarding. The men became brighter and fitter and some, apparently, plumper. The new eating system, concluded Fletcher, brought both the fat and the thin to an ideal weight and cured disease. Disorders helped included indigestion, haemorrhoids, catarrh and pimples.[42] Personal experience led Van Someren to add diabetes and 'morbid sexual cravings' to the list and Chittenden added 'bad knee', possibly gout. As the years passed the number of conditions curable by chewing grew. In 1912, a pamphlet issued by the National Food Reform Association, a British organisation to which Fletcher belonged, told schoolchildren that, if they Fletcherised, 'colds and other so-called "minor ailments", such as indigestion, toothache, headache ... [would] become *the exception* and good health ... *the rule*'.[43] Fletcher had by then put adenoids, anaemia, appendicitis, colitis, alcoholism and insanity on the list, and by 1913 anything was fair game. He demanded: 'What wears out the kidneys? ... What causes biliousness? ... That tired feeling? Blues? Bad breath? ... Bright's disease? ... Paralysis? Rotten teeth? Ulcerated gums? Premature death?' The answer, of course, was improperly chewed food.[44]

Such statements would not have struck contemporaries as outrageous as they sound today. The advances in physiology and nutritional science were confirming definite links between diet and disease, even though the causes of many disorders remained unidentified. The medical community tended to agree that malnourishment of any sort, whether through over- or under-eating, left one more vulnerable to sickness.[45] Not only laymen but doctors found Fletcher's promise of nutritional equilibrium plausible. Other dietetic fads similarly claiming to cure a wide variety of ills by restoring the body's natural physiological balance also benefited from the new awareness of the complex role that nutrition played in health. For example, after a slow start in the 1880s, Alexander Haig's teaching on uric acid attracted a huge following in the Edwardian period, and the yoghurt fad, fuelled by Elie Metchnikov's research, took Europe and the United States by storm in 1907.[46]

The prospect of effecting a revolution in national health through diet excited some social reformers in Britain. Although warnings about the physical condition of the working classes had been voiced as far back as the 1830s, the level of concern had risen dramatically in recent years.[47] Report after report told of stunted growth, muscular weakness, bone deformities, dental decay and pale, haggard looks – deficiencies all too easy to spot. 'Even a casual visitor to London must be struck with the great number of inferior, deteriorated looking people whom he meets on the streets,' wrote an American doctor in 1904, 'This great centre of civilization seems to be also a centre of human degeneracy'.[48] To give just a few statistics: wealthy men aged 23–30 were on average 2½ in. taller and 16 lb heavier than relatively fortunate artisans; in Glasgow, girls from families living in only one room were 11 in. shorter than their cohorts from families occupying four rooms.[49] One-third of all deaths of men aged 15–44 were due to tuberculosis; the incidence of rickets was fifty-four per thousand in 1904, up from twenty-two per thousand in 1885; kidney disease and intestinal disorders were rife.[50] What would be the consequence for national efficiency if such physical defects were inherited rather than acquired? The sturdy and thrifty middle classes were producing proportionately fewer children than the spindly creatures in the poorer strata.

Observers in the United States were just as worried about conditions there. Despite a tremendous outpouring of charity, John Spargo's book *The Bitter Cry of the Children*, issued in 1906, showed little had changed since Jacob Riis had published *The Children of the Urban Poor* fourteen years earlier.[51] Both painted a shocking picture of half-starved little ragamuffins whose moral depravity all too often matched their physical wretchedness. As in Britain, the words 'city' and 'poor' connoted not only debility but lawlessness, drunkenness and unmannerly behaviour – a worrying outlook for a crowded industrial democracy. Riis warned of the political costs if the situation continued. 'As we mould the children of the toiling masses in our cities', he wrote, 'so we shape the destiny of the State in which they will rule in their turn . . .'.[52] If Western countries were to be governed and defended by healthy, upright citizens rather than by physical and moral defectives, the links between urbanisation and poverty, sickness and crime, had to be broken.

In June 1898, Horace Fletcher was one of America's Progressive Era reformers tackling this problem. He was determinedly optimistic and had written several books of New Thought philosophy, teaching that one's frame of mind governed physical circumstances. Witnessing the arrest of a 4-year-old thief in the still busy heart of Chicago one midnight made him realise there was more to it. Fletcher's solution was published as *That Last Waif; or, Social*

Quarantine in September. Dismissing claims that there existed naturally bad people, Fletcher argued that negative behaviour was learned. To eradicate vice, separate infants from vice and teach them virtue. Just as America was protected by quarantine laws from imported diseases, so people could be screened 'at the entry port of birth' from 'malarial conditions' infecting the social atmosphere. He proposed 'Character-Building and Habit-Forming schools or institutions to meet the needs of all apprentice citizens'. The cost would be recovered as the crime rate fell and well-being rose. The end result: 'a rational and civilized environment' filled with 'the joyous consciousness of usefulness, efficiency, progress, hope and happiness'.[53] Fletcher's sociological theories reflected the influence of the Chicago settlement house movement. Reformers at Hull House and sister institutions differed from traditional charity workers in believing there were no undeserving poor, that factors other than character affected behaviour, and that people should be encouraged to 'do' rather than lectured about 'don'ts'. Fletcher borrowed the method that Stanton Coit, the founder of the movement, used to teach new ways. Called 'the family idea of co-operation', it trained recruits from the targeted group to spread information through contact with family and acquaintances.[54] According to Fletcher, it needed only 'one serious and earnest person in any community' to set the ball rolling and just ten years for results to become evident.[55]

That Last Waif met with a gratifying response. That autumn, Fletcher gave forty talks to kindergartens, town councillors, industrialists, officials from the penal system, and leaders of the women's movement. By the turn of the year, four towns were considering introducing social quarantines. It was at this high point in the campaign that Fletcher took himself off to Europe in dudgeon. His colleagues simply could not see what by then was so obvious to him: that the crucial factor in character formation was proper nutrition. 'Knowing *how* to eat and eating as one should', he later explained, 'is really the universal pass-key to comfort, satisfaction, temperance, morality, good citizenship, amiability, respectability, and all the details of normality'.[56]

A simple diet technique that promised to stretch working-class diets, cure diseases *and* eliminate moral turpitude was bound to catch reformers' attention, especially when its founder had links with the scientific community. Although state and local governments on both sides of the Atlantic launched remedial programmes such as school meals during this period, there was still a great need for charitable endeavour, and no consensus on what would work. One American reformer believed that if every family adopted Fletcherism 'there would be such a reduction in the numbers of the impoverished that the problem of the poor might be regarded as solved ...'. Fletcher himself expected the Nobel prize in economics.[57]

Fletcherism promised to improve behaviour in several ways. The sheer length of time spent chewing taught patience and perseverance, while knowing that one's own masticatory efforts made food go further encouraged a responsible attitude. Fletcherites often gave up alcohol, since it tasted nasty when masticated. Similarly, they ate less meat. That was good for working people too. Meat was not only expensive but was believed to instil an aggressive attitude. Too much, wrote Fletcher, 'excites lust, intemperance, and savagery in man and gives explosive, non-enduring force'.[58] To claim as a general principle that specific foods induced bad behaviour was to invite ridicule. When Bishop Fallows of Chicago announced in 1906 that 'vice can be fed into children through their stomachs', *Punch* responded with a satirical poem entitled 'Dietetic Ethics'. Warning against Welsh rarebit and pickles, the writer advised that the only safe food for a child was boiled rice.[59] The idea that good behaviour and good nutrition were two sides of the same coin was nevertheless in the air. How much this was due to Fletcher's influence – if at all – is impossible to say. Fletcherism itself surely benefited from the trend. 'Are You Lovable?' asked an article by one of Fletcher's American followers. If not, you were not eating properly. 'Moral and mental qualities, psychologists now tell us, turn largely on our physical condition,' claimed the writer.[60] In Britain, *Hints toward Diet Reform* was issued in 1909 by the National Food Reform Association 'to make known the intimate connection of diet with ... moral and physical well-being ...'.[61] Several speeches given at a schools' conference in London in 1912 suggest similar beliefs. W. A. Nicholls, former president of the National Union of Teachers, held that 'physical, mental, moral and spiritual education are no longer separate ... We may hope for a higher *morale* if the material condition of our boys and girls is improved'.[62] Indeed, the Board of Education encouraged this attitude by advising school authorities, for example through regulations issued in 1908, that the provision of school meals should result not only in better bodies but in better manners.[63]

Horace Fletcher tried to accomplish this in his inimitable fashion at the Kindergarten of Vital Economics, which he ran for a year in a New York City slum. By using the settlement house approach to reform, he planned to train local children to spread his dietetic ideas to the family and then the community – the message, in his words, 'working outward in progressively-radiating effectiveness until social disorders shall be only a memory of blemish on civilization'.[64] This training occurred at free Politeness Parties, soon dubbed kindergarten muncheons, which supplemented the three Rs with the three Ms – Munching, Manners and Music. Often, dozens of children were turned away for lack of space. Given the menus, this is not surprising. The inaugural meal consisted of milk toast, chocolate, nuts and peanut brittle. Fletcher always served his favourite snacks. Just before the children sat down to eat, he gave a brief lecture on basic manners and explained that good looks came from chewing food until all the taste in it was gone. Far from being turned off by this homily, he found that the children reacted positively. The lessons also stuck: trainees met on the street invariably demonstrated their newly acquired grasp of civilised behaviour.[65]

While a well trained child promised the greatest returns for society, an individual was never too old to be morally improved by Fletcherism. Several religious denominations and temperance groups in the United States endorsed Fletcherism as a way of inculcating virtue among adults. In 1908, after chewing had cured him of influenza and depression, the Reverend F. E. Clark, head of the United Society of Christian Endeavor, appointed Fletcher associate editor of the *Christian Endeavor World*, a post he held for several years. Fletcher ran a correspondence School of Health and Efficiency through the paper, and produced a slew of articles with titles like 'Careful Eating and the Abolition of the Slum', 'The Saloon Slouch' and 'Don't be a Drone'.

Correction officials in Europe thought Fletcherism might help in the rehabilitation of criminals and other wastrels. In March 1906, Isaac Marcosson, the Fletcherite editor of *World's Work*, wrote of a Belgian prison that had recently put inmates on a restricted diet and taught them to 'eat properly' – that is, to Fletcherise. The prisoners became more docile, allowing even some of the worst to be paroled. Britain too, he said, was thinking of introducing 'the principles of Fletcherism' to convicts and paupers on relief.[66] There was indeed some support for this, although Marcosson meant not the mechanical process of chewing food to a cream but the idea that, if one stopped wasting food by bolting it, one could become healthier and purer on less food than was generally thought to be required. In April 1906, the doctor serving Salop County Council told a meeting of Medical Officers of Health that Fletcher's teaching on calories and protein meant that prisons, workhouses and asylums would all have to change their dietaries.[67] In fact, Fletcher had testified before a departmental committee on vagrancy the previous August, though not about the ethics of super-mastication, but about Chittenden's experiments. Hopkins was also there to explain scientific details and Foster provided a written memorandum advising the adoption of the Chittenden rather than the Voit figures. The committee subsequently set the daily standard for an adult male in a casual ward at 3,000 kcal and 70 g of protein, which would supposedly save ratepayers money. Summarising the report, the British Medical Journal expressed the hope that 'the bias of the discipline and diet would all tend to the reformation of the vagrant . . . '.[68]

The only known case of a criminal claiming to have been morally uplifted by Fletcherism comes from the United States. It concerns a marvellously Uriah Heep-like character named Edgar Burnz, in Sing Sing prison for murder. He blamed his downfall partly on his juvenile diet. As a child he had been allowed to eat 'a miscellaneous lot of fodder, of which meat formed a large percentage'. Fletcherism enabled him to break the bad habits of a lifetime, whereupon he found that dietary righteousness went hand in hand with spiritual well-being.[69]

FLETCHERISM AND WAR

The last significant manifestation of Fletcherism in Britain was associated with national defence. In 1898, one of Fletcher's friends suggested that his dietetic discovery might solve the army's food problems.[70] The Boer War offered an opportunity to put this to the test. Van Someren had not yet given his paper on Fletcherism when he and Fletcher approached British army medical staff and a parliamentary commission on military victualling about trying super-mastication in South Africa. Would the War Office, they asked, provide troops for experiments that would show why rations should be reduced by one-third? During the winter of 1899, the forces in South Africa had suffered terribly from typhoid fever, caused (said Fletcher) by 'putrid excreta'. Fletcherism would ensure no more lumps of food rotted in the troops' intestines. After two months of silence, the War Office replied that 'for political reasons' it was not considered safe to tamper with the men's rations. The parliamentary commission was just as short-sighted. Fletcher spent a whole day with the head of the commission, Dr J. S. Haldane, a professor of physiology at Oxford, only to find him 'both dull and steeped in academic fallacies relative to nutrition'.[71]

By 1908, the British military were reconsidering their position. Several armies had made limited trials of the Chittenden standards. Chittenden's experiments at Yale in 1903–4 had used soldiers as test subjects, Fletcher having pulled strings through his friend General Leonard Wood. According to the *Daily Express*, those troops doubled their strength and endurance by Fletcherising their low-calorie/low-protein meals and developed into 'unusually fine athletic specimens of humanity'.[72] Their lack of complaints contributed to Chittenden's confidence in his findings, which were publicly sanctioned by the army when it put the troop on display at the St Louis World Fair. Physicians who met the men near the end of the experiment paint a bleaker picture, however. One wrote that the soldiers were 'so eager to get back to regular rations' that they 'would say *anything* about their feelings which would tend to bring the experiment to a close'.[73] Fletcher inspired further, voluntary, trials of Fletcherism at the US Military Academy at West Point, where he lectured to cadets in July 1907. Fletcher also penned instructions for 'attaining economic assimilation of nutriment and immunity from disease, muscular soreness, and fatigue' which were distributed in US Army medical schools.[74]

Chittenden's claims that soldiers improved their physical efficiency on his dietetic standards raised the tantalising prospect of hardier, cheaper armies. In 1906, France conducted low-protein experiments during autumn manoeuvres. Part of the meat ration was replaced by sugar, with excellent results: the men showed greater physical resistance to fatigue and sustained fewer accidents.[75] In August 1908, Major Robert Blackham of the Royal Army Medical Corps suggested in the *British Medical Journal* that the time had come for Britain to make some trials. As with prison diets, calories and protein were the prime concern. However, Blackham gave Fletcher full credit for raising the issue and stressed that, with troops on active duty who were often forced to subsist on limited, tough and uninteresting rations, it was 'especially important that officers and soldiers should be instructed in the importance of perfect mastication and insalivation of food'. He cited Foster's endorsement of Fletcherism as evidence that super-mastication did effect both food economy and 'a remarkable improvement in the condition of the whole gastro-intestinal tract'. British military rations contained more meat than those of other European countries and Japan. Yet Britain imported much of its meat – indeed, the bulk of its food. In 1905, a Royal Commission had reported on the threat this posed to the security of the nation in the event of war. By testing a modified dietary, Blackham argued, military doctors might do 'some epoch-making work' of value to the nation as well as the army. 'The whole question of food values', he concluded, 'is ... a matter of supreme economic importance to every nation on the globe, but especially so to this ... Island Kingdom, where the food supply of the people, in peace and war, is the burning question of the hour'.[76] Fletcher, incidentally, believed that Britain could feed itself without imports if the whole population chewed properly.[77]

A test by the RAMC was reported in the *British Medical Journal* two years later. Twenty men were observed on a twelve-day march during which they carried kits, set up and struck their own camps, slept under canvas and played sports in the evenings. In contrast to Chittenden's warm laboratory, bad weather added another component affecting metabolism. The protein ration for the first six days was 190 g, of which 100 g came from corned beef and the rest from biscuit; 145 g of fresh meat and bread were served subsequently in unspecified proportions. The average 3,481 gross kcal a day proved insufficient. The men all lost weight, officers suffering most. The investigators concluded that troops engaged in strenuous activity required at least 5,000 gross kcal a day and warned that the protein level tried was as low as it was safe to go under stressful circumstances.[78]

When World War I broke out, Britain's armed forces were spared any more such threats to their rations. Not so civilians. Chittenden became scientific adviser to Herbert Hoover, the US Food Administrator, and in 1917 tried to persuade the European allies to adopt his dietary standards for compulsory rationing. He estimated that if they reduced daily *per capita* consumption by 400 kcal, they would save 5 to 6 million tons of shipping space a year and see greater physical efficiency in the people. The Royal Society's Food (War) Committee, of which Hopkins was a member, successfully deflected this scheme, which would have lowered average consumption in Britain by one-third.[79] Other attempts to spread Fletcherism came from within the country. The Director of Food Economy at the Ministry of Food from December 1916 to June 1917 was Kennedy Jones, co-founder of the *Daily Mail* and former editor of the *Evening News*. Jones was a Fletcherite, and several official publications reflect his views. Both *Little Food Economies*, a pamphlet by Dr E. I. Spriggs, and *The Win-the-War Cookery Book* urged lengthy mastication so that the intestines could utilise food efficiently. The former stressed the urgency of chewing starches, digestion of which started in the mouth. The latter, the more blatantly Fletcherite piece, claimed that 'half-chewed food gives half its nourishment [because] it is not absorbed, but gives the stomach DOUBLE TROUBLE; and the chewer has to eat DOUBLE THE AMOUNT of it to get his nourishment'. It would be difficult for adults to break bad habits – 'to eat slowly requires real force of character, real power of concentration' – but children would pick the idea up readily and enjoy the benefits for the rest of their lives.[80] The Royal Society protested to the Prime Minister that such advice was best left to the pages of *Punch*.[81] Soon afterwards, both Kennedy Jones and Lord Devonport, the Food Controller, were replaced for this and other blunders. It seems, however, that at A. V. Hill's prompting the Royal Society reconsidered the possible worth of Fletcherism later that year because of the bread shortage.[82] Spriggs's pamphlet also got a new lease of life when it was incorporated into *Food and How to Save It*, issued by the Ministry of Food in 1918.[83]

Meanwhile some local campaigns were launched to spread Fletcherism through schoolchildren. During the week of 23 April 1917, following a lecture at Holy Trinity School by Councillor George Holden, the initiator of the scheme, all 7,000 students in Darwen, Lancashire, received daily instruction in masticating squares of dry bread. By June, reportedly, this resulted in a 25 per cent drop in bread consumption in the area and school officials and the Medical Officer of Health found children not only looking brighter and healthier but attending school more regularly. As Fletcher had predicted, with this approach, the children had taught the rest of Darwen's 40,000 population to make the most of their food. Holden hoped London's 750,000 pupils would follow suit and spread the message to another 4 million people in the capital.[84] In a smaller programme, pupils at the Dundee Industrial Schools also learned the art of Fletcherism in 1917.[85]

The campaigners' hopes were, of course, disappointed. Working people in any number were not going to Fletcherise, war or not. As one physiologist commented, the general state of their teeth alone precluded it.[86] Besides, few had time and surely fewer still were attracted by the promise that their diet would become simpler and sparser. The war allowed many workers to earn decent money for the first time in their lives and their instinct was to increase both amount and variety in their diet. Despite food shortages, the government actively promoted this through new factory canteens. The high level of industrial unrest in 1917, much of it associated with food problems, also made the Fletcherites' campaign incredibly poorly timed and rendered it unlikely to be taken seriously by anyone other than fanatics.

An obituary of Fletcher by a friend deplored this missed opportunity for Britain to adopt an effective and beneficial method of food economy. Even so, said the writer, Fletcher should be considered 'among those who had helped most to win the war'.[87] A more balanced assessment of Fletcher's career emphasised his achievements over the longer term. 'He was laughed at, but he was followed,' it pointed out; indeed, he 'almost revolutionised the science of dietetics'.[88] So ludicrous do some of Fletcher's teachings seem today, it is easy to overlook his contribution to the lowering of the recommended level of protein in the diet and the assistance he gave, as test subject and donor, to professional research. Many ordinary people also gained their first exposure to dietetics from him and other faddists of the age. As the preceding pages suggest, though, even this encomium would not have satisfied Fletcher. To him, Fletcherism was a philosophy of life that entailed 'getting the most good out of everything ... of pictures and of music and of landscapes and of atmospheres and of all opportunities to improve one's self in all branches of human economy'.[89]

NOTES

1 'A praiseworthy fad', *The Lancet*, 30 January 1904, p. 318.
2 H. Fletcher, 'How I made myself young at sixty', *Ladies' Home Journal*, September 1909, p. 9.
3 G. Warren, 'Horace Fletcher is teaching the East Side how to eat', *New York Herald*, 10 January 1909, section 1, p. 2.
4 'Definite rules of diet evolved by interesting scientific experiments', *New York Times*, 9 June 1907, section 5, p. 9.
5 H. Fletcher, *The A.B.–Z of our Own Nutrition*, New York, 1906, p. 92.

6 H. Fletcher, *The New Glutton; or, Epicure*, New York, 1912, pp. 121, 201.

7 H. Fletcher to P. Waddell, 7 October 1898, Fletcher Papers, shelf mark bMs Am 791, Houghton Library, Harvard University. The references to, and quotations from, the Fletcher papers in this article are included by permission of the Houghton Library; 'Fat get thin; the thin fat', *New York Times*, 3 August 1907, p. 1.

8 Warren, 1909, op. cit., section 1, p. 1.

9 Fletcher, 1909, op. cit.

10 F. W. Crowninshield, *Manners for the Metropolis. An Entrance Key to the Fantastic Life of the 400*, New York, 1908, p. 40.

11 E. Pawel, *The Nightmare of Reason. A Life of Franz Kafka*, New York, 1984, p. 208.

12 E. Miles, 'Horace Fletcher. An Appreciation', *National Review*, April 1919, p. 274; 'Definite rules of diet . . .', 1907, op. cit.

13 Fletcher, 1912, op. cit., pp. 272–3.

14 Ibid., p. 60.

15 *Punch*, 14 March 1906.

16 See A. E. Wilson (ed.), *The Plays of J. M. Barrie*, London, 1942.

17 'The recent progress of Fletcherism in England', *Good Health*, September 1909, p. 665.

18 H. Fletcher to Mr Murray, 23 April 1913, Fletcher Papers.

19 M. Williams, 'Fletcherizing with Fletcher', *Good Housekeeping*, May 1908, p. 505.

20 H. Fletcher, *What Sense? or, Economic Nutrition*, Chicago, 1898.

21 For an account of Atwater's activities see N. Aronson, 'Nutrition as a social problem: a case study of entrepreneurial strategy in science', *Social Problems*, 1982, vol. 29, pp. 474–87.

22 E. Van Someren, 'Was Luigi Cornaro right?', *British Medical Journal*, 10 August 1901, pp. 389–92; Fletcher to Maj. Barrett, 16 March 1901, Fletcher Papers.

23 E. Van Someren, 'Was Luigi Cornaro right?', *British Medical Journal*, 12 October 1901, pp. 1082–4.

24 H. Fletcher to J. H. Patterson, 5 January 1901, excerpt in Patterson, 'What Horace Fletcher, an old friend of the "N.C.R.", writes me about health', *The N.C.R.*, 1 February 1902, p. 14; M. Foster to H. P. Bowditch, 25 January 1901, Bowditch Papers, B Ms c7.2, Countway Library of Medicine, Boston; M. Foster, 'Experiments upon human nutrition', 26 April 1902, in Fletcher, 1906, op. cit., pp. 50–1.

25 H. Fletcher to L. Wood, 27 March 1906, Fletcher Papers.

26 Fletcher, 1906, op. cit., pp. 48–52.

27 H. Fletcher to I. Fisher, 26 February 1908, Fletcher Papers.

28 R. H. Chittenden, 'Sixty years of service in science: an autobiography', typescript, 1936, pp. 101–2, 212, Box 2, Chittenden Papers, Sterling Library, Yale University.

29 See K. J. Carpenter, *Protein and Energy*, Cambridge, 1994, pp. 100–18, for an account of this controversy.

30 'Aran Coirce', 'The ideal diet', *British Medical Journal*, 7 April 1906, p. 829.

31 One exception was Otto Folin, who used Van Someren as a test subject.

O. Folin, 'Laws governing the chemical composition of urine', *American Journal of Physiology*, 1905, vol. xiii, pp. 66–105.

32 F. G. Benedict, 'Metabolism during inanition', *New York Medical Journal*, 21 September 1907, pp. 527–30.

33 H. Fletcher to J. Brennan, 7 July 1913; H. Fletcher to I. Fisher, 13 August 1913; H. Fletcher to Mr Murray, n.d. [1913], Fletcher Papers.

34 Written between 18 March and 19 April 1902: Van Fletch [pseudonym], 'With Prince Henry', *Argonaut*, 14 April 1902, p. 229; 'The capital of Bohemia', 12 May 1902, p. 314; 'The Magyar capital', 19 May 1902, p. 331; 'A night train trip', 26 May 1902, p. 346; 'Football in Hungary', 2 June 1902, p. 361.

35 H. Fletcher, 'Congress of Physiology', *Argonaut*, 11 November 1901, p. 311.

36 'Proposal to found an international laboratory of research for the study of nutrition in all its aspects', in H. Fletcher, 1906, op. cit., pp. 55–66. The ten signatories were M. Foster, A. Mosso, H. Kronecker, N. Zuntz, P. Heger, A. Dastre, H. P. Bowditch, R. H. Chittenden, W. H. Welch and J. P. Pavlov.

37 S. G. Kohlstedt, 'Institutional history', in S. G. Kohlstedt and M. W. Rossiter (eds), *Historical Writings on American Science*, special edition of *Osiris*, second series, 1985, vol. I, p. 17.

38 M. Foster to H. P. Bowditch, 26 October 1901, Bowditch Papers.

39 M. Foster to H. P. Bowditch, 6 October 1902, Bowditch Papers.

40 W. O. Atwater to A. C. True, 30 October 1902, Box 6A, Atwater Papers, Wesleyan University, Middletown, CT; H. Fletcher to Mr Patterson, 18 October 1904, Fletcher Papers.

41 Benedict found Fletcher's metabolism to be no different from anyone else's. Despite being almost completely inactive during the four-day experiment, Fletcher burned an average 1,896 kcal a day. His failure to lose weight on an average daily intake of 1,357 kcal, Benedict explained, was due not to his more efficient extraction and use of nutrients from the food but to the retention of water in body tissues, the result of the high-carbohydrate diet Fletcher himself chose for the test. See F. G. Benedict, 'The nutritive requirements of the body', *American Journal of Physiology*, 1906, vol. xvi, pp. 432–4; F. G. Benedict and R. D. Milner, *Experiments on the Metabolism of Matter and Energy in the Human Body, 1903–1904*, US Department of Agriculture, Office of Experiment Stations, Bulletin No. 175, Washington: Government Printing Office, 1907.

42 H. Fletcher to P. Waddell, 7 October 1898, Fletcher Papers.

43 Schools Committee of the National Food Reform Association, 'Aids to Fitness (No. 1)', in C. E. Hecht (ed.), *Rearing an Imperial Race*, London, 1913, pp. 305–6.

44 C. Geisel, 'Some diseases that possibly may be prevented by Fletcherization', *Good Health*, January 1909, p. 57; H. Fletcher to J. Brennan, 7 July 1913, Fletcher Papers.

45 See J. Wheatley, 'The advancement of the principles of diet as a branch of public health work', *Public Health*, June 1906, pp. 572–82, and H. W.

Wiley, 'Diet as a Prophylactic and Therapeutic', speech given at a meeting of the American Therapeutic Society, 6–8 May 1909, Box 201, Wiley Papers, Library of Congress.

46 See L. M. Barnett, '"Everyman his own physician": dietetic fads, 1840–1914', in H. Kamminga and A. Cunningham (eds), *The Science and Culture of Nutrition, 1840–1940*, Amsterdam, 1995, pp. 155–78.

47 See T. E. Jordan, *The Degeneracy Crisis and Victorian Youth*, New York, 1993.

48 J. H. Kellogg, 'Deterioration in Great Britain', *Good Health*, 1904, p. 332.

49 *After Bread Education. A Plan for the State Feeding of School Children*, Fabian Tract No. 120, London, 1905, pp. 4–5; L. Mackenzie and A. Foster, 'Report on the Physical Condition of Children Attending the Public Schools of the School Board of Glasgow', 1907, p. v, in M. E. Bulkley, *The Feeding of School Children*, London, 1914, pp. 172–3.

50 L. Bryder, *Below the Magic Mountain. A Social History of Tuberculosis in Twentieth-Century Britain*, Oxford, 1988, p. 1; 'Food and food preservatives', *British Medical Journal*, 18 August 1906, p. 352.

51 J. Riis, *The Children of the Poor*, New York, 1971, orig. 1892, and J. Spargo, *The Bitter Cry of the Children*, Chicago, 1968, orig. 1906.

52 Riis, 1971, op. cit., p. 1.

53 H. Fletcher, *That Last Waif; or, Social Quarantine*, Chicago, 1898, pp. 41–2, 181–2, 270; Fletcher to unknown correspondent [1910], Fletcher Papers.

54 W. I. Trattner, *From Poor Law to Welfare State*, New York, 1979, pp. 139–41.

55 H. Fletcher, 'Department of Social Quarantine – the movement is begun', *Kindergarten Magazine*, December 1898, p. 231; H. Fletcher to G. Taylor, 31 August 1898, Fletcher Papers.

56 Preface to the 1903 edition of *That Last Waif*, New York, 1903, pp. xiv, xxi; H. Fletcher, 'The warrant for optimism', *Good Health*, January 1910, p. 29.

57 M. J. Higgins, circular to members of Immaculate Conception Parish, Germantown, Philadelphia, 12 January 1909, reprinted in H. Fletcher, 'Fletcherizing the W.C.T.U.', *Good Health*, May 1911, p. 410; H. Fletcher to A. W. Erickson, 21 December 1910, Fletcher Papers.

58 H. Fletcher, 1912, op. cit., 121 (footnote).

59 'Dietetic ethics', *Punch*, 28 November 1906; 'Bishop Fallows on diet', *Good Health*, July 1907, p. 359.

60 Elbert Hubbard, 'Are you lovable?', in *Selected Writings of Elbert Hubbard. His Mintage of Wisdom, Coined from a Life of Love, Laughter, and Work*, New York, 1922, vol. 9, p. 284.

61 'Notes on books', *British Medical Journal*, 2 October 1909, p. 990.

62 W. A. Nicholls, 'Feeding of public elementary school children: how far an educational function?', in Hecht, op. cit., p. 81.

63 Board of Education, *Code of Regulations for Public Elementary Schools in England*, 1908, p. ii, quoted in Bulkley, p. 83.

64 H. Fletcher to A. W. Erickson, 10 January 1911, Fletcher Papers.

65 H. Fletcher, 'Politeness to the stomach', *Christian Endeavor World*, 27 May 1909, p. 735; H. Fletcher, 'The kindergarten muncheons', *Christian Endeavor World*, 6 May 1909, p. 675.

66 I. F. Marcosson, 'The growth of Fletcherism', *World's Work*, March 1906, p. 7326.

67 This was also stressed in Wheatley, 1906, op. cit., p. 576.

68 See *Parliamentary Papers*, 1906, vol. ciii, 'Report of the Departmental Committee on Vagrancy', vol. 2, pp. 361–8, and vol. 3, pp. 143–4; 'Vagrancy, diet, and disease', *British Medical Journal*, 17 March 1906, p. 635.

69 'Why I am a Life Prisoner in Sing Sing prison', *Ladies' Home Journal*, March 1910, pp. 15, 93; Sing Sing Admission Registers, Series B0143, Box 13, New York State Archives.

70 H. Fletcher to A. Whiting, 10 November 1898, Fletcher Papers.

71 H. Fletcher, 'One meal a day', *Argonaut*, 19 August 1901, p. 1275; Fletcher to W. E. Berry, 18 November 1912, Fletcher Papers.

72 'Do we eat too much?', *The N.C.R.*, September 1904, p. 176. Reprint of article in *Daily Express*, 3 August 1904.

73 W. Hutchinson, *Instinct and Health*, New York, 1908, p. 19.

74 'Instructions issued by the United States Army Medical Department for the students of the army medical schools', in Fletcher, 1912, op. cit., pp. 325–8.

75 'Low-protein ration experiments in the French army', *Modern Medicine*, August 1908, p. 210; M. Joly, 'Value of sugar in the ration of the infantry soldier during manoeuvres', *Archives de Médicine et de Pharmacie Militaire*, April 1907. English title cited by R. J. Blackham, 'The feeding of the soldier in barracks, in hospital, and in war', *British Medical Journal*, 8 August 1908, pp. 310–17.

76 Blackham. op. cit., passim; see also *Parliamentary Papers*, 1906, vols xxxix, xl, 'Royal Commission on the Supply of Food and Raw Material in Time of War'.

77 'Fletcherism', *Daily Express*, 14 May 1909.

78 Lt-Col. Melville, 'Discussion on food requirements for sustenance and work. Opening paper', *British Medical Journal*, 29 October 1910, pp. 1337–41.

79 L. M. Barnett, 'The impact of "Fletcherism" on the food policies of Herbert Hoover during World War I', *Bulletin of the History of Medicine*, 1992, vol. 66, pp. 250–1.

80 Both in the John Johnson Collection of Printed Ephemera, Bodleian Library, Oxford University.

81 Food (War) Committee, 'A Tragic Muddle', n.d. [1917], Box 527, Food (War) Committee Papers, Royal Society.

82 D. N. Paton to W. B. Hardy, 28 October 1917, Box 530, Food (War) Committee Papers, Royal Society. The Royal Society's 'Fletcherism' file has since disappeared.

83 E. I. Spriggs, *Food and How to Save It*, London, 1918; a public notice issued by health authorities in Crumpsall in June 1917 also contains a hint of Fletcherism. It urged people to chew food thoroughly to ensure

all nutrients were extracted from it. 'Limited outbreak of scurvy', City of Manchester, *Report of the Medical Officer of Health*, 1917, pp. 49–51.

84 Holy Trinity (Seniors) Log Book, April 1917, SM Da 18/2. Lancashire Record Office; '7,000 children Fletcherizing', *Daily Mail*, 11 July 1917; 'An open letter from a Lancashire cotton manufacturer to London teachers', *London Teacher*, 29 June 1917. Typescript copy with comments by Horace Fletcher. United States Food Administration (USFA) Papers, Box 127 F–H, Hoover Institution on War, Revolution and Peace, Stanford University.

85 W. Mackenzie to H. Hoover, 19 November 1917, USFA Papers, Box 127 F–H.

86 D. N. Paton to W. B. Hardy, 28 October 1917, op. cit.

87 Miles, 1919, op. cit., pp. 271–2.

88 'Horace Fletcher taught the world to chew', *Literary Digest*, 8 February 1919, pp. 95–6.

89 H. Fletcher, 'Open letter to physical directors', *Good Health*, December 1909, p. 947.

2

THE FOUNDATION AND EARLY YEARS OF THE DUNN NUTRITIONAL LABORATORY

Mark W. Weatherall

In the 1920s and 1930s, the major source of funding for nutritional studies in Britain was the Medical Research Council (MRC). The council's first 'external' research laboratory was devoted to nutrition: founded in Cambridge in 1927, it was christened the Nutritional Laboratory. 'Dunn' was added to the title in recognition of the donation of funds by the trustees of the estate of Sir William Dunn.[1]

After a brief outline of previous attempts to set up a nutrition laboratory in Cambridge, the main sections of this chapter detail the foundation and early development of the Dunn Laboratory, focusing on the strategies employed by successive Secretaries of the MRC, Walter Morley Fletcher and Edward Mellanby, to put into practice their visions of the contribution that the laboratory should make to nutrition science. These strategies aimed first of all to persuade the director of the laboratory, Leslie Harris, to orientate its research programme towards the areas that Fletcher and Mellanby considered appropriate. The proper role of the laboratory was eventually established through a series of negotiations involving Fletcher, Mellanby, Harris, the Cambridge Professor of Biochemistry, Frederick Gowland Hopkins (under whose control the laboratory nominally rested), and other scientists into whose areas Harris had strayed. Defining a role for the laboratory became equivalent, therefore, to defining a role for Harris; the outcome of this process is considered in the concluding section.

29

CAMBRIDGE'S FIRST NUTRITION LABORATORY: THE INSTITUTE OF ANIMAL NUTRITION

The study of nutrition in Cambridge did not begin with the foundation of the Nutritional Laboratory. Before the First World War, two Cambridge scientists were regularly carrying out feeding experiments: the agricultural chemist Thomas Barlow Wood and the biochemist F. G. Hopkins.[2] Around 1904, when Hopkins was the holder of a readership in chemical physiology, he began to investigate qualitative differences in dietary requirements. In 1906, Hopkins and the physiologist Edith Willcock published a paper which showed that mice fed maize protein as their sole source of protein failed to thrive, and soon died. Adding tryptophane, an amino acid which Hopkins and his colleague Sydney Cole had recently isolated,[3] led to a significant increase in the average length of time that the mice survived.[4] At the 1906 meeting of the British Association, Hopkins was reported to have claimed that:

> Science had not yet given attention to the fact that to get the best qualitative constituents of food for growing children was of the utmost importance. If we knew more we could by studying details of children's food profoundly affect their condition and very much raise their normal standard.[5]

Hopkins's work on qualitative differences in dietary protein was of immediate interest to Wood, who had worked on animal nutrition since the mid-1890s, conducting feeding trials with bullocks and investigating the nutritive value of common feedstuffs. In 1907 Wood became Professor of Agriculture, and the following year took out a bank loan with the parasitologist G. H. F. Nuttall and the pathologist G. S. Woodhead for the erection of a series of Field Laboratories. These three scientists invited Hopkins to join them on a committee of management. Wood believed that Hopkins's work provided a basis for the practical differences in feeding value long known to stock breeders, and that it promised to lead to many an 'economic advance in the science of feeding'.[6] Running the Field Laboratories proved expensive, however, and only two projects were carried out in them: Nuttall's work on tick-borne diseases and Stanley Griffiths's work on tuberculosis.[7]

In 1909, however, a new source of funding became available. Lloyd George's 'People's Budget' included a proposal to establish a fund for national economic development. The Development Fund, disbursed by a body of commissioners, was to be used for a

variety of purposes, including the promotion of agricultural education and research.[8] Robert Olby's recent account of the Development Commission's organisation of agricultural research rightly
stresses the importance of Daniel Hall, Director of the Rothamsted
Experimental Station, in fashioning the programme of research
institutes, but he does not do justice to the role of the civil servants
of the Board of Agriculture and Fisheries (BAF) in establishing
where support should be given.[9] The BAF was already supporting
research and most of the institutes set up by the commission were
based on existing laboratories which were receiving grants from the
BAF. The chief architect of this policy was the Assistant Secretary to
the BAF, Thomas Middleton, who had previously been Professor of
Agriculture at Cambridge. In a memorandum drawn up in March
1910 Middleton suggested that the best policy would be to support
research at a local level, and recommended the establishment of an
Advisory Committee on Agricultural Science which would consider
applications for funding.[10] Hall, on the other hand, believed that the
commissioners should be in sole charge of the disbursement of their
fund, and that they should create new institutes.[11] Negotiations
resulted in a compromise. Hall's plans for institutes remained, but
the BAF's Advisory Committee was to recommend where they should
be and what work should be supported.

Two institutes were created at Cambridge: the Institute of Plant
Breeding, directed by R. H. Biffen, and the Institute of Animal
Nutrition, co-directed by Wood and Hopkins. Biffen's work was an
obvious choice: it was well known and highly regarded. Animal
nutrition was a less obvious choice; in 1910, Hall had despaired of
the subject: 'More than anything else an Institute for the investigation of animal nutrition is called for, but we possess no nucleus for
such work nor any men acquainted with more than the externals
of such investigation'.[12] The BAF Advisory Committee probably
selected Cambridge as the site of the Animal Nutrition Institute as
a result of the applications made by the university that had been
considered and approved in 1910. Among these were applications
for £640 for apparatus for Wood's work on the chemistry of flour
and farm crops, and for £2,000 for the Field Laboratories, which
were called the 'Animal Institute' in the application. The choice of
Cambridge was approved by the commissioners in August 1911; in
an internal BAF memorandum Middleton speculated that around
£3,000 would be spent establishing the institute.[13] Wood and
Hopkins had grander ideas, however, and in November 1911

submitted plans for an extension of the School of Agriculture to provide a home for the Animal Nutrition Institute, as well as extra space for plant breeding research, and teaching. This extension, in fact, nearly doubled the size of the school. It was estimated that it would cost in the region of £20,000. The commissioners provided £14,500 and the university economised by reducing the space available for teaching, but provided more research space. There was room for twenty-two researchers: thirteen in chemistry (including nutrition), six in botany, and three in physiology.[14] Building began in early 1913, and was completed later that year. Wood and Hopkins were appointed co-directors, and research was begun on the quantitative study of proteins of agricultural importance, the factors underlying variations in the nutritive value of rations, and the nutritive value of non-protein nitrogen.[15]

In the event, however, Hopkins had little more to do with the institute. In 1914 he was appointed Professor of Biochemistry and given his own department. Hopkins became closely involved with the war work of the Medical Research Committee and the Royal Society Food (War) Committee. After the war Hopkins's energies were devoted to his own department, and he resigned the directorship of the institute. Hopkins's drift away from the institute may have also been due to the scepticism with which the agriculturists treated his other nutritional interest of this period: during the course of his protein feeding experiments, Hopkins had become convinced that a complete diet comprised more than protein, fat, carbohydrates and salts, and hinted at the existence of accessory food factors – vitamins, as they became known – in public lectures given in 1906 and 1909, while carrying out experiments to determine the nature of these factors.[16] He finally rushed his results into print when the *Daily Mail* gave unwanted publicity to his views in its financially and politically motivated campaign for an 80 per cent wholemeal 'standard bread' in mid-1911: the paper Hopkins penned the following year for the *Journal of Physiology*, 'Feeding experiments illustrating the importance of accessory substances in normal dietaries', was destined to become widely acknowledged as the 'classical' work on vitamins, and to win him a share of a Nobel prize in 1929.[17] This was partly due to the strikingly effective way in which Hopkins used simple graphs to make his case – one commentator even suggested that the paper ranked 'aesthetically beside the best short stories of H. G. Wells'[18] – but was primarily due to the fact that his work appeared as the centrepiece of the historical introduction to the *Report on the Present State of Knowledge Concerning the Accessory Food Factors (Vitamines)*, the first, hugely influential monograph, issued in 1919 by a committee chaired by Hopkins, the Accessory Food Factors Committee of the MRC and the Lister Institute.[19]

Recalling the foundation of the institute over twenty years later, Hopkins remembered that he 'at least hoped that vitamins would receive their share of attention'.[20] If Hopkins's work on dietary protein had earned him the respect of Wood and the other agricultural scientists, his views on accessory food factors found less favour. Wood was openly sceptical: as late as 1921 he was reported to be ridiculing the whole idea of vitamins.[21] Wood had good reason to be sceptical: he and his colleagues worked very closely with bodies such as the National Association of British and Irish Millers, on topics such as the chemistry of flour and the breeding of new strains of wheat. These millers were the very people whose livelihood was threatened by the *Daily Mail* standard bread campaign. Hopkins's enlistment in that campaign therefore threatened to become a source of discord between the millers and the academics. Indeed, in *The Story of a Loaf of Bread*, written in 1913, Wood very publicly played down the significance of Hopkins's experiments.[22] In the 1920s scientists at the Animal Nutrition Institute quickly lost interest in researching the qualitative differences in diet, and concentrated on the energy requirements of animals.

HOPKINS, FLETCHER, AND THE CREATION OF THE DUNN NUTRITIONAL LABORATORY

Hopkins was one of the first British scientists to study nutrition using experimental animals. Having made his fame in that field, he subsequently acquired a biochemical institute of his own, endowed by the trustees of the estate of Sir William Dunn, largely owing to the patronage of the Secretary of the MRC, Walter Morley Fletcher.[23] However, he also gave up the work that had made him famous. Hopkins's interest in the subject began to wane during and after the war as he became more interested in other subjects such as biological oxidation and catalysis. Feeding experiments were long, difficult, messy and expensive, and the financial position of Hopkins's department was precarious. In the late 1910s, and the early 1920s, Hopkins received money from at least five companies – the Planters' Margarine Company, the Maypole Dairy Company,

Virol, J. & J. Colman and the Co-operative Wholesale Society – for work in connection with the nutritive value of their products; when their funding ceased, Hopkins told Fletcher that he could no longer afford to do feeding experiments.[24]

Hopkins's reluctance to push vitamin work frustrated Fletcher, who was tremendously excited by the potential of fundamental research into vitamins. Fletcher was happy to see other centres pick up some of the work – for example, the MRC supported research on vitamin C by S. S. Zilva at the Lister Institute, on vitamin A by Jack Drummond at University College, London, on rickets and dental disease by Edward and May Mellanby in Sheffield – but Fletcher was determined to try to reserve what he considered the most exciting research for his *alma mater*. In April 1920 he told William Bate Hardy:

> Though Hopkins was the pioneer, he has now so many outside jobs that he has little free energy to push this business on, and Cambridge is letting the work slip away to other places. It is one of the biggest new things in biology, and may turn out to be more fundamental than we guess, even now. As for medicine, it is out and away the biggest thing ... I should like to see Hopkins pushing ahead on a much bigger scale, without special reference to any medical or other applications at the moment.[25]

A general reconstellation of the MRC's nutrition research gave Fletcher the opportunity to goad Hopkins into action.[26] Announcing the reform of the council's Human Nutrition Committee in 1926, Fletcher signalled that the new committee would frame a 'comprehensive and co-ordinated programme' of nutrition re-search.[27] While laying the groundwork for this programme, Fletcher began to persuade Hopkins that Cambridge would be the best place to pursue basic biological research into nutrition.[28] In January 1927, Fletcher told A. V. Hill that:

> The only job I seem to be doing ... is to drive Hopkins towards finding some lieutenants to run a real patch of work upon nutrition ... I told Hopkins that, having somehow bagged the credit for inventing vitamins, he spends his time in collecting gold medals on the strength of it, and yet in the past ten years has neither done, nor got others to do, a hand's turn of work in the subject. His place bristles with clever young Jews and talkative women, who are frightfully learned about

protein molecules and o-r potential and all that. But they all seem to run away from biology. The vitamin story is clamouring for analysis, if only as an intriguing scientific puzzle. It happens also to be damned important for practical purposes. Yet not a soul in Cambridge will look at it, either in Hopkins's place or in the so-called Institute of Animal Nutrition, where Capstick warms up his pigs.[29]

In January 1927 Hopkins submitted proposals for a new nutritional laboratory to be situated at the Field Laboratories, and to be constructed out of the cheapest possible material. Six buildings were planned: one laboratory and five animal houses. Hopkins put the cost at about £3,000, and warned Fletcher that the annual expenditure would be of the same order. 'The cost of feeding experiments is astonishingly great,' he wrote, 'and I think the Centre should be prepared to do everything on a proper scale'.[30] Hopkins suggested that the laboratory should have four members of staff in the first instance: one senior researcher, one junior and two attendants. He suggested a former student of his, Leslie Julius Harris, for the senior job, and a current student, Tommy Moore, as the junior. Harris had undertaken Ph.D. research on the physico-chemical properties of proteins and amino acids under Hopkins's supervision between 1921 and 1923. In 1924 he was appointed by the Norwich-based company J. & J. Colman to develop research laboratories and carry out investigations connected with the development of a baby food called Almata.[31] Hopkins must have thought highly of Harris, for Sir Jeremiah Colman, the director of the company, was a good friend whom he had first met when Colman was chairman of the Dunn trustees. Colman had subsequently donated £1,000 towards the cost of the Biochemistry Library. Recommending Harris to Fletcher, Hopkins noted that, besides his excellent technical credentials, Harris was 'essentially a man of enterprise', and confessed himself 'struck' with the quality of the work that he had done for Colman's.[32] Tommy Moore, who Hopkins believed showed 'great promise', was the son of Benjamin Moore, who had held chairs in biochemistry at Liverpool and Oxford before his death in 1922. Before moving out to the Field Laboratories, Moore had been investigating the possible vitamin A activity of the plant pigment xanthophyll, which involved drying huge quantities of stinging nettles. These covered the floors of Hopkins's institute; Moore's colleagues may not have been too sad to see him move out.[33]

NEGOTIATING NUTRITION RESEARCH,
1927–33

Once the sanction of the Council of the MRC had been given to the Nutritional Laboratory scheme, Harris, Hopkins and Fletcher met to discuss the plans. The destiny of the Nutritional Laboratory was in the hands of these three men but, from the beginning, each held different views of what research the laboratory should undertake. In summer 1927, Harris toured British research centres in order to 'obtain helpful views' on how best to design a nutritional laboratory.[34] Harris's 'building first' approach consisted of drawing up detailed comparisons of systems of animal feeding, housing and recording at centres such as the National Institute for Medical Research, the Lister Institute, the Rowett Institute in Aberdeen, and so on – though he does not seem to have visited the Mellanbys in Sheffield, a major omission, considering the fact that he went just about everywhere else where animal experiments were done. He also made an effort to acquire details of foreign laboratories.

Fletcher, on the other hand, wanted Harris to think about work first, and start worrying about a building only when work was progressing satisfactorily; he quickly became frustrated with Harris's peregrinations, and attempted to imbue him with a 'work first' attitude:

> it is the progress and success of new work that alone can justify all ambitious plans for building. Moreover, the very design of the building should follow the lines of work that call for it and ought to determine it . . . The worst thing to do with a baby is to put it into tight swaddling clothes . . .[35]

Work was begun at the Field Laboratories and in the Institute of Biochemistry in August 1927. This arrangement involved Harris shuttling to and fro in his car. Meanwhile, Fletcher set to work to raise the funds for a building, having seen for himself that the existing accommodation at the Field Laboratories was inadequate. He obtained money from the resources remaining in the coffers of the Dunn trustees.[36] The sum expended – £6,000 – was sufficient to build and equip a basic laboratory which was ready for occupation by the end of 1929.

In his original proposals, sent to Fletcher in January 1927, Hopkins had outlined four areas which he considered could be followed with profit in Cambridge: a study 'of the functional failures, and of actual lesions, displayed by individual organs and tissues as a result of individual specific deficiencies in the diet'; the effect of deficiencies on resistance to infection; the testing of statements in the literature (he gave the example of the supposed influence of a specific vitamin upon fertility); and the effects of environmental variations on metabolic needs. When in May 1927 Fletcher officially informed Harris of the MRC's offer that he should take charge of the laboratory, he was more succinct:

It is the intention of the Council that, for the present at least, the work here should consist chiefly in the analytic study of the part played by vitamins in nutrition, rather than in the extension of the common empirical studies of the general results of vitamin presence or neglect.[37]

When work began in Cambridge in August 1927, Harris sent Fletcher a list of preliminary minor investigations being carried out in the Field Laboratories and the Institute of Biochemistry. Not one of the six topics listed could be regarded as fulfilling Fletcher's desire to promote fundamental research into the biology of vitamins (Table 2.1). Over the following few years, however, Fletcher's close interest in the laboratory was rewarded by an increase in the amount of research being done along lines of which he approved. These developments are outlined in Tables 2.1–2.4, which outline the research proposed for the laboratory between 1927 and 1935; the outlines are drawn from Harris's original programme of 1927, his correspondence with the MRC in February 1930 and February 1932, and an outline of work at the laboratory prepared by Sir Charles Martin in March 1935.[38] By 1932 half the research proposed for the laboratory was of the nature that Fletcher had envisaged.

The strategies used by Fletcher to guide Harris are clearly demonstrated by the negotiations surrounding Harris's proposed research into the effects of prolonged vitamin C deficiency on the teeth and gums. This topic also shows how Harris's relations with other nutrition scientists impinged upon his relationship with Fletcher, and thereby upon the research carried out. Harris had become interested in the effects of vitamin C deficiency on the teeth and gums by considering the changes in dental tissue found in scurvy. One of his original proposals was to study the effect of slight vitamin C deficiency on pre-natal development and dentition in guinea pigs, and its possible bearing on the prevention of human dental disease.[39] This work was begun with the Cambridge

Table 2.1 Original plans for work in the Nutritional Laboratory

F.G. Hopkins, January 1927
1 Functional failures and tissue lesions in deficiency
2 Effect of deficiencies on resistance to infection
3 Repetition and control of statements in the literature
4 Effects of environmental variations on metabolic needs

Walter Fletcher, May 1927
'. . . the work here [the Dunn] should consist chiefly in the analytic study of the part played by vitamins in nutrition, rather than in the extension of the common empirical studies of the general results of vitamin presence or neglect'

Leslie Harris, August 1927
1 Changes in teeth in prolonged vitamin C deficiency   *
2 Effect of deficiencies on susceptibility to tuberculosis   *
3 Effect of manuring on vitamin content of crops
4 Stability of B vitamins under refrigeration
5 'Quality' of proteins in feeding
6 Work on nutrition and cancer (*never begun*)

* These fall under one of Hopkins's original categories.

Table 2.2 Work being done, February 1930

1	Changes in teeth in prolonged vitamin C deficiency	*
2	Effect of deficiencies on susceptibility to tuberculosis	*
3	Immunological effects of dietary irregularities	*
4	ECG diagnosis in dietary abnormalities	*
5	Moore's work on carotene and vitamin A	†
6	Proposed work on tissue culture as affected by nutrition	†
7	The role of vitamin D in controlling calcium and phosphorus absorption	†
8	Hypervitaminosis and 'vitamin balance'	
9	Appetite and the choice of food	
10	Role of the thymus in calcification	
11	Coalfield dietaries (*never begun*)	

* These proposals fall under one of Hopkins's original categories.
† These proposals fall under Fletcher's definition.

Table 2.3 Research proposed, February 1932

1	Changes in teeth during prolonged vitamin C deficiency	*
2	Dietary factors influencing final form of vitamin A deficiency	*
3	Determination of vitamin B levels using ECG test	*
4	Determination of the alleged basic nature of vitamin C	*
5	Carotene and vitamin A	†
6	Tissue culture work	†
7	Actions of vitamin D and parathormone on calcium and phosphorus metabolism	†
8	Function of vitamin B, using ECG investigation technique	†
9	Human reserves of vitamin A (and transfer from mother to child)	†
10	Constitution of crystalline vitamin B	†
11	Effects of soil treatment on nutritive value of plant tissues	
12	Hypervitaminosis and 'vitamin balance'	

* These fall under one of Hopkins's original categories.
† These fall under Fletcher's definition.

Table 2.4 Research proposed, March 1935

1	Changes in teeth in prolonged vitamin C deficiency	*
2	Diagnosis of vitamin C deficiency by urine analysis	*
3	Determination of vitamin B_1 distribution using ECG test	*
4	Determination of distribution of vitamins B_6 and H, and flavin	*
5	Vitamin A assay	*
6	Measurement of vitamin C in human milk	*
7	Influence of vitamin D, calcium and phosphorus on bone development *in vitro*	†
8	Influence of vitamin D and parathormone on 'net absorption'	†
9	Human reserves of vitamin A (*continued* with special reference to liver disease)	†
10	Connection of co-enzyme systems and lactic dehydrogenase with vitamin B_1 action	†
11	Influence of dietary factors on redox systems in the lens of the eye	†
12	Relationship of pellagra-producing and anti-anaemia factors	†
13	Influence of vitamin E on chick embryo development	†
14	Attempted isolation of vitamins B_6 and H by electrodialysis	†
15	Attempted isolation of vitamin E	†
16	Transformation of fats to absorptive forms *in vitro* and *in vivo*	

* These fall under one of Hopkins's original categories.
† These fall under Fletcher's definition.

histologist J. R. M. Innes, and with Wilfred Fish from the Research Laboratories of the Royal Dental Hospital in London.[40] Clinical investigation into the effect of vitamin C deficiency went well beyond the brief that Fletcher had given Harris in 1927. None the less, these proposals went unchallenged for four years until, in March 1931, Harris indicated that he wished to extend the investigation by undertaking a study of pyorrhoea (gum disease) in dogs.[41] Perhaps it was the mention of dogs that set alarm bells ringing, bringing to mind the work of May Mellanby in Sheffield. Harris's letter, with the words 'overlaps Mrs Mellanby', was brought to Fletcher's attention. Fletcher, in turn, quizzed Harris about the possible overlap.[42]

Harris replied with an extensive justification of his proposal, beginning with the original observations of dental changes in scorbutic guinea pigs, made in 1920 by P. R. Howe, Professor of Dental Research at Harvard. Harris stated that he wished to continue his histological investigations of guinea pig teeth, and also to begin some small-scale investigations of gum disease in dogs. He did not specify why he wished to start such work, though he did say that he wanted to bring more dental work into the Nutritional Laboratory, as his collaboration with the Royal Dental Hospital was being hampered by the distance between Cambridge and London, and also by what he called the 'orthodox dental view . . . that vitamins are of "little practical consequence"'.[43] Harris stated that his work did not overlap May Mellanby's, as she was not concerned with vitamin C, nor he with vitamins A or D, but this reply did not satisfy Fletcher. While Harris's proposal interested him, Fletcher was not convinced that it was either economical or practicable that the work should be done in Cambridge. He arranged with the MRC's Dental Committee for Harris to discuss his proposals with them, and wrote to May Mellanby to ask if she would go and 'talk "teeth"' with Harris.[44] When he sent an extract from Harris's proposal May Mellanby responded at once, confirming Fletcher's doubts:

> I did not realise . . . that he [Harris] thought of working on dogs; these animals as you know are not susceptible to a lack of vitamin C. I tried many experiments both with deficient and abundant vitamin C (with and without A and D) and came to the conclusion that in these animals vitamin C plays little or no part in the normal development of the dental tissues . . .[45]

Here May Mellanby was talking about her research into the calcification of teeth.[46] Harris had not, however, been proposing to investigate the effect of vitamin C on the teeth, but on the gums, a subject not covered in May Mellanby's published work. But in her letter to Fletcher, May Mellanby had set little store by the possibilities of such work:

> with prolonged deficiency there might be some effect on the development of 'pyorrhoea'; so far, however, my experiments show no such effect but one cannot tell what will happen ultimately.

May Mellanby believed that vitamins A and D were '*the* important factors in dental disease', and when she visited Harris she seems to have dissuaded him from working on dogs. Soon after, when Fletcher enquired of Harris whether his plans had changed, the latter replied that his general purpose remained the same and that, because he was working primarily with guinea pigs, he would not be overlapping with May Mellanby.[47] Fletcher let the matter rest until after the meeting of the Dental Committee in June 1931. The committee recommended that Harris should do experiments on pyorrhoea if funding permitted, and that it would be best if he could use monkeys. But Fletcher had yet to be convinced that the work should be done in Cambridge. He questioned Harris whether, as a matter of policy, the work was suitable for the Nutritional Laboratory, that is, whether it counted as the 'analytical study of the mode of actions of vitamins'. Suggesting that Harris should consult Hopkins, Fletcher concluded, in typically homiletic style, 'It is now, at the beginning of the road, that a wrong turn matters most'.[48] He also wrote back to May Mellanby, imploring her to say what she really thought of Harris's ideas.[49] She replied that

> It is rather difficult for me to advise about Dr Harris's proposed work. I certainly do not want to discourage any one from doing dental research, and yet I agree with you that there does not seem much justification for beginning a new centre for work on vitamins and dentition at the present time, especially as Dr Harris does not seem to have any new ideas to test and there are so many other vitamin problems to be unravelled.[50]

But Harris had already got the message. He wrote to Fletcher to say that his plans had changed, that he would merely be supplying material to be examined by his collaborator, and would henceforth be responsible only for feeding the experimental animals. He was able to salvage something from the wreckage of his proposal, however. He brought forward the possibility of linking the vitamin C work with some work on the histological effects of vitamin A deficiency just being completed at the laboratory, making a case for investigating the activity of both vitamins using tissue culture techniques. It was a clever move. Honor Fell, the director of the largely MRC-funded Strangeways Research Laboratory at Cambridge, had offered to direct the work, but had no one free to do it. Would it be possible, Harris inquired, for the MRC to fund someone? Fletcher could hardly refuse; it was, after all, exactly the sort of work that he wanted Harris to be doing.[51]

This incident highlights the ways in which Fletcher and Harris negotiated over the nature of the research to be undertaken at the Dunn. Fletcher was clearly interested in Harris's proposed research. It was the kind of research which, if it were carried out successfully, could have major social implications. Such an outcome would have provided a first-rate example of Fletcher's maxim, stated in a BBC broadcast in 1931, that 'there can be no proper government of this or any other country, there can be no sound statecraft, that does not take full account of the science of living things and act under its guidance'.[52]

Although Fletcher certainly considered that the work ought to be done, his view about *where* it should be done was conditioned by his assessment of the relative goals, abilities and merits of the members of his staff, and of the overall shape of MRC policy. He always had to bear in mind the economics of organising a coherent programme without undue duplication. In this case Harris's curiosity was admirable but, as it had taken him on to someone else's patch, Fletcher was bound to step in and guide him away. Avoiding unnecessary duplication was particularly important in the early 1930s, when the MRC's budget was strained. At the time of the events described, the unfolding financial crisis of 1931 led to the fall of the Labour government, the creation of the National Government, and economies in public expenditure.

The early development of the Dunn cannot be understood without considering the personal relationships of the three men in whose hands its direction lay: Fletcher, Hopkins and Harris. We have already seen how Fletcher and Hopkins held subtly differing views about what counted as fundamental biochemical research. The relationship between Fletcher and Harris (of which we have a relatively good understanding because of the frankness of Fletcher's letters) was often stormy: they clashed several times over seemingly inconsequential issues such as Harris's failure to make full use of library facilities, his commissioning stationery without approval, and his assumption of the title of 'Director' before it had been officially bestowed upon him, which led to a particularly stern rebuke:

> I hinted to you in talk some time ago that my strong advice to you would be to avoid most carefully any aggrandisement of yourself or the laboratory at the start ... To do anything now that seems to claim a position still waiting to be won merely gives an unnecessary hostage to fortune and, human nature being what it is, is likely to put up the backs of your colleagues elsewhere.
>
> ... I have already noticed, however, that some of the possible dangers to which I pointed have not been wholly avoided. You must remember that I have various diplomatic difficulties here, of which you cannot be fully aware, and if you will not lie low at the beginning for your own sake ... you must do it for mine.[53]

Harris's relationship with Hopkins is less transparent, as few of their discussions were recorded. It appears that, once the Nutritional Laboratory was founded, Hopkins had relatively little to do with the negotiations about the research done there. It was not in his nature to do so; he tended instead to allow his colleagues and students to follow whatever scientific leads interested them. Both Fletcher and Harris attempted to recruit Hopkins to their cause, but Hopkins was never a powerful ally because of his unwillingness to take sides and because of the distractions of his own institute and of his presidency of the Royal Society.[54] The Nutritional Laboratory was essentially Fletcher's creation, and he devoted a disproportionate amount of his time to it. His patronage was important in protecting Harris from the criticisms of outsiders; after Fletcher's death in 1933, however, Harris found himself involved in an altogether more difficult set of negotiations over the direction of the laboratory.

NEGOTIATING NUTRITION RESEARCH:
HARRIS AND MELLANBY, 1933–39

Fletcher's successor as Secretary of the MRC was Edward Mellanby, a former pupil of Hopkins who from 1920 to 1933 now held the chair in pharmacology at the University of Sheffield. Mellanby's assessment of the Nutritional Laboratory was scathing. He complained that little work of fundamental importance had been done, and noted the discord caused by Harris's habit of, as he put it, 'rushing into publication after following up other people's work . . . usually in the form of a letter to *Nature* on all manner of problems which other people are trying to develop'. Mellanby did not wish to spend his time guiding Harris, and attempted to bring Harris's activities under tighter control by imposing a committee of management. This was to consist of Hopkins, Mellanby, and the former head of the Lister Institute, Sir Charles Martin, who had retired to live in Cambridge. Mellanby believed that Martin would have 'just the requisite knowledge and wisdom to introduce an entirely new atmosphere into the laboratory'.[55] Mellanby recommended that the committee of management should read all publications, and have the right to stop or alter them, and that it should exercise strict control over expenditure and the recruitment of new workers.

Mellanby's criticism of Harris's style of working probably originated in the incident with his wife discussed in the previous section, but his distaste for Harris's publishing tendencies was intensified in 1932 and 1933 by the clashes between Harris and other scientists over the elucidation of the nature of vitamin C. Mellanby was delegated by the unanimous vote of the Accessory Food Factors Committee (of which Harris was not a member) to approach Fletcher about Harris's publication record.[56] This criticism was repeated in a memorandum on the future of the laboratory prepared by Mellanby in summer 1934. The minutes of the Accessory Food Factors Committee do not record the delegation, but they do reveal that as early as February 1932 its members were concerned that scientists at the Dunn were needlessly duplicating work being done elsewhere. At the end of the outline of 'Proposed Programme of Vitamin Work and Budget for 1932' a brief note was made that:

The work proposed on Vitamin C . . . [proof or disproof of the alleged basic nature of vitamin C by I. Mills] appeared

44

to be similar in aim and scope to that at present being carried out by Dr Zilva at the Lister Institute. The Committee, therefore, recommended that Dr L. J. Harris be asked to get into close touch with Dr Zilva in order to prevent overlapping and unnecessary expenditure.[57]

Worse was to come, for later that year the Dunn became embroiled in the heated disputes raging over the nature of vitamin C between Zilva and the Hungarian scientist Albert Szent-Györgyi. In 1928, Szent-Györgyi had proposed that hexuronic acid, a highly reducing substance that he had isolated from oranges, cabbage and adrenal glands, was responsible for the anti-scurvy properties of fruit and vegetables, that is, that hexuronic acid *was* vitamin C. Zilva disagreed, citing work that he had done showing that vitamin activity and reducing power were independent of one another. There the matter lay for four years until, in 1932, Szent-Györgyi carried out experiments to see whether hexuronic acid would protect guinea pigs from scurvy. In April that year, he published an interim report in *Nature* to the effect that hexuronic acid did indeed have that property.[58] Zilva disagreed again, stating that the protection could as easily have come from a vitamin contaminating Szent-Györgyi's hexuronic acid sample. In response to this challenge, Szent-Györgyi sent Zilva some of the sample, and asked him to repeat the experiments. This Zilva did, but, though he obtained the same result, he still refused to draw the same conclusion.[59]

It was as this point that Harris became involved, for Szent-Györgyi also sent him a sample of hexuronic acid. It is not clear why he did this; Harris had not published any work on vitamin C whatsoever. It is possible that Szent-Györgyi reached Harris through Hopkins, in whose institute he had first isolated hexuronic acid.[60] Harris and his colleagues came down firmly on Szent-Györgyi's side, publishing their conclusions in *The Lancet*, the *Biochemical Journal* and *Nature*.[61] The paper in *The Lancet* was particularly galling for Zilva, as it presented results of experiments on the anti-scurvy activity of suprarenal glands which were virtually identical to those which Zilva had been doing himself. Zilva could only respond by rushing a one-page paper into print in the *Biochemical Journal* with his own results, but it appeared months after the offending paper from the Dunn.[62] Matters were compounded by the tone of the discussions which accompanied the Nutritional Laboratory's experiments, which implied either that Zilva's influence had unduly held up the true recognition of affairs, or that he was unable to interpret his own results correctly.[63] Worse still, the Dunn's workers received the credit for suggesting that hexuronic acid (now renamed ascorbic acid) was a better standard for vitamin C activity than lemon juice.[64]

The committee of management does not seem to have had much effect on Harris's activities. Even though all the laboratory's papers had to be vetted by Martin before publication, Mellanby received further complaints from Zilva in 1935 that Harris had misunderstood his work, failed to cite it properly, and unfairly claimed priority for himself in discussions of methods for determining the 'saturation' of subjects with vitamin C, published in *The Lancet* and *Annual Review of Biochemistry*.[65] In a memorandum sent to Landsborough Thomson, the Assistant Secretary of the MRC, Zilva summarised the findings published by his and Harris's groups:

> Harris did *not* mention, nor did he appreciate, the phenomenon of 'saturation' in his first paper. (I don't think he *fully* appreciates it even now!) ... Yet in publishing in the *Lancet* 'the technique of our diagnostic test' [*sic*], 'in view of the current interest of clinical and other workers' [*sic*], which rests on the saturation theory ... he not only does not give credit to us, but, using his inimitable literary artistry, implies that we have confirmed him! He further holds forth upon what we have already discussed in our paper in the most pontifical, and not always intelligent, way.[66]

Zilva was clearly exasperated. As his private covering letter to Thomson put it:

> I may be a prejudiced party, but the egotism & disingenuousness of the paper seems to me to be strikingly evident ... Even if I was really to have 'confirmed' Harris's findings & adopted all his 'methods' as he ambiguously insinuates, he might have referred to it more generously, as we are colleagues, at least on paper, & both serving the Council.[67]

This incident led to the appointment of another expert (the chemist Otto Rosenheim) to the committee of management. This appointment made little difference to Mellanby's opinion of Harris: at the end of 1937, he still thought that Harris was chasing up other people's leads.[68]

DEFINING THE PROPER ROLE OF THE DUNN

In his initial diagnosis of the situation at the Nutritional Laboratory, Mellanby blamed the fact that Harris was occupying 'the time of his workers chasing after problems which are being investigated by other workers' on the absence of any scientists with medical, pathological or physiological knowledge.[69] The idea of what the role of the Nutritional Laboratory should be had changed: Mellanby's complaints about Harris were quite different from those of Fletcher. Fletcher had wanted Cambridge biochemists to work on the biochemistry of vitamins without immediate reference to practical problems, and in relative isolation from practical people, but Mellanby believed that the lack of contact with, and respect for, such people was producing trivial results. Both Fletcher and Mellanby were products of the Cambridge physiological laboratory, which prided itself on its freedom from the necessity to concentrate on medical or pathological problems, but Mellanby had actively fostered links between the laboratory and the clinic during his period in Sheffield. In a book entitled *Nutrition and Disease. The Interaction of Clinical and Experimental Work*, published in 1934, Mellanby celebrated the way in which the two kinds of research could 'react on one another to their mutual advantage'.

Harris's personal relationship with Mellanby continued to be poor throughout the 1930s and 1940s,[70] although in the late 1930s Harris began to direct part of the programme of the Dunn towards the more practical nutritional concerns of the wider medical and scientific community. Harris and his colleagues designed blood and urine tests for various vitamin deficiencies, including a test for vitamin C status based upon the vitamin C 'saturation' studies. Harris discussed the value of these tests, and other means of assessing malnutrition, in a five-part article in *Medical Officer* in 1937. This was a field of work which offered considerable returns: the development of objective tests for malnutrition would permit intervention in the disputes about malnutrition which raged between doctors, scientists, health administrators, politicians and political activists.

In his articles for *Medical Officer*, Harris attempted to put forward a 'purely scientific statement' of the causes, incidence and treatment of malnutrition.[71] He highlighted the problems of clinical assessment of malnutrition, and presented biochemical techniques as a solution to some of the uncertainties of clinical methods. When considering evidence for the incidence of malnutrition, Harris drew upon the research of economists, dietitians, doctors and sociologists, as well as that of experimental scientists, to present a comprehensive picture of contemporary views of the subject.[72] The message of Harris's articles was that accurate and specific scientific knowledge about nutrition – the product of a laboratory such as his own – was vital if nutritional theory was to be translated into practice. Harris illustrated the potential of the application of the 'basic scientific facts' of nutrition by drawing a parallel between the contemporary position of nutrition science with that of bacteriology in the 1860s.

During the Second World War, the Dunn turned even more directly towards practical matters, addressing the nutritional problems that were thrown up by wartime measures such as rationing. Harris was also busy outside the laboratory. The mixture of expertise that he had drawn upon in his *Medical Officer* articles was characteristic of the Nutrition Society, founded in 1941, of which Harris was the first honorary secretary, and president 1953–6. During his tenure of the secretary's post, according to the reminiscences of R. C. Garry, Harris 'planned ... [and] organized until every aspect of the work of the Society occupied its proper niche'.[73] Harris's articles on malnutrition, and his work within the Nutrition Society, epitomise the way in which biochemists came to assume their 'proper niches' within the multi-faceted community of British nutrition scientists. In the post-war era the Dunn Nutritional Laboratory, with continued support from the MRC, became the natural home of the experimental study of nutrition, as scientists at the Dunn concentrated upon the kind of fundamental studies that Fletcher had originally envisaged. Harris and the Dunn had found their proper roles at last.

NOTES

I would like to thank David Smith and Harmke Kamminga for their valuable comments on drafts of this chapter.

1 That is, a laboratory not part of the National Institute for Medical Research. This was not the first external MRC laboratory, but two earlier examples were for purposes other than research. See A. L. Thomson, *Half a Century of Medical Research*, London, 2 vols, 1973/1975, vol. 1, pp. 133–9, vol. 2, p. 352, and A. A. Paul (ed.), *The First 60 Years. History and Publications of the MRC Dunn Nutrition Unit, 1927–1987*, Cambridge, 1987.

2 Existing accounts of Hopkins present contradictory pictures of his research and its connection with his vision of biochemistry. Compare J. Needham and E. Baldwin (eds), *Hopkins and Biochemistry, 1861–1947*, Cambridge, 1949, with R. E. Kohler, *From Medical Chemistry to Biochemistry*, Cambridge, 1982. For an attempt to resolve these contradictions, see H. Kamminga and M. W. Weatherall, 'The making of a biochemist I: F. G. Hopkins' construction of dynamic biochemistry', and 'II: 'The construction of F. G. Hopkins' reputation', in *Medical History*, 1996, vol. 40.

3 F. G. Hopkins and S. W. Cole, 'A contribution to the study of proteids' I, *Journal of Physiology*, 1901, vol. 27; II, ibid., 1903, vol. 29.

4 E. G. Willcock and F. G. Hopkins, 'The importance of individual amino acids in metabolism', ibid., 1906, vol. 35.

5 'British Association', *The Times*, 9 August 1906.

6 T. B. Wood, 'The chemistry of the proteins', *Transactions of the Highland Agricultural Society of Scotland*, 1911, fifth series, vol. 23.

7 See the minutes of the Management Committee of the Field Laboratories in the University of Cambridge Archives.

8 B. K. Murray, *The People's Budget, 1909/10. Lloyd George and Liberal Politics*, Oxford, 1980, p. 146.

9 R. Olby, 'Social imperialism and state support for agricultural research in Edwardian Britain', *Annals of Science*, 1991, vol. 48.

10 T. H. Middleton, memorandum, 12 March 1910, Public Record Office (hereafter PRO) MAF 33/63 A13129/1910.

11 A. D. Hall, memorandum, 2 December 1910, PRO D 4/1.

12 Ibid.

13 T. H. Middleton, memorandum, 27 September 1911, PRO MAF 33/7 A 17894/1912.

14 R. F. Scott to Development Commissioners, 1 March 1912, PRO MAF 33/7 A 17894/1912.

15 Board of Agriculture and Fisheries to Development Commission, 9 May 1913, PRO MAF 33/7 A 17348/1913.

16 M. W. Weatherall, '"A revolution in the science of food": how "standard bread" sold newspapers', in H. Kamminga and A. R. Cunningham (eds), *The Science and Culture of Nutrition, 1840–1940*, Amsterdam, 1995, pp. 179–212.

17 F. G. Hopkins, 'Feeding experiments illustrating the importance of accessory factors in normal dietaries', *Journal of Physiology*, 1912, vol. 44.

18 W. R. Aykroyd, *Vitamins and Other Dietary Essentials*, London, 1933.

19 Kamminga and Weatherall, op. cit.

20 F. G. Hopkins, 'Vitamins and agriculture', 1938?, manuscript in Hopkins Reprint Collection, Wellcome Unit for the History of Medicine, University of Cambridge.

21 M. J. Rowlands told the Royal Society of Medicine that, after reading the work of Hopkins and others, he fed his pigs on vitamin-rich diets, and they swept the board at the 1920 Smithfield Show. But in 1921, when Rowlands read a paper to the Farmers' Club, 'T. B. Wood . . . ridiculed all my experiments, and the whole idea of vitamins . . .':

M. J. Rowlands, 'Rheumatoid arthritis: is it a deficiency disease?', *Proceedings of the Royal Society of Medicine*, 1926–7, vol. 20.

22 T. B. Wood, *The Story of a Loaf of Bread*, Cambridge, 1913.

23 R. E. Kohler, 'Walter Fletcher, F. G. Hopkins, and the Dunn Institute of Biochemistry: a case study in the patronage of science', *Isis*, 198, vol. 69.

24 F. G. Hopkins to W. M. Fletcher, 22 April 1920, PRO FD 1/89.

25 W. M. Fletcher to W. B. Hardy, 20 April 1920, PRO FD 1/89

26 For an account of Fletcher's views on the importance of nutrition research see C. Petty, 'Primary research and public health: the prioritization of nutrition research in inter-war Britain', in J. Austoker and L. Bryder (eds), *Historical Perspectives on the Role of the MRC*, Oxford, 1989.

27 Medical Research Council, *Report of the Medical Research Council for the Year 1926–27*, London, 1928.

28 David Smith notes Fletcher's impetus, and provides an account of how the Human Nutrition Committee came to be formed: D. F. Smith, 'Nutrition in Britain in the Twentieth Century', unpublished Ph.D. thesis, University of Edinburgh, 1987, pp. 100–1, 336–7.

29 W. M. Fletcher to A. V. Hill, 20 January 1927, PRO FD 1/1948.

30 F. G. Hopkins to W. M. Fletcher, 8 January 1927, PRO FD 1/3806.

31 S. Horrocks, 'Consuming Science. Science, Technology and Food in Britain, 1870–1939', unpublished Ph.D. thesis, University of Manchester, 1993.

32 F. G. Hopkins to W. M. Fletcher, 8 January 1927, PRO FD 1/3806.

33 T. Moore, 'Vitamin A and carotene', in Paul, 1987, op. cit., p. 27.

34 L. J. Harris to W. M. Fletcher, 6 May 1927, PRO FD 1/3806.

35 W. M. Fletcher to L. J. Harris, 15 July 1927, ibid.

36 W. M. Fletcher to J. Colman, 9 July 1928, PRO FD 1/1836.

37 W. M. Fletcher to L. J. Harris, 3 May 1927, PRO FD 1/3806.

38 L. J. Harris to W. M. Fletcher, 10 August 1927, PRO FD 1/3806; L. J. Harris to A. L. Thomson, 13 February 1930, PRO FD 1/3807; L. J. Harris to A. L. Thomson, 15 February 1932, PRO FD 1/3809; C. J. Martin to E. Mellanby, 27 March 1935, PRO FD 1/3810.

39 L. J. Harris to W. M. Fletcher, 10 August 1927, PRO FD 1/3806.

40 Fish also received MRC support for his investigations of the structure of normal teeth throughout this period.

41 L. J. Harris to F. H. K. Green, 3 March 1931, PRO FD 1/3808.

42 W. M. Fletcher to L. J. Harris, 31 March 1931, ibid. May Mellanby had recently published 'Diet and the teeth: an experimental study. I, Dental structure in dogs', *Medical Research Council Special Report Series*, 1929, No. 140.

43 L. J. Harris to W. M. Fletcher, 15 April 1931, PRO FD 1/3808.

44 M. Mellanby to W. M. Fletcher, 26 April 1931, ibid.

45 M. Mellanby to W. M. Fletcher, 30 April 1931, ibid.

46 M. Mellanby, op. cit.

47 L. J. Harris to W. M. Fletcher, 22 May 1931, PRO FD 1/3808.

48 W. M. Fletcher to L. J. Harris, 12 June 1931, ibid.

49 W. M. Fletcher to M. Mellanby, 12 June 1931, ibid.

50 M. Mellanby to W. M. Fletcher, 15 June 1931, ibid.

51 L. J. Harris to W. M. Fletcher, 17 June 1931, ibid.
52 W. M. Fletcher, *Biology and Statecraft. The Seventh of the Broadcast National Lectures delivered on 23 January 1931*, London, 1931.
53 L. J. Harris, W. M. Fletcher and F. G. Hopkins, September and October 1929, and March 1930, PRO FD 1/3807; L. J. Harris to W. M. Fletcher, 7 May 1932; W. M. Fletcher to L. J. Harris, 9 May 1932, PRO FD 1/3809.
54 See the draft of a memorandum, probably by Mellanby, for the Council of the MRC on the future of the Dunn Nutritional Laboratory, n.d. (June/July 1934), PRO FD 1/3810.
55 E. Mellanby to H. S. Raper, 4 April 1934, PRO FD 1/3809.
56 Ibid.
57 Minute (5) of the Accessory Food Factors Committee, 25 February 1932, PRO FD 1/7069.
58 A. Szent-Györgyi, *Nature*, 1932, vol. 129.
59 S. S. Zilva, *Nature*, 1932, vol. 129.
60 R. W. Moss, *Free Radical. Albert Szent-Györgyi and the Battle over Vitamin C*, New York, 1988.
61 L. J. Harris, I. Mills and J. R. M. Innes, 'The chemical identification of vitamin C: confirmation of activity of a preparation of hexuronic acid', *The Lancet*, 1932, vol. ii; L. J. Harris and S. N. Ray, 'Vitamin C and the suprarenal cortex I.: Antiscorbutic activity of ox suprarenal', *Biochemical Journal*, 1932, vol. 26; T. W. Birch, L. J. Harris and S. N. Ray, 'Hexuronic (ascorbic) acid as the antiscorbutic factor and its chemical determination', *Nature*, 1933, vol. 131.
62 S. S. Zilva, 'The antiscorbutic activity of the cortex of the suprarenal gland of the ox', *Biochemical Journal*, 1932, vol. 26.
63 Harris and Ray, op. cit.; W. J. Dann, 'Hexuronic (ascorbic) acid as the antiscorbutic factor and its chemical determination', *Nature*, 1933, vol. 131. Dann's paper drew a reply from Zilva which he also sent to the MRC: S. S. Zilva to A. L. Thomson, PRO FD 1/3786. This file also contains Zilva's accounts of the discovery of vitamin C, written in 1933 and 1935, which accord credit to Szent-Györgyi, and denigrate the work done at Cambridge.
64 K. M. Key and B. G. E. Morgan, 'The determination of the vitamin C value of ascorbic acid', *Biochemical Journal*, 1933, vol. 27.
65 E. Mellanby to C. J. Martin, 15 February 1935, PRO FD 1/3809; E. Mellanby to C. J. Martin, 12 July 1935, PRO FD 1/3810.
66 S. S. Zilva, memorandum on 'saturation' of vitamin C, PRO FD 1/3786.
67 S. S. Zilva to A. L. Thomson, 15 January 1935, ibid.
68 E. Mellanby to C. J. Martin, 22 December 1937, PRO FD 1/3811.
69 E. Mellanby to H. S. Raper, 4 April 1934, PRO FD 1/3809.
70 See, for example, Mellanby's concern about letters Harris wrote to the *Daily Herald* and the *Yorkshire Weekly* in May 1935 about the malnutrition of children: E. Mellanby to C. J. Martin, 20 May, 5 June 1935, PRO FD 1/3611.
71 L. J. Harris, 'The incidence and assessment of malnutrition: a critique and review', *Medical Officer*, 1937, vol. 58.

72 In these articles Harris does not privilege his own views, except in one area. Every opinion is backed up by a reference to other authorities. This fact, and Harris's acknowledgements, which thank (among others) Martin, Hopkins and Rosenheim for their comments, suggest that the articles appeared with the approval of the committee of management. The exception is Harris's discussion of techniques for estimating vitamin C deficiency, in which he does not cite the work of Zilva and devotes space to his own publications on the subject.

73 Interview with R. C. Garry recorded with E. M. Widdowson in E. M. Widdowson (ed.), *The Nutrition Society, 1941–1991. Presidents and Honorary Members: Their Stories and Recollections*, London, 1991. See also Smith, op. cit.. chapters 4 and 5.

3

NUTRITION SCIENCE AND THE FOOD AND PHARMACEUTICAL INDUSTRIES IN INTER-WAR BRITAIN

Sally M. Horrocks

Vitamins occupy so important a place in nutrition that no food manufacturer can ignore them.[1]
    (Arthur Knapp, chief chemist of Cadbury's, 1938)

By the end of the 1930s scientists employed by Britain's largest and most innovative food and pharmaceutical manufacturers were convinced of the important role that nutritional knowledge had come to play in their industry. While the connection between nutrition theory and commercial profit had been successfully exploited during the Victorian age by individual entrepreneurs such as Justus von Liebig and T. R. Allinson,[2] during the inter-war years the focus moved from individuals developing and exploiting their own discoveries to salaried researchers working within the confines of large and well established enterprises. By this time nutrition research had come to be dominated by a focus on micronutrient content and especially vitamins, what E. V. McCollum referred to as the 'Newer Knowledge of Nutrition'.[3] In addition there had been widespread attempts to disseminate the new ideas to the general public. These three factors combined to expand and change the ways in which nutritional knowledge was developed and applied in the commercial sector.

The historiography of nutrition science in Britain has, however, had relatively little to say about these commercial aspects of its development, concentrating instead on state-funded research and the role of nutrition science in health policy.[4] While there are a few studies of the commercialisation of nutrition theories, especially those of Liebig, which ante-dated the emergence of the vitamin concept, the period since then has received only fragmentary treatment. Recent work in the business history of the inter-war years has, however, indicated the importance of vitamin products in the evolution of the British pharmaceutical industry, as well as pointing to their role in food manufacturing and marketing.[5] These studies of the British situation, along with research into this period which discusses the United States,[6] indicate the important role played by commercial factors in bringing nutrition science into the public domain.[7] This chapter reinforces this suggestion by examining in detail some of the different ways in which the commercial exploitation of nutrition science operated to increase its presence in the world beyond the laboratory door. It does so by looking first at those factors which underpinned the emergence of nutrition as an important component of organised industrial science in both the food and the pharmaceutical industries – the recruitment of trained scientists from the 1890s onwards and their identification of the commercial possibilities of nutritional knowledge. Second, it considers how the subsequent exploitation of this knowledge was shaped by competing interests and alliances within industry, academic nutrition research and the medical establishment.

THE GROWTH OF COMMERCIAL INTEREST IN NUTRITIONAL KNOWLEDGE, 1900–39

The employment of trained scientists in British industry became commonplace in the final decades of the nineteenth century, although some industries, especially those related to chemical manufacture, had started the practice much earlier. In both food and pharmaceuticals the first scientists to be employed were analytical chemists, whose work was closely related to production. Gradually these chemists extended the range of their work beyond the application of routine testing procedures and began to carry out investigations into new analytical techniques and to improve existing products and processes. By 1914 it was the norm for large food and pharmaceutical manufacturers to employ their own scientists, and many regarded them as essential to future commercial success. The contributions made by scientists persuaded several of the largest firms, including Cadbury, Rowntree and Burroughs Wellcome (hereafter Wellcome), that an active commitment to research would pay dividends, and it became an integral part of their operations before the First World War. They were, however, the exceptions, and research was carried out by only a small minority of firms.[8]

Events during the First World War led to the formal establishment of research departments in many more enterprises. During the inter-war years extensive research facilities were set up by a small number of firms in the food industry, most notably Lyons, Cadbury, Rowntree, United Dairies, Lever Brothers, Metal Box and Glaxo. While many other enterprises employed scientists they did so on a much smaller scale, with only a few staff and a limited capacity for research.[9] There was a similar concentration of resources in the pharmaceutical industry, with Boots, Wellcome, May & Baker and British Drug Houses (BDH) establishing themselves as the leading employers of scientific personnel.[10]

In the food industry the most common areas of scientific investigation were new techniques of quality control, improving the efficiency of production, and finding profitable uses for waste materials. New product development was undertaken, but it was often less important than finding more efficient ways of producing existing lines.[11] Greater importance was attached to new products in the pharmaceutical industry, but here too there was a considerable amount of routine work, especially production control.[12] Only limited resources were available for what was regarded as fundamental research, but even these investigations were usually related in some way to the interests of the enterprise.[13] It became common for leading industrial scientists to publish results regarded as of general interest, but knowledge considered to have commercial significance remained within the firm.[14]

It is difficult to obtain an accurate picture of the total number of scientists employed in these industries prior to the 1930s, although evidence at the level of the individual firm indicates that there had been a substantial increase since the late nineteenth century.[15] For the 1930s we can draw on figures collected in 1943 as part of a survey of the research and development efforts of British firms carried out by the Federation of British Industries, although the figures relate to research and development only, and do not include scientists engaged solely on routine testing and production control. By combining the results of this survey with data from elsewhere we can get an idea of the extent of research in leading firms in both industries (Table 3.1).[16]

The establishment of significant internal research capabilities

Table 3.1 Employment of qualified staff for research by firms in the food and pharmaceutical industries, 1930–41

Firm	Sector	1930	1935	1938	1941
Lever Bros	f	30	57	79	85
Lyons	f	71	70	84	80
Boots	ph	34	34	45	80
Wellcome	ph	n.a.	n.a.	n.a.	66
Glaxo	f	7	12	21	64
May & Baker	ph	n.a.	n.a.	n.a.	58
Rowntree	f	28	34	40	34
Metal Box	f	n.a.	4	28	19
BDH	ph	n.a.	n.a.	14	16
Cadbury	f	21	21	23	15

Notes: f = food, ph = pharmaceutical. All figures are from CBI Predecessor Archive, University of Warwick, Modern Records Centre (hereafter CBI), MSS 200 F/3/T1/127c, except for those for May & Baker and Wellcome, which are from J. Liebenau, 'The British success with penicillin', *Social Studies of Science*, 1987, vol. 17, pp. 69–86. The figures for these two firms are thus not strictly comparable with those for the others, and relate to total employment of qualified scientists rather than to just those engaged on research and development. 'Qualified' meant holding a degree or professional qualification, usually an Associateship of the Institute of Chemistry. For a fuller discussion of the limitations of these figures see D. E. H. Edgerton and S. M. Horrocks, 'British industrial research and development before 1945', *Economic History Review*, 1994, vol. 67, pp. 213–38.

did not mean that these firms relied wholly on their own scientific and technological capacity. Instead scientific staff acted as an interface with the world outside the firm, constantly alert to the commercial potential offered by new ideas emerging from external sources. Formal and informal contacts were maintained with scientists working for other firms. Professional organisations, which included general societies as well as more specialist groups such as the Society of Chemical Industry's Food Group, brought together researchers from universities, industry and government research establishments. Many firms maintained close links with particular university departments or academic researchers.[17] In addition they had access to a wide range of publications. Lyons, for example, regularly received ninety journals.[18] This role as gatherers and processors of information concerning new developments taking place outside the firm alerted industrial scientists to the possibilities offered by the rapidly developing field of nutrition research. An example of just how important this role could be comes from the work of Harry Jephcott, who was initially hired by Glaxo as a quality control chemist, but later became the driving force behind the firm's transition from food to pharmaceuticals. Jephcott attended the International Dairy Congress in the United States in 1923 and took the opportunity to visit American scientists to discuss their research. He also secured the manufacturing rights to processes that the Americans had developed. These proved to be very profitable for his employers.[19]

While the employment of trained scientists ensured that firms were in a position to understand and appreciate the technical and marketing possibilities offered by the 'Newer Knowledge of Nutrition', this ability would have been of little long-term importance to them in the absence of efforts to encourage the public to follow the prescriptions emerging out of new research. In the case of vitamins, however, the extensive efforts of nutrition researchers and other enthusiasts to stimulate public awareness helped to create a climate which made it possible for industrial scientists to secure resources to exploit these new developments. It is, of course, very difficult to measure directly the extent to which the general public was aware of the findings of nutrition research, or the influence such awareness had on their buying habits. Instead recourse must be made to indirect sources, which in the case of inter-war Britain yield ambiguous evidence. The League of Nations Mixed Committee on the Relation of Nutrition to Health, Agriculture and Economic Policy reported in its final communiqué:

> The amount of space which the newspapers of the United Kingdom, the British Dominions and the Continent of Europe now devote to the discussion of food problems and values and to the publication of balanced menus is a striking testimony to the growth of public interest in these questions.[20]

This view is supported by anecdotal comment such as that presented in *The Long Weekend*, first published in 1940, which claims that 'vitamins were the all-weather favourites . . . and before the end of the Thirties were lettered from A to E in the hearts of even the most backward villager'.[21] Other sources, notably William Crawford's survey of national dietary habits published in 1938, give a different impression. This investigation concluded that only a minority of housewives were actually interested in dietetic subjects.[22] What is beyond dispute, however, is that there was a considerable volume of information about nutrition entering the public domain from all sections of the media.

Several scientists involved in nutrition research, including V. H. Mottram, Professor of Physiology at King's College of Household and Social Science, and R. H. A. Plimmer, Professor of Chemistry at St Thomas's Hospital Medical School, produced books for a popular audience. Mottram wrote *Food and the Family*, as well as articles for *Homes and Gardens* magazine and the scripts for his own radio broadcasts. Plimmer and his wife Violet wrote *Food, Health, and Vitamins* in 1925. In 1938 the eighth edition appeared. The sheer volume of books published on nutrition, especially during the late 1930s, caused a reviewer in *Food Manufacture* to complain that 'it is with something akin to despair that one opens a new book on nutrition, as these have been precipitated by printing presses in almost alarming numbers during the last year or so'.[23]

This barrage of information did not come only from scientists who were themselves engaged in nutrition research. Advocates of the 'planning' of science to ensure the maximum social return such as Julian Huxley and J. D. Bernal promoted nutrition theory as an important example of how scientific research could be used to improve the quality of human life.[24] The British Medical Association produced a cookery book, *Family Cookery and Catering*, based on the principles of contemporary nutrition science. Extracts from it appeared widely in the popular press.[25] The extent of this publicity fuelled a widespread belief among scientists in industry that a 'diet-conscious public' had emerged, and that 'no food manufacturer could afford to underestimate' the commercial potential of this development.[26] Acting on this belief, research directors in industry began to devote resources to a range of nutrition investigations which led to the introduction of new products and the modification of existing lines, and encouraged references to the nutritional properties of products in advertising material.

Evidence of growing commercial interest and involvement in nutrition research in both the food and the pharmaceutical sectors emerges from a range of sources. From its inception the Food Group of the Society of Chemical Industry included papers on nutrition in its programme. By 1938 interest in this topic was considered sufficient to justify a separate Nutrition Panel within the group. This was the first scientific organisation which focused exclusively on nutrition.[27] Firms began to employ scientists with specific expertise in nutrition,[28] or more frequently encouraged existing employees to develop an interest in the field.[29] These scientists began to contribute articles on nutrition to academic journals such as the *Biochemical Journal*. In some firms, including Lever Brothers, Cadbury's and Glaxo,[30] separate sections devoted to nutrition research were established. Smaller firms without their own resources could purchase the expertise of private consultants. Vitamins Ltd, founded in 1927, offered its services to clients who required vitamin assays carried out by chemical, biological, micro-biological or spectroscopic means, as well as other consultancy services and technical advice. From a staff of six in 1935 it grew to eleven in 1946, qualified in sixteen specialities.[31] The Nutrition Department of the Pharmaceutical Society's Pharmacological Laboratories, directed by Katherine Coward, could also be consulted.[32] In addition manufacturers of scientific apparatus began to produce specialised equipment for testing vitamin preparations during commercial production.[33]

A measure of the development of this interest in nutritional issues can be derived from the number of articles in the trade technical press which dealt with the subject. *Food Manufacture*, which served scientists working in the food industry, included a substantial article on 'The present state of our knowledge of the vitamins' by R. F. Hunwicke of Glaxo in its first volume in 1927, on the grounds that 'the importance attached to the presence of vitamins in foodstuffs' had brought repeated enquiries on the subject, which the editor hoped would be answered thereby.[34] Both the number of articles and the range of topics grew steadily, peaking in the late 1930s (see Table 3.2).

Pharmaceutical Journal, which was aimed at the retail pharmacist, contained news of developments in medical research and therapeutic possibilities, and included an extensive section of advertisements through which manufacturers brought their wares to the attention of the retail trade. Reporting on nutrition took the form of short notes on new discoveries and products, and more extensive articles which presented new research findings, or related them to the pharmaceutical trade. Here too there is clear evidence of a growth in interest, reaching its height in the late 1930s (see Table 3.3).

EXCLUSIVE KNOWLEDGE BECOMES STANDARD PRACTICE

While the increasing number of articles on these topics, especially vitamins, gives an indication of growing interest in this field, it says

Table 3.2 Articles on vitamins and nutrition appearing in
Food Manufacture, volumes 1–13, 1927–38

Volume	Date	Vitamins	Nutrition	Total
1	05–10/27	4	–	4
2	11/27–04/28	2	–	2
3	05–12/28	2	3	5
4	1929	3	–	3
5	1930	6	–	6
6	1931	10	–	10
7	1932	9	–	9
8	1933	7	1	8
9	1934	11	1	12
10	1935	2	2	4*
11	1936	6	11	17
12	1937	13	–	13
13	1938	11	7	18

Notes Figures obtained by counting the number of index entries for each volume.
The journal was first published in 1927, hence this is the first year considered. In
1939 the journal amalgamated with Food Industries Weekly, and the figures are not
comparable.
* The low figure for 1935 can probably be attributed to the inclusion of a series of
papers presented at a conference on canned food and nutrition as a single item in
the index.

Table 3.3 Articles on vitamins and nutrition appearing in
Pharmaceutical Journal, 1910–1939, selected years

Year	Vitamins	Nutrition	Total
1910	–	2	2
1915	2	–	2
1920	4	–	4
1925	6	1	7
1930	9	–	9
1935	16	3	19
1939	19	2	21

Notes: Two volumes of the journal were produced each year – the figures give the
combined total from both.

little about the nature of that interest, of how it changed over time
or the reasons for the changes. Closer examination of these articles,
along with evidence from the archives of individual firms and other
sources, suggests that developments in the commercial exploitation
of vitamins can be divided into three phases. To start with, the
presence of scientists in a few firms led to the development of new
products which were formulated in line with the findings of

nutrition scientists. Heavy investment in both resources and personnel was required to overcome the technical problems they encountered in pioneering a new field. However, once standard techniques were established, and especially after vitamin concentrates became commercially available, the barriers to entry fell, and competition quickly became fierce. The number and variety of products grew steadily, as did the volume of advertising which included vitamins as part of the promotional message. The high public profile brought criticism of industrial practices from those who saw them as potentially damaging, putting profits before health considerations. Large manufacturers countered it by seeking to distance themselves from smaller and less technically sophisticated enterprises, by drawing attention to their own research programmes, and by pointing to their investment in scientific research as proof of responsible and reliable behaviour. They began to attack other enterprises which did not themselves follow this strategy, so that by the mid-1930s criticism of irresponsible commercial exploitation of vitamins came from within the ranks of industry as well as from outside.

Initial interest in nutrition science from within industry came from firms which had already established scientific laboratories, such as Lever Brothers and Cadbury. While interest within Cadbury at this point did not lead to any sustained programme of investigations,[35] at Lever Brothers research started during World War I into the vitaminisation of margarine and led to a prolonged interest in nutrition. Lever Brothers' experience indicates that any firm wishing to take advantage of new developments by adding vitamins to its products faced a complex task, involving the investment of considerable financial and human resources. By 1919 annual expenditure on the project had reached several thousand pounds, a large sum in terms of industrial research spending during this period.[36] Efforts centred on the production of a concentrate to add to margarine which would make its vitamin content comparable with that of butter. Initial research centred on fish liver oils, but the taste was hard to disguise, and it was not until 1927 that a marketable product emerged. To start with it had little commercial success, and not until several years later did vitaminised margarine begin to show a profit for the firm.[37]

Lever Brothers were not alone in discovering that turning nutritional knowledge into marketable products was a lengthy process. Colman's established a research department specifically to develop a new vitaminised infant food, initial attempts in the early 1920s having been condemned by Frederick Gowland Hopkins, Professor of Biochemistry at Cambridge University. He suggested to the firm that it should employ Leslie Harris, a Cambridge-trained biochemist, who joined Colman's in 1924.[38] After several years' work Harris and his research team produced 'Almata', which they claimed was a perfect substitute for mother's milk. Unfortunately for the firm, however, the technical merits of the product did not guarantee it high sales.[39]

While the commercial success of these pioneering projects was far from spectacular, other new vitamin products, notably those of Glaxo Laboratories, fared better. The strategy adopted by this firm, which involved exploiting processes developed initially by others, pointed to the dominant future trends more strongly than the experience of Lever Brothers and Colman's. Glaxo launched Ostelin Liquid, a vitamin D concentrate, in 1924, probably the first standardised vitamin preparation to appear in the United Kingdom. The firm had been involved in vitamin research for some years in relation to its dried milk business, and used contacts from this to take out a licence for a process developed in the United States by Theodore Zucker. This enabled Glaxo to produce a vitamin concentrate from cod liver oil. In 1929 it was replaced by irradiated ergosterol, a far more concentrated form of vitamin D, which was again produced under licence, this time using a process developed by Harry Steenbock, a biochemist working at the University of Wisconsin.[40] The development of the Steenbock process heralded a new stage in the commercialisation of vitamins. It meant that firms no longer needed to have access to their own sources of expertise or to invest in research to the extent that Lever Brothers and Colman's had done earlier. Instead they needed the financial resources to pay the licence fee demanded by the Wisconsin Alumni Research Foundation.[41] In 1932 pure crystalline vitamin D, calciferol, became widely available, and since only very small quantities were needed, the price of £6 per gram ensured that it was accessible to many firms. This further simplified the process of adding vitamin D to existing products, as calciferol was purer, chemically more stable, and easier to standardise than irradiated ergosterol had been.[42] Glaxo quickly adopted it for its vitamin D products.[43]

The decline in the cost and technical difficulties associated with vitaminisation made it feasible for an increasing number of firms to produce vitaminised products. There is evidence too that the potential of advertising campaigns was an added attraction for firms considering the possibility of using the process.[44] Products containing vitamin D, dubbed the 'sunshine vitamin', were particularly prominent. This vitamin received specific mention in advertisements for six of the twelve products promoted by drawing attention to their vitamin content in the *Daily Express* during one month in 1929.[45] Analysis of this publicity material provides an indication of the range of products to which vitamins were being added by that date, as well as revealing the way in which manufacturers and distributors of existing foodstuffs had begun to draw attention to vitamin content in order to boost sales.

A total of seventeen display advertisements for twelve different products which included the word 'vitamin' in their text appeared in the *Daily Express* during May 1929. These were for infant foods (Nestlé, Libby's, Cow & Gate, Allenbury's), food drinks (Allenbury's Diet, Postum), breakfast cereals (Muffets, Grape Nuts), fruit and vegetables (Sunkist oranges and Farrow's peas), bread (Turog) and Yeast-Vite, a dietary supplement. The vast majority of these advertisements were moderate in tone, pointing in a matter-of-fact way both to the presence of vitamins in the product and to the benefits that they would bring to the consumer. Vitamins were described as 'wonderful', 'precious body-building elements', 'essential for bone and muscle growth', and able to 'ensure the perfect formation of bones and teeth', but claims were fairly specific and generally reflected closely the kind of dietary advice given by academic nutrition researchers. The majority of the advertisements informed as well as persuaded, reinforcing the general association between vitamins and good health.

The advertisements for Yeast-Vite, however, adopted a very different tone. They were not only by far the largest, but they also made claims which went well beyond those used to promote other products. These included the speedy relief of a host of conditions ranging from rheumatism to constipation, insomnia and anaemia. Yeast-Vite was said to replace missing 'vitamin energy', contain 'powerful vitamin nutrition which cannot fail to benefit every nerve and fibre: every organ of the body, and every gland and cell' and Yeast-Vite represented a 'World's Record Fair-Play Good Health Offer'. These claims for a product whose credentials as a source of vitamins were loudly trumpeted fuelled the suspicions of scientists working outside industry, who already mistrusted commercial food processors, and they began to voice concern over manufacturing techniques.[46] Anxiety was expressed that the public was being misled by unsubstantiated claims and duped into buying preparations of dubious value rather than being educated to consume a balanced diet which would provide sufficient nutrition without recourse to expensive supplements. This attitude was summarised by V. H. Mottram, who wrote that 'for general purposes it is best to take an all-round, well-chosen, mixed diet rather than to rely on some special article of food, commercial preparation or drug'.[47] His views were echoed by other scientists in their popular texts. Critics of commercial practices were concerned that they would ultimately undermine the credibility of nutrition science as a whole in the public mind, since the unwary consumer would be unable to distinguish between information from reliable and unreliable sources.

Efforts were made by the academic nutrition establishment to retain some control over commercial developments by moving to establish the means by which vitamin preparations could be standardised and controlled. The Accessory Food Factors Committee of the Medical Research Council and the Lister Institute coordinated this work, which proved complex. Researchers at the Pharmaceutical Society laboratories provided the first success when in 1930 they devised a quantitative standard for vitamin D using irradiated ergosterol.[48] These efforts took on an international dimension with the establishment in 1931 of a League of Nations Committee on Vitamin Standards under the auspices of the Permanent Committee on Biological Standardisation. An initial conference in 1931 established preliminary standards, known as international units, which came into operation in 1932. Their success was reviewed by a second conference in 1934, which noted significant progress as well as some difficulties in the implementation of previous recommendations.[49]

The developing controversy over the proper manner in which to exploit nutritional knowledge was fuelled by a divergence of opinion both among nutrition researchers and between them and the health-care establishment regarding the best way to use nutrition science to improve the health of the nation. While academic nutrition researchers voiced concern about the commercial exploitation of nutrition science, a significant proportion of them at least shared with those working in industry the common goal of promoting the role of vitamins in public health.[50] This view of the fundamental importance of vitamins was not, however, shared by Sir George Newman, chief medical officer at the Ministry of Health, who favoured a more holistic approach to tackling health problems which included environmental concerns such as housing and sanitation as well as diet.[51] The attack which Newman launched in 1933 on the commercial exploitation of vitamins should thus be seen in the context of this reluctance to submit to pressure from those nutrition researchers who sought a more central role in public health for their emerging discipline.

In his report for 1932 Newman challenged what he regarded as 'a new problem in food adulteration', which he defined as 'the scientific "treatment" of food (sometimes described as "sophistication") at the hands of skilled chemists'. In this he included the '"fortification" of foods by artificially added vitamins', criticising what he regarded as the

> tendency at the present for manufacturers to avail themselves of the publicity value of recent vitamin research by adding [vitamins] empirically to a variety of foods without due consideration of the results which may accrue from such haphazard practices. If a halt is not called to this indiscriminate dosing of foods with vitamins there is a possibility of a disturbance in the balance of nutrition which may have wide-reaching effects and which it is not unreasonable to contemplate with some uneasiness.[52]

Newman also expressed concern about the problem of hypervitaminosis which might arise from the unregulated addition of vitamins to common foodstuffs.

Initial reaction from industrial chemists to Newman's remarks was angry. Leslie Lampitt, who as chief chemist of Lyons presided over one of the largest laboratories in the food industry, claimed that they had been unfairly characterised as 'diabolical' figures intent on the harmful sophistication of foods, and argued that in fact industrial chemists were the guardians of quality and purity, acting in the interests of the consumer to provide a cheap, hygienic food supply for the nation.[53] Larger manufacturers, including Cadbury's, began to draw attention to their research facilities in advertising material. This public commitment to research was one way in which enterprises could distance themselves from those commercial practices which had been attacked as irresponsible, linking their products instead with the image of science as a reliable protector of consumer interests.

This commitment to research was publicly demonstrated in a number of ways. Firms began to refer to their laboratories in advertisements, and some even included pictures of white-coated scientists surrounded by test tubes and microscopes. The long-standing practice of seeking the endorsement of products by individual members of the medical profession was modified to include the use of fictitious figures who extolled the virtues of vitamins or otherwise linked vitaminised products with good health.[54] Some firms, including Fyffe's, even designed their advertisements around the presentation of analytical data on food composition.[55] Industrial scientists were encouraged to publish the results of their work in academic and technical journals, providing publicity as well as demonstrating independent assessment of the quality of their work. At Cadbury's, for example, papers reporting the findings of research into the vitamin content of cacao shell and its use as a cattle fodder were published in *The Analyst, Biochemical Journal* and *Journal of the Society of Chemical Industry*.[56] Particularly worth noting in this context are the investigations carried out by scientists working for BDH into standardisation techniques, which resulted in a number of publications.[57] Not only were these used effectively for publicity purposes by the firm, but in 1935 two members of its scientific staff served on the Committee on Vitamins of the British Pharmacopoeia,[58] an acknowledgement of the expertise which had been built up in industry on this topic. Scientists working for Glaxo were also active contributors to the scientific literature, and Alfred Bacharach, a leading figure in industrial food science and later the first honorary treasurer of the Nutrition Society, was another member of this committee.[59] Another way in which producers could draw attention to their scientific credentials was by listing the vitamin potency of their products in terms of international units, and referring to standards laid out in the British Pharmacopoeia.[60]

As well as adopting a strategy which drew attention to their scientific credentials and which distanced their practices from those of less reputable firms, industrial scientists in both the food and the pharmaceutical industries sought to enforce their own procedures as standard practice throughout industry. To this end they prepared papers which stressed the advantages to be gained by the manufacturer adopting techniques such as standardisation. This topic was discussed by K. Culhane, S. W. F. Underhill and A.

L. Bacharach at a Food Group meeting in Manchester in 1933. The first two authors encouraged manufacturers to adopt standard-isation as an aid to economising on production costs.[61] Both *Food Manufacture* and *Food Industries Weekly*, which had a tradition of promoting the high technical standards associated with the largest manufacturers, encouraged other firms to adopt what they regard-ed as best practice. They held up as positive examples such practices as a requirement for the advertising department to submit all its material to the research department before any scientific claim could be used for publicity purposes.[62]

Signs soon began to appear that this strategy was paying off and that criticism from outside industry was being targeted on specific practices rather than indiscriminately. In 1933, in an exchange of correspondence in *Food Manufacture*, Jack Drummond, Professor of Biochemistry at University College London, defended the industry against the criticism that each manufacturer was exploiting 'an ignorant, fear-ridden public of his own creation' through 'advertise-ments shrieking from every hoarding concerning vitaminised foods'.[63] Drummond stated in response that while 'few would deny that the commercial exploitation of vitamins has often been abused . . . nowadays one rarely encounters a flagrant case of the public being misled'. He went on to add that 'it would be ungenerous to ignore the fact that many of the commercial firms have expended large sums of money on scientific research in order to improve the food value of their products'.[64]

While Drummond's support for the policy adopted by large manufacturers suggests some success, the increasing ease with which firms could enter this market meant that established enter-prises, which had invested heavily in research, continued to feel threatened by new competitors, and they maintained their efforts to define the boundaries of the legitimate commercialisation of nutritional knowledge. An article in *Food Manufacture* in 1936, for example, suggested that the public was being exploited by manufacturers who offered vitamins as a cure for 'numerous vague, borderline states of ill-health which often puzzle the physician and disable the patient'.[65] The following year in *Pharmaceutical Journal* the value of vitamin creams was questioned, with the author indicating that 'emphatic statements as to their cosmetic utility are to be found in trade and technical literature', but 'one seeks in vain for detailed reports of adequately controlled experiments'.[66] Arthur Knapp of Cadbury's, in a paper presented to the Society of

Chemical Industry annual meeting in Canada in 1938, argued for the adoption of a definite policy on the addition of vitamins to foodstuffs to ensure adequate diets, pointing out that

> if food manufacturers were to add one or more vitamin concentrates to foodstuffs in general the position would become confused. If the addition of vitamins to foodstuffs should develop without due consideration, the producer or manufacturer, in order to claim the presence of vitamin D, might add a mere trace which was so small as to be of no dietetic consequence.[67]

To guard against this possibility Knapp offered his support for the initiative of the American Medical Association, which sought to provide guidelines for manufacturers.[68] His words suggest that by that stage some industrial scientists had come to regard outside regulation as the best way of securing public confidence in their products and protecting their own market share.

The situation which had been reached after a little over two decades of commercial interest in vitamins can be summed up by considering the reaction to the opening by the Swiss firm, Roche, of a new plant to produce synthetic vitamin C and B_1 in Welwyn, Hertfordshire, in 1938. It was hailed as a 'landmark in the era of re-adjustable foods',[69] since the synthetic vitamins which it was to produce would significantly increase the scope for vitaminisation. The following year *Food Industries Weekly* encouraged its readers to take advantage of the new facility, since the addition of synthetic vitamins to their products 'would undoubtedly show good returns for the outlay involved'.[70] At the same time as they were making it easier for manufacturers who had not themselves been involved in extensive research to add vitamins to their products, Roche advertising stressed the availability of their own research chemists to assist such enterprises. Vitaminisation had developed from a process open only to a few to one accessible to manufacturers both large and small. At the same time those enterprises which had invested significant resources in scientific research continued to draw attention to the commitment as an important legitimation of their own actions, and sought to protect their investment by defining the boundaries of acceptable practice.[71]

CONCLUSION

By 1939 nutrition science, and especially the vitamin concept, had firmly established its place in both the food and the pharmaceutical industries. Scientists acknowledged as experts in the field were employed by leading enterprises, which devoted significant research resources to the production of new knowledge. As well as contributing to the growth of nutritional knowledge, industrial scientists had used that information to produce new products, modify existing lines and create new images for yet more. This commercialisation and the accompanying pursuit of nutritional knowledge brought the ideas of nutrition science into the public domain in two ways: first, by incorporating its findings within commodities which were bought and sold, and, second, through advertising, which was both educational and promotional. While the popularisation of the new ideas on nutrition had helped to create a market for such products in the first place, the activities of the commercial sector themselves formed a significant element within the process by which nutritional knowledge moved from the laboratory into the public domain. Control over this process was, however, contested as nutrition researchers in universities and government research establishments criticised commercial practices, leading to controversy and debate. Tension was heightened by those in the health establishment who were not convinced that vitamins played the vital role in health claimed for them by the commercial sector and nutrition researchers. Industrial scientists in large firms responded by adopting a strategy which drew attention to their research commitments, pointed to their shared interests with academic researchers, and emphasised the distance between themselves and smaller firms.

These events suggest the important role played by the commercial sector in the process by which scientific research into nutrition became widely known, accepted and adopted, pointing to the active role played by industry in determining both the way in which information was conveyed, and those aspects which received the most coverage. In particular they highlight the multiple functions which advertising served. For the manufacturers it was useful not only as a means of selling their products but also as a way of portraying a positive image of business practices. To the consumer it acted as a source for information about nutrition in general as well as drawing attention to specific products. For nutrition researchers in academic posts and government-funded institutes it was perceived as a threat, undermining their efforts to put their own message across. No single group was able by itself to determine precisely what entered the public domain, or in what manner it did so, leaving the consumer to make sense of a range of often conflicting messages and perspectives.

NOTES

The author wishes to thank conference participants, the editor and Paolo Palladino for comments on drafts of this chapter. The assistance of several archivists is also gratefully acknowledged.

1 A. W. Knapp, 'Vitamin D in foodstuffs: a discussion of policy', *Chemistry and Industry*, 1938, vol. 57, pp. 558–61.

2 M. Finlay, 'Quackery and cookery: Justus von Liebig's Extract of Meat and the theory of nutrition in the Victorian age', *Bulletin of the History of Medicine*, 1992, vol. 66, pp. 404–18; P. S. Brown, 'Medically qualified naturopaths and the General Medical Council', *Medical History*, 1991, vol. 35, pp. 50–77; R. D. Apple, '"Advertised by our loving friends": the infant formula industry and the creation of new pharmaceutical markets, 1870–1910', *Journal of the History of Medicine and Allied Sciences*, 1986, vol. 41, pp. 3–23.

3 E. V. McCollum, *The Newer Knowledge of Nutrition. The Use of Food for the Preservation of Vitality and Health*, New York, first edition 1918. McCollum's title was chosen to contrast the new era of nutrition investigations which began with the emergence of the vitamin concept with previous theories.

4 Examples include M. Mayhew, 'The 1930s nutrition controversy', *Journal of Contemporary History*, 1988, vol. 23, pp. 445–64; E. C. Petty, 'Primary research and public health: the prioritisation of nutrition research in inter-war Britain', in L. Bryder and J. Austoker (eds), *Historical Perspectives on the Medical Research Council*, Oxford, 1989, pp. 83–108; D. F. Smith, 'Nutrition in Britain in the Twentieth Century', unpublished Ph.D. thesis, University of Edinburgh, 1987.

5 R. T. P. Davenport-Hines and J. Slinn, *Glaxo. A History to 1962*, Cambridge, 1992; G. Tweedale, *At the Sign of the Plough. Allen & Hanburys and the British Pharmaceutical Industry, 1715–1990*, London, 1990; R. Fitzgerald, *Rowntree and the Marketing Revolution, 1862–1969*, Cambridge, 1994, p. 381; S. M. Horrocks, 'Consuming Science. Science, Technology and Food in Britain, 1870–1939', unpublished Ph.D. thesis, University of Manchester, 1993, chap. 5.

6 R. Apple, '"They need it now": science, advertising and vitamins, 1925–1940', *Journal of Popular Culture*, 1988, vol. 22, pp. 65–83, and 1986, op. cit.

7 The role of commercialisation in the 'popularisation' of science has rarely been discussed, a fact reflected in the analysis of the issue in R. Cooter and S. Pumfrey, 'Separate spheres and public places: reflections on the history of science popularization and science in popular culture', *History of Science*, 1994, vol. 32, pp. 237–67.

8 J. Liebenau, 'Corporate structure and research and development', in J. Liebenau (ed.), *The Challenge of New Technology*, Aldershot, 1988, pp.

30–42; D. E. H. Edgerton, 'Industrial research in the British photographic industry, 1879–1939', in Liebenau (ed.), pp. 106–34; E. M. Tansey and R. C. E. Milligan, 'The early history of the Wellcome Research Laboratories, 1894–1914', in J. Liebenau, G. J. Higby and E. Stroud (eds), *Pill Pedlars. Essays on the History of the Pharmaceutical Industry*, Madison, WI, 1990, pp. 91–106; Horrocks, 1993, op. cit., chap. 4.

9 Horrocks, 1993, op. cit., chap. 4.

10 J. Liebenau, 'The British success with penicillin', *Social Studies of Science*, 1987, vol. 17, pp. 69–86.

11 Horrocks, 1993, op. cit., chap. 4.

12 Liebenau, 'Corporate structure'. On the industry as a whole during this period see note 5 above and J. Slinn, *A History of May & Baker*, Cambridge, 1984; M. Robson, 'The Pharmaceutical Industry in Britain and France, 1919–39', unpublished Ph.D. thesis, London School of Economics, 1993.

13 Making distinctions of this kind is a problematic exercise, and they are used here to reflect contemporary perceptions and designations as to the nature of the work done in research departments.

14 Horrocks, 1993, op. cit., chaps 4 and 5, and Tansey and Milligan, 1990, op. cit.

15 For example, Annual Reports of the Chief Chemist, 1901–39, Cadbury Archives, Bournville (hereafter CA).

16 D. E. H. Edgerton and S. M. Horrocks, 'British industrial research and development before 1945', *Economic History Review*, 1994, vol. 67, pp. 213–38, table 3, p. 223. Liebenau, 'Corporate structure', p. 39, notes that during the five-year period 1936–41 Wellcome staff were responsible for 220 of the 307 publications which were authored by all staff at May & Baker, Wellcome, Glaxo, BDH and Boots.

17 These included Colman's and Cadbury; see Horrocks, 1993, op. cit., chap. 4.

18 L. H. Lampitt, *Laboratory Organisation*, London, 1935, p. 11.

19 Davenport-Hines and Slinn, 1992, op. cit., pp. 73–5.

20 League of Nations, *Final Report of the League of Nations Mixed Committee on the Relation of Nutrition to Health, Agriculture and Economic Policy*, Geneva, 1937, p. 146.

21 R. Graves and A. Hodge, *The Long Weekend*, London, reprinted 1985, pp. 189–90.

22 J. Burnett, *Plenty and Want*, London, third edition, 1989, p. 281.

23 T. Crosbie-Walsh, review of A. B. Callow, *Food and Health*, in *Food Manufacture*, 1938, vol. 13, p. 422.

24 J. Huxley, *Scientific Research and Social Needs*, London, 1934; J. D. Bernal, *The Social Function of Science*, London, 1939. P. G. Werskey, *The Visible College*, London, second edition 1988, is a collective biography of several of the leading socialist scientists of the 1930s, including Bernal.

25 British Medical Association Archives, Contemporary Medical Archives Centre, Wellcome Institute for the History of Medicine, BMA SC 33 and 33A.

26 Review of *Food, Health and Income* in *Food Manufacture*, 1936, vol. 11, p. 140. A similar sentiment was widely expressed during this period in this and other journals, including *Food Industries Weekly* and *Industrial Chemist*.

27 H. D. Kay, 'A short history of the Food Group', *Journal of the Science of Food and Agriculture*, 1972, vol. 23, pp. 127–60, and Horrocks, 1993, op. cit., chap. 7.

28 For example, Leslie Harris at Colman's, see below.

29 A. Churchman at Cadbury and Kathleen Culhane at BDH were examples of this trend. On Churchman see Horrocks, 1993, op. cit., chap. 5. For Culhane see R. Bramley, 'Kathleen Culhane Lathbury', *Chemistry in Britain*, May 1991, pp. 428–31.

30 The organisation of research at Cadbury is discussed in Horrocks, 1993, op. cit., chap. 5. On Lever Brothers see K. MacLennan, 'The evolution of margarine: Lever Brothers and vitamin research', *Progress*, 1928, No. 28, pp. 47–51 (*Progress* was the company magazine), and R. S. Morgan, 'Vitamins and health: Port Sunlight experience analysed', *Food Industries Weekly*, 12 July 1935, pp. 12–13. On Glaxo see Davenport-Hines and Slinn, 1992, op. cit., chap. 4.

31 The contribution of consultants to the technical development of British industry has been neglected by historians, and we have no clear idea of their number or activities. Details of the work of Vitamins Ltd are contained in 'Responses to Questionnaire B from Vitamins Ltd' and 'The Research Laboratories, Vitamins Limited', CBI MSS 200/F/T2/7/2 and MSS 200/F/3/T1/17.

32 On Coward see 'A new honorary member', *Pharmaceutical Journal*, 1937, vol. 84 (fourth series), p. 484. On the work of the laboratories see F. Wokes, 'Vitamins in relation to pharmacy', *Pharmaceutical Journal*, 1930, vol. 71 (fourth series), pp. 478–80. Its early history is discussed in S. W. F. Holloway, 'Producing experts, constructing expertise: the School of Pharmacy of the Pharmaceutical Society of Great Britain, 1842–1896', in V. Nutton and R. Porter (eds), *The History of Medical Education in Britain*, Amsterdam, 1995, pp. 116–40.

33 'Hilger Vitameter A', *Pharmaceutical Journal*, 1934, vol. 79 (fourth series), p. 478, discusses the fifth edition of a pamphlet detailing the use of the firm's apparatus for spectrophotometric testing of vitamin A concentration.

34 R. F. Hunwicke, 'The present state of our knowledge of vitamins', *Food Manufacture*, 1927, vol. 1, pp. 97–8.

35 Minutes of the Research Committee, 1919, CA, contains discussions concerning feeding experiments undertaken on rats which were not followed up or used for publicity purposes.

36 Food Investigation Board Committee on Oils and Fats, Minutes of Meeting, 21 May 1919, Public Record Office DSIR 6/94.

37 On this project see C. Wilson, *The History of Unilever. A Study in Economic Growth and Social Change*, London, 1954, vol. 1, pp. 306–7, and vol. 2, p. 338; MacLennan, 1928, op. cit.; 'Vitaminised margarines', *Industrial Chemist*, 1929, vol. 4, pp. 97–104.

38 See Chapter 2 of this volume for further details of Harris's career.

39 S. M. Horrocks, 'The business of vitamins: nutrition science and the food industry in interwar Britain', in H. Kamminga and A. Cunningham (eds), *The Science and Culture of Nutrition*, Amsterdam, 1995, pp. 235–58.

40 Glaxo's early research into vitamins and the products it produced are discussed in Davenport-Hines and Slinn, 1992, op. cit., pp. 68–97.

41 On Steenbock see R. Apple, 'Patenting university research: Harry Steenbock and the Wisconsin Alumni Research Foundation', *Isis*, 1989, vol. 80, pp. 375–94. In the mid-1930s the royalties paid by Glaxo for the use of the process were the fourth highest of thirty-one firms.

42 *Food Manufacture*, 1932, vol. 7, p. 4.

43 Davenport-Hines and Slinn, 1992, op. cit., p. 80.

44 Annual Reports of the Chief Chemist, 1929, CA.

45 *Daily Express*, May 1929.

46 Academic nutrition researchers in inter-war Britain frequently expressed the view that the commercial processing of foodstuffs lay at the heart of nutrition problems; for example, Plimmer and Plimmer, *Food, Health, and Vitamins*, London, 1925, p. 8, state that 'Machines and commercial processes have denatured common foodstuffs in such a way as to jeopardise health', while Jack Drummond singled out the introduction of roller milling as a commercial innovation which had done much harm to health. J. C. Drummond, *The Englishman's Food. A History of Five Centuries of English Diet*, London, reprinted 1991, pp. 388–90.

47 V. H. Mottram, *Food and the Family*, London, 1925, p. 34.

48 K. H. Coward was the author of the standard text on the subject, *The Biological Standardisation of Vitamins*, London, 1938. The adoption of the Pharmaceutical Society standard for vitamin D was reported in *Pharmaceutical Journal*, 1930, vol. 71 (fourth series), pp. 222–3.

49 K. H. Coward, 1938, op. cit., appendix 1.

50 This is not meant to imply that their motivations for promoting this goal were the same, simply that different interests pointed to similar conclusions in this case.

51 Petty, 1989, op. cit.

52 G. Newman, *On the State of the Public Health, 1932*, London, 1933, pp. 135–42.

53 *Chemistry and Industry*, 1933, vol. 52, pp. 965–7.

54 Examples include Cadbury's, Stork margarine and Trufood. See Horrocks, 1993, op. cit., chap. 5, and *The Times*, 5 May 1937, p. 18, and 7 May 1937, p. 21.

55 *The Times*, 19 May 1939, p. 12.

56 Full details of these papers are given in Cadbury Bros, *The Cadbury Laboratories*, Bournville, 1937.

57 British Drug Houses seems to have been one firm particularly active in the field of standardisation. See Bramley, 1991, op. cit., pp. 429–30, and F. J. Griffin, 'Obituary of Francis Howard Carr', *Chemistry and Industry*, 1969, vol. 88, p. 196. Carr was research director of BDH from 1920 to 1948. Standardisation featured in the firm's advertising to pharmacists. *Chemist and Druggist*, 15 January 1938, p. iv.

58 This committee was established in 1935 to produce an addendum to the 1932 Pharmacopoeia which took into account developments in the knowledge of vitamin structure and synthesis which affected the extent to which vitamin preparations were regarded as drugs rather than as foods. It sought to ensure that therapeutic preparations were properly standardised.

59 Obituaries appeared in *British Journal of Nutrition*, 1967, vol. 21, pp. 235–6, and *Chemistry and Industry*, 1966, vol. 85, pp. 1651–3.

60 In early 1934 *Pharmaceutical Journal* drew attention to calls made by Jack Drummond in *The Lancet* for manufacturers to use international units when expressing vitamin potency rather than vague terms such as 'rich in vitamins'. *Pharmaceutical Journal*, 1934, vol. 78 (fourth series), p. 80.

61 'The need for standardisation of products containing added vitamins', and 'The vitamin content of natural products', *Chemistry and Industry*, 1933, vol. 52, pp. 66–8 and 68–71.

62 *Food Manufacture*, 1935, vol. 10, pp. 54–5, and Annual Reports of the Chief Chemist, 1939, CA.

63 R. Whymper, 'Good food and vitamins', *Food Manufacture*, 1933, vol. 8, p. 276.

64 Letter from J. C. Drummond, *Food Manufacture*, 1933, vol. 8, p. 354.

65 'Vitamin pills', *Food Manufacture*, 1936, vol. 11, p. 118.

66 The latter provoked some debate as to its merits. See H. S. Redgrove, 'Vitamin creams', *Pharmaceutical Journal*, 1937, vol. 84 (fourth series), p. 399.

67 Knapp, 1938, op. cit.

68 'Permissible claims for vitamins: American medical recommendation', *Pharmaceutical Journal*, 1936, vol. 82 (fourth series), p. 659.

69 'Synthetic vitamins at Welwyn', *Food Manufacture*, 1938, vol. 13, p. 423.

70 '"Vitaminise" your foods and watch sales soar', *Food Industries Weekly*, 19 May 1939, p. 13.

71 'Roche synthetic vitamins: their significance to manufacturers of food products', *Food Industries Weekly*, 16 September 1938, p. 8. The advertisement goes on to say that 'Roche research chemists are experimenting on the practical application of these vitamins in the food industry and invite the co-operation of manufacturers and canners interested in increasing the health-giving qualities of their manufactured products and prepared foods'.

4

KING'S COLLEGE OF HOUSEHOLD AND SOCIAL SCIENCE

and the origins of dietetics education

Nancy L. Blakestad

King's College of Household and Social Science (KCHSS) – or, as it was renamed in 1953, Queen Elizabeth College, London – is most widely known in the historiography of nutrition in Britain as the backdrop to Edward Mellanby's pioneering experiments on the role of vitamins in rickets, which led to the discovery of vitamin D, and for instituting the first British B.Sc. in nutrition in 1953.[1] None the less, little has been written about KCHSS and its connection with the development of nutritional science in Britain, or about its contributions to the development of dietetics education and professionalisation.[2] KCHSS was the first to establish a college diploma in dietetics in 1933 and the first university to offer a postgraduate dietetics diploma in 1936. The B.Sc. in nutrition was only the final chapter in KCHSS's long history of teaching applied nutrition as part of its three-year 'household and social science' course – an applied science discipline focusing on the domestic sphere – which began in 1908 at King's College for Women and was established as a London B.Sc. course in 1920. In terms of the college's original ideals, the development of dietetics as a branch of household and social science (hereafter 'household science') was a more positive development than the nutrition B.Sc., which soon eclipsed household science in popularity and ultimately led to its demise in 1967. This chapter documents this neglected episode in the history of nutrition in Britain, tracing the origins of the discipline of household science in the context of the Edwardian women's movement and contemporary concern about the reform of 'the home' as an institution, the development of dietetics as a branch of household science in the inter-war period, and the influence of KCHSS in the early professionalisation of dietetics in Britain.

ORIGIN OF 'HOUSEHOLD SCIENCE'

KCHSS originated as a department of King's College for Women (KCW) in 1908, when a three-year course in 'home science' was inaugurated as a university training aimed at women working in 'social welfare' – whether as housewife/mother or in the many public health occupations opening to women such as factory and sanitary inspection and health visiting.[3] As stated in the first syllabus, the object was to provide 'a thoroughly scientific education in the principles underlying the whole organisation of Home life, the conduct of institutions, and other spheres of civic and social work in which the same principles are applicable'. The course was constructed around a core of sciences relevant to the domestic sphere (chemistry, biology, physiology, bacteriology and hygiene) together with economic history, practical cookery and housewifery, business methods, and an elective element (divinity, psychology, logic, English literature, ethics or another approved course).[4] In 1915 the course took on a more professional approach – the humanistic elements were abandoned in order to augment the scientific content and to introduce a third-year specialisation according to three career options: science and/or domestic science teaching, household and institutional administration, and social work.[5] Although initial enrolment numbers were small (only twelve students completed the course in 1911–13), a separate 'Home Science and Economics Department' was created as an independent university department in 1914 – largely because it had its own sizeable endowment fund – following the decision of the Royal Commission on the University of London (1909–13) to merge KCW's relatively impoverished art and science departments with King's College, Strand.[6] The home science department, which moved in that year into the new premises originally intended for KCW in Campden Hill Road, Kensington, was eventually given collegiate status, becoming 'King's College of Household and Social Science' in 1928, as it was known until 1953.[7] Following the introduction of the B.Sc. in household science in 1920 the annual number of household science graduates grew steadily over the inter-war period, from six in 1920 to a peak of forty-five in 1939.[8]

The concept of an applied science of the household as a

university subject was imported from the American Midwest, where the mid-nineteenth-century influx of immigrants into the prairie territories had caused concern in federal circles about the development of agriculture. The (Morrill) 'Land Grant' Act of 1862 and its supplement in 1890 provided federal funding for each state or territory to maintain or develop a college of agriculture and mechanical arts as a means of supporting rural life.[9] These 'Land Grant' colleges and universities were co-educational, and 'home economics' courses were introduced as an applied science for women. Originally many of these courses, generally elective elements of a broader 'liberal arts' curriculum, aimed only at increasing the efficiency of rural housewives through practical lessons in baking, canning and pickling.[10] Towards the end of the century, however, home economics developed into an academic discipline in its own right and aimed to foster research into the principles underlying the physical and social aspects of domestic life.[11] For example, the University of Chicago's Department of Household Administration, created in 1904, embodied one of the most scientific and research-based home economics programmes, which included courses on the social origins of the family, sociology, economics, physiology, food chemistry, and even the legal and economic position of women.[12] This shift towards a science-based discipline was in part due to the numbers of women scientists researching domestic-related such as topics in sanitation, water purity and food adulteration. Although some historians have noted that such topics were considered to be 'appropriate' subjects for women scientists, and that many women scientists were forced to work in home economics departments, others have pointed out that they were, nevertheless, frequently motivated by the same social reform ideals which informed their more traditional sisters in social work, teaching and nursing.[13]

The idea of establishing a 'home economics' course in Britain was the brainchild of Alice Ravenhill, a one-time hygiene lecturer and the first woman Fellow of the Royal Sanitary Institute, who was involved in many social welfare initiatives in late nineteenth- and early twentieth-century England.[14] Ravenhill, who had first heard about American home economics at the Paris Exhibition in 1900, was commissioned by Michael Sadler, head of the Board of Education's Department of Special Reports, to write a report on home economics in America in 1901.[15] Her fact-finding tour was organised by Ellen Swallow Richards, a chemist working in sanitation at the Massachusetts Institute of Technology who became the first president of the American Home Economics Association in 1908. Ravenhill visited many schools and universities across the Northeast and Midwest and parts of Canada, bringing her into contact with progressives such as Jane Addams of Hull House and John Dewey, the 'learn by doing' educational theorist. Ravenhill was so impressed with the American movement that she considered returning to train there herself:

> I was strongly disposed to resign my appointment and to enter myself as a student in one of the American university courses, thinking I might sooner attract the attention of those in England upon whom it depended to secure university recognition of household economics if I could present its claims from inside personal experience... But [Sadler] strongly dissuaded me from taking this step, confident that I should accomplish more by remaining in England.[16]

Upon her return Ravenhill was able to tap into a groundswell of support among a circle of women academics at the University of London who were critical of mainstream higher education and who believed it should be reformed to make it more relevant to modern life. Although Ravenhill provided the initial inspiration for the household science course, it was Thereza, Lady Rücker, wife of Sir Arthur Rücker, FRS, Principal of the University of London 1901–8, who provided the public leverage needed for its eventual realisation at KCW in 1908.[17] Lady Rücker, who had studied at Bedford College, had been inspired to campaign for a 'home science' course after hearing a speech on women's education by a friend of Ravenhill, Arthur Smithells, FRS, Professor of Chemistry and Pro-vice-chancellor of Leeds University, at a meeting of the British Association for the Advancement of Science in 1906. Lady Rücker believed that there should be a university course for women who wished to train as institutional administrators or teachers, or for the many new social reform careers.[18]

Although Lady Rücker had ties with Bedford College, King's College for Women provided a more fertile ground for the launching of the household science 'experiment'. Begun in 1871 to provide non-degree lecture courses for local 'ladies', KCW had not only continued to provide non-degree courses much longer than the other, more academically oriented London women's colleges, but had also instituted a popular 'household management' class in

1897 at the request of its students.[19] The Vice-principal of KCW from 1894 to 1907, Lilian M. Faithfull (a student of Somerville College, Oxford, who had taken a first in English in 1887), was receptive to the idea of extending these lectures into a full three-year course.[20] She resigned in 1907 to become headmistress of Cheltenham Ladies' College, but was replaced by another Somervillian and supporter of the household science ideals, Hilda D. Oakeley, who had taken a first in Literae Humaniores in 1898 and later a master's degree from McGill University in Montreal. Like Ravenhill, Oakeley had been influenced by visits to American women's colleges and universities. She had met both Alice Freeman Palmer, president of Wellesley, who had introduced practical housekeeping into the Wellesley curriculum, and Marion Talbot, proponent of the scientific home economics model at the University of Chicago.[21]

University women such as Oakeley, Rücker and Faithfull who were involved in the household science movement were critical of the masculine values enshrined in the universities and traditional disciplines. They believed that the universities had failed to address significant social and public health problems such as nutrition and hygiene because these problems related to the traditional sphere of women. Lady Rücker argued in 1910:

> The need for efficiency in technical affairs had forced the educational authorities to give degrees for the professions of Law, Medicine, Engineering, Veterinary Surgery, and Agriculture. Was it therefore too much to hope that the University would go a step further and recognise that inefficiency in women was as great a danger to the State as quackery in medicine?[22]

Lady Rücker and the other women promoting household science urged that the new generation of university women should challenge masculine values by taking 'the home' into the academy. Mabel Atkinson, an economics graduate of Glasgow University and suffrage campaigner who taught economics and ethics at KCW from 1908 to 1914, argued that the early women's higher education movement had conformed to a 'system of education framed for men and not for women' which consequently led to an 'undervaluation of domestic pursuits'.[23] Faithfull explained in her autobiography:

There seemed no reason why men should be able to take a degree in the special study which they required for their future work in life, such as agriculture or engineering, and women be debarred from obtaining the same recognition after pursuing an ordered course . . . of a university standard, specially designed to fit them for the work in life which most often falls to their share. Furthermore, a more rational treatment of the problems of the home was urgently demanded, and it was hoped that encouragement would be given to research in Chemistry, Bacteriology and other sciences which would prove to be of very real value.[24]

These university women – themselves products of the early women's higher education movement – were loath to criticise the pioneers of women's higher education for seeking to prove that women could compete intellectually with men, but they maintained that women had already 'won' their point and that the women's higher education movement urgently needed to reassess its goals in the light of twentieth-century social problems. As Atkinson argued, the first generation had followed the only acceptable path at the time but 'the problems which call for solution . . . have assumed a new form'.[25] Lady Rücker maintained that the high rate of infant mortality was a 'blot' upon the women's higher education movement:

[Women] have had to prove that they were capable of working on exactly the same lines as men; but thanks to the splendid band of university trained women, we have proved this up to the hilt, and we have now . . . to go further, and to carry the highest research into that field of activities which must ever occupy women.[26]

Oakeley and her colleagues stressed repeatedly that household science did not imply an attempt to limit women's choices in higher education; it merely aimed to provide the opportunity for *some* women to specialise in the subject under university auspices. The household science movement thus constituted a new dimension in women's higher education: it entailed, Oakeley argued, no 'backward-looking, no break in continuity or change' from the original ideals of the movement but merely a 'spreading or extension of their illumination'.[27]

The movement drew support from a number of progressive

male academics who were interested in modernising higher education and gained momentum through their involvement. Arthur Smithells was highly critical of 'pure' science and advanced the cause of the applied sciences, which he believed were more in touch with the needs of modern British industry.[28] Smithells's main interest in household science was to establish a scientific training course of university standard for domestic science teachers who were, at the time, also teaching general science to girls. He served as the chief scientific adviser to the household science Board of Studies from 1907.[29] Other supporters included Halford Mackinder (Principal of the London School of Economics), Herbert Jackson (FRS and Professor of Organic Chemistry at King's College) and Sir Arthur Rücker – all of whom were keenly interested in making higher education more relevant to the demands of the modern world.[30]

The interest of these women and men in creating an applied science of the household must be considered in the context of Edwardian preoccupation with the problems of the domestic sphere and how to reform it. The atmosphere of alarm about working-class health which led to the appointment of the Interdepartmental Committee on Physical Deterioration, together with the publication of George Newman's book on infant mortality in 1906, only served to heighten a more general national concern about a decline in 'home life' across *all* classes of society.[31] This theme occurred frequently in the Edwardian press and elicited much public discussion. The Bishop of Kensington declared at a meeting in 1909, for example, that English home life was 'disappearing', a trend which he blamed not only on the increasing number of women taking up paid work, but also on London society through an infatuation with hotel and club life.[32] The implications of industrialisation for domestic and social life were also beginning to be discussed in a more reflective vein. *The Times*, for example, commented in 1909 on how the home's traditional functions were being taken over by commercial firms – in catering, laundering and food processing – and how this affected domestic economics and organisation.[33] Other contemporary factors, such as suffragette militancy and the increasing numbers of women pursuing professional careers, provoked debate as to whether the modern woman was neglecting her domestic responsibilities.[34] Although this 'decline' in home life was largely an illusion created, as Jose Harris points out, by the rising 'moral and practical standards by which families were judged', the anxiety nevertheless prompted a new realisation of the importance of 'the home' to society.[35] Liberals and conservatives agreed that the home and family were the warp of society's moral fabric and the locus of national and even imperial stability, especially in an age of declining religious belief. In Jane Lewis's words, the household was regarded as the 'fundamental unit of the polis and as such the agent of social progress as well as the object of social reform'.[36]

However, anxiety about the quality of home life did not necessarily result in a back-to-the-home traditionalist crusade against the modern woman. Although there were some (largely male anti-suffragists) who believed this to be the best solution, others were supportive of the changes in women's social position and prepared to consider potentially radical solutions to domestic problems. For example, *The Times Woman's Supplement* commented in 1910 that although the English home was 'not what it used to be' it was wrong to blame the 'advanced woman':

> It must be remembered that, when conditions change, it is not always through neglected duties or increased self-seeking. . . [T]he duty of each generation is not to render stubborn resistance to inevitable change, but to make the best use of its own conditions.[37]

There was much discussion in the Edwardian period about 'co-operative' living, whereby families would dine in communal kitchens and share cleaning, laundry and child-care arrangements. The concept was not new in England, but was revived in the early 1900s by the American feminist Charlotte Perkins Gilman, whose books provided a radical critique of 'the home' and the social position of women.[38] Although she was actually opposed to families 'co-operating' in housekeeping duties (advocating instead that housework should be done by paid professionals), Gilman's campaign for 'kitchenless' houses was taken up by those promoting communal housing developments and inspired other schemes of household reorganisation in Britain. A 'Society for the Promotion of Co-operative Housekeeping and House-Service' was created in 1911 by Alice Melvin, an enthusiast of the 'garden city' movement.[39] The Fabian Society appointed a 'Committee to Reorganise Domestic Work' in 1914, and H. G. Wells enshrined the 'kitchenless' concept in his book *A Modern Utopia* (1905).[40]

Supporters of household science at King's College for Women likewise subscribed to the Gilmanesque view that 'the home' was 'not fulfilling its function' as a social institution and that reforms were necessary. Ravenhill argued in 1903 that the household had somehow been bypassed by the technological and scientific revolution which had transformed industry, and that habit and custom were thwarting the 'legitimate changes consequent upon social development'.[41] Nevertheless, the household science movement embodied a more theoretical approach to domestic problems than that of Gilman. Ravenhill and others of the 'inner circle' believed that it was society's failure to discover and apply the underlying scientific principles of domestic life that was at the root of domestic inefficiency, ill health and, ultimately, social disharmony. Ravenhill wrote in 1910:

> To waste time, energy and money merely on the palliation of symptoms is now recognised as false economics and misplaced philanthropy; therefore, the duty of tracing symptoms to causes must become paramount, and the knowledge must be acquired [of] how to remove these causes with courage, tact, and resource; otherwise the balance wheel of human efficiency, instead of being redressed by the regulators of our social machinery, will be but further, though perhaps less obviously, disturbed.[42]

Supporters of household science believed that domestic reforms must thus be based on firm scientific and social-scientific principles; reforms which merely focused on improving women's housewifery skills or 'reorganising' household functions, they argued, treated the symptoms rather than the causes of domestic ills and might even reinforce harmful, unscientific 'rule-of-thumb' practices.[43] This view found support in the press. *The Times* proclaimed in 1907, 'The time has gone by for instructing merely in details ... the hour has come for studying broad underlying principles'.[44] An editorial in *Education* observed:

> [L]ittle encouragement or facility has been afforded to ... delve into the scientific foundations of arts strongly tinctured with the flavour of drudgery, or to raise their study to a plane which would permit a truer estimate to be formed of their intimate connexion with national efficiency or which would allow their wide scope to be seen in true perspective.[45]

Ravenhill, who had met Frederick Gowland Hopkins, the pioneer of vitamin research, at a University Extension meeting at Cambridge in 1903, argued that no attempt was being made to apply new advances in nutrition to the everyday problems faced by women in feeding their families.[46] The idea of 'household science' was thus to bring together the relevant scientific disciplines (biology, physiology, chemistry, physics), combining them with elements of economics, ethics and other social sciences, and to teach them with special emphasis on their domestic applications: food and nutrition, personal and domestic hygiene, housing, and social and civic life.

THE DEVELOPMENT OF DIETETICS AS A BRANCH OF 'HOUSEHOLD SCIENCE'

Although intended to address the scientific problems of the domestic sphere in all its many facets, the household science discipline nevertheless developed a strong emphasis on applied nutrition during the inter-war period. This was due to a number of factors. There was, for example, a steady growth in demand for women with a solid training in cookery and dietary principles in domestic science teaching, school meal services, hospital diet kitchens, the food-processing industry and factory canteen management. In addition, there was continuing public concern about the nutritional status of the working-class population. Finally, the household science approach to the problems of social welfare, based predominantly upon the natural sciences, was quickly eclipsed by the London School of Economics and other university social science departments which emphasised socio-economic aspects of social welfare.[47]

The emergence of applied nutrition as the predominant focus of the discipline owed much to the influence of Vernon Henry Mottram, Professor of Physiology at KCHSS from 1920 to 1944. Like his predecessor, Edward Mellanby, Mottram had also studied at Cambridge and had worked as a demonstrator for Hopkins, but, in contrast to Mellanby's laboratory and clinical research, Mottram's interests were closer to the kitchen – the correct preparation of food to maintain nutritive quality, the construction of special diets, and low-cost alternative foods for working-class budgets. These interests, which reflected Mottram's long-standing socialist sympathies, were characterised in a KCHSS student poem:

> Good temper triumphed in his face,
> And in his heart he found a place
> For all the ailing human race –
> And every wretched fellow.

> It made him very sad to think
> That some get fat while others shrink.
> Now what to eat or what to drink,
> It's *food* that builds the body.[48]

Mottram, like Mellanby, later became involved in the nutrition controversies of the 1930s. Mottram was a member of both the British Medical Association's Nutrition Committee and the Ministry of Health's Advisory Committee on Nutrition,[49] but he was most widely known for his public lectures and BBC radio broadcasts, and for popularised versions of his research such as *Food and the Family* (1925), *Sound Catering for Hard Times* (1932), and *A Manual of Modern Cookery* (1927), co-written with Jessie Lindsay, head of KCHSS's Household Arts Department.[50]

Mottram's interest in practical nutrition had been kindled across the Atlantic in 1915 after hearing the nutritionist Graham Lusk give an account of the caloric value of food served in a popular restaurant chain. Mottram later recalled:

> It was the first, and rather electric, time that I'd seen any practical application of the study of nutrition to practical affairs of life. I was enormously impressed. . . I was still full of the idea when I came back to England & when I saw the advertisement of the Chair in Physiology . . . tenable at KCW . . . I leapt at the idea of putting in for it with a view to plugging nutrition.[51]

Despite this enthusiasm Mottram found it difficult to persuade KCHSS's Academic Board to develop a separate professional dietetics course. Mottram made several attempts in the late 1920s, but later noted that the Board was 'always scared of expense . . . and new ideas':

> There were difficulties all round. Money was tight. People in the College and in the department even were agin the idea. I know that it was difficult going and I wish I'd kept a letter from Graham Lusk in which he characterised my attitude about dietetics in Great Britain as one of 'humorous despair'.[52]

The academic reasoning of those 'agin the idea' is not recorded; it appears, however, that money may have been the deciding factor. The college had recognised its failure to keep pace with American standards in nutrition education as early as 1913. Following a tour of North America, the Warden, Janet Lane Claypon (a medical doctor who was active in the child welfare movement), reported to the college executive committee that KCW was 'deficient, and very markedly deficient, in the teaching of nutrition in its widest sense'.[53] None the less, the precariousness of the college's finances in the 1920s, as KCHSS struggled under the burdens of developing the site in Campden Hill, placed severe constraints on the college in developing the curriculum, promoting research or introducing new courses.[54]

KCHSS's reluctance to institute a special dietetics course was also due to the success of its household science graduates in carving out a strong professional niche in hospital dietetics, where their combined training in physiology, biochemistry and food preparation was increasingly being recognised. However, dietetics had originated as a specialisation within the nursing profession, as the feeding of patients fell within a nurse's responsibility, and many of the early hospital dietetics departments in Britain had been established by sister dietitians. Edinburgh's Royal Infirmary created the first in 1924 (headed by Ruth Pybus), followed in 1925 by the London Hospital (Rose Simmonds), and St Thomas's Hospital (W. Tancred).[55] As the work became more technical, hospitals began to recruit science graduates to organise dietetics departments. University College Hospital appointed the first graduate, Elspeth M. Marshall (KCHSS 1922–5), in 1928, followed shortly afterwards by St Bartholomew's Hospital, where an Oxford graduate, Margery Abrahams, was appointed at Mottram's suggestion.[56] KCHSS graduates rapidly built up a professional reputation and were much sought after by hospital administrators. In the early 1930s no fewer than seven prominent hospitals opened dietetic departments with household science graduates at their heads: the Royal Northern, Holloway (O. Clendinnen, KCHSS 1923–8); David Lewis Northern Hospital, Liverpool (F. J. Keay, KCHSS 1925–8); Radcliffe Infirmary, Oxford (A. M. Waterhouse, KCHSS 1928–32); Addenbrooke's Hospital, Cambridge (J. I. Mills, KCHSS 1927–30); Royal Masonic Hospital, London (B. J. Jamieson, KCHSS 1928–32); Royal Infirmary, Manchester (M. R. Muriel, KCHSS 1929–31); and Middlesex Hospital (established by Marshall and developed by M. V. Scott Carmichael, KCHSS 1929–32).[57]

Yet, despite this apparent success, Mottram had been sending his protégées to the United States for additional professional training, where dietetics education was more advanced. The American Dietetic Association had been formed in 1917, and most American home economics departments offered dietetics courses by the early 1920s.[58] Abrahams was sent by Mottram to study at Columbia University, where she received a master's degree in nutrition and institutional management.[59] Abrahams, Marshall and Tancred's successor at St Thomas's, M. C. Broatch (KCHSS 1919–21), as well as the three pioneering sister dietitians (Pybus, Simmonds and Tancred), were all awarded travelling fellowships by the Rockefeller Foundation to study for a year or more in North America.[60] Marshall's fellowship enabled her to observe dietetics teaching and practice in various centres throughout the North-east and Mid-west, and she studied briefly at Teachers College, Columbia University, under the eminent nutritionist Mary Swartz Rose.[61]

In the end it was only external pressure which allowed Mottram to establish a professional dietetics course. In March 1930 Helene Reynard (KCHSS Warden 1925–45) reported to the academic board that 'requests were continually being received from various sources for the establishment of a course in dietetics', and asked Mottram to draw up a syllabus.[62] Mottram originally prepared a postgraduate syllabus, but the scheme launched in 1930 was a modest venture, consisting of a term-long evening course providing twenty hours of lectures and forty hours of practicals as an introduction for nurses, domestic science students, social welfare workers and caterers. By 1932, however, KCHSS's executive committee was coming at last to recognise the necessity of consolidating the college's unique position in dietetics education in Britain in the face of growing competition from hospitals and domestic science colleges, many of which were organising their own dietetics courses. The Royal Infirmary, Edinburgh, accepted both domestic science teachers and science graduates for a six-month training course, and both St Thomas's and the London Hospital offered dietetics training for nurses in 1928. Short courses were also being set up at domestic science colleges to train women for positions in school meal services and institutional catering.[63] The Glasgow and West of Scotland College of Domestic Science was the first to inaugurate a systematic course in 1927, and the Gloucestershire Training College of Domestic Subjects instituted a diploma in dietetic therapy in collaboration with a London hospital (c. 1930).[64] The type of training offered on these courses varied considerably, especially with regard to scientific content. Glasgow's course required only one term's study of chemistry and physiology, for example, whereas KCHSS's B.Sc. course required three.[65] A report in October 1932 that a 'London School of Dietetics' providing short practical courses had sprung up on KCHSS's doorstep thus caused great consternation among the graduate dietitians and spurred the college into action. KCHSS swiftly inaugurated a one-year college dietetics diploma in 1933.[66]

CHALLENGES FROM THE MEDICAL AND NURSING PROFESSIONS

Reconsideration of KCHSS's position was also hastened by the stirring of professionalisation among both graduate and nurse dietitians, who were concerned about the growing tendency for the title 'dietitian' to be used by persons with what they considered substandard qualifications. Some 'dietitians' held a three-year degree as well as dietetics and catering certificates; at the other extreme, some had only a domestic science certificate with six weeks' worth of nutrition.[67] In order to safeguard the profession from the latter type, the four leading London dietitians (Marshall, Simmons, Abrahams and Broatch) set up a working committee in 1932 to discuss the creation of a professional dietetics association. The committee included members of the medical profession and was chaired by Dr John McNee, a noted pathologist and Professor of Medicine at Glasgow University.[68]

The immediate threat to KCHSS's pre-eminent position in dietetics education came not from among the dietitians themselves, however, but from the medical profession. McNee, who had championed the graduates' cause for an academic training, was forced to relinquish the chair to Lord Dawson of Penn, president of the Royal College of Physicians (RCP) and honorary physician at the London Hospital, who suddenly appeared at one of the meetings.[69] Dawson had been informed about the committee's discussions by Rose Simmonds, the head nurse dietitian at the London Hospital, who was anxious to secure influential support for the nurses.[70] Dawson set up a dietetics committee in October 1933 under the auspices of the RCP, inviting representatives from the nursing and medical professions, graduate dietitians and academics in order to establish standards for training within the budding profession. The involvement of the medical profession in negotiations was ostensibly to 'secure its rightful practice by giving the subject recognition and guidance'; however, Dawson's pre-occupation with establishing a 'portal of entry' for nurses in the profession was also motivated by a desire to ensure that dietitians remained subordinate to doctors, as they would do if dietetics remained within the nursing profession.[71]

The point of dispute between the graduate and nurse dietitians on the RCP committee was not the issue of a creating a 'portal of entry' for nurses within the profession itself – relations between Simmonds and her three graduate colleagues were congenial, although there was a difference of opinion between the two groups about the relative merits of the nurse's training in bedside manner and the graduate's scientific knowledge.[72] The dispute centred rather on the length of the scientific training for intending nurse dietitians as well as the status of the graduate dietitian within the hospital hierarchy. The graduates were concerned to ensure the dietitian's professional independence from the nursing profession, as in some hospitals the dietitian worked under the charge of ward matrons.[73] Marshall, for example, had encountered open hostility at University College Hospital from the ward nurses, who thought it 'terrible' that a young graduate should be allowed to completely take over the feeding of certain patients.[74] The graduate dietitians were also anxious that their pay and status would be reduced to that of a nurse – a level that was not commensurate with the graduate's longer and more costly education. One unsigned memo, for example, charged the London Hospital with making a 'gorgeous convenience' of Simmonds by failing to give her an appropriately high status.[75] Fearful that the RCP committee would undermine the strong position established by KCHSS graduates in hospital dietetics, the graduate dietitians succeeded in having Helene Reynard seconded to the committee to reinforce Mottram in protecting their interests.[76]

The protracted discussions in Dawson's RCP committee revolved around establishing the length of the scientific training which should be given to nurse dietitians. This was a particular concern for both KCHSS and the graduates, as Dawson was pushing to create a separate dietetics diploma for nurses, domestic science teachers, factory canteen managers and others working in food-related occupations, which would have undermined the status of KCHSS's own household science degree and the college dietetics diploma.[77] The graduates maintained that nurse dietitians should undergo at least a two-year scientific training if not a three-year degree course, but Simmonds pointed out that most nurses could not afford this and suggested that a one-year science course would be sufficient.[78] There was considerable pressure to make some allowance for the nursing profession: the London County Council, anxious to train some of its nurses, threatened to establish its own course if nothing could be agreed.[79] Although a compromise was eventually reached, based on an eighteen-month theoretical course (plus one year of practical training) for nurse dietitians, Mottram and Reynard succeeded in bringing this course under the auspices of KCHSS by arranging a one-year preliminary science course which would enable non-graduates to receive the KCHSS dietetics diploma in two years.

Despite the concessions made to the nursing profession, KCHSS was unwilling to sacrifice its autonomy in pursuing its own objectives in dietetics education. Quite independently of these negotiations KCHSS's executive committee applied to the university senate for the institution of a university postgraduate diploma based on the existing college diploma and open only to approved university graduates, medical practitioners or others who had the requisite science education and experience.[80] This infuriated Lord Dawson, who had assumed that the RCP committee was working to create a new joint dietetics diploma under the auspices of KCHSS and the Royal Colleges.[81] He charged Reynard and Mottram with duplicity, but Reynard countered that she and Mottram had been sitting on his committee in a private capacity and that KCHSS's administration had never been approached officially about any joint proposal.[82] Dawson continued to press for a joint KCHSS/RCP non-graduate diploma but it was never instituted, in part because the Royal College of Surgeons baulked at the idea of awarding non-medical diplomas.[83]

The new postgraduate diploma, inaugurated at KCHSS in 1936, involved two terms of theoretical work and six months of practical work in diet and general hospital kitchens. Examinations were held in chemistry and the physiology of nutrition, the principles of dietetics, diet and disease, and large-scale catering, together with a six-hour practical exam in cookery and the construction of special diets.[84] Nurses and domestic science students were not altogether excluded from the profession, however, as they were still eligible for the diploma if they held the requisite science credentials, and training continued to be given at the various hospitals – for example, at the Royal Infirmary, Edinburgh, where Miss Pybus had opened a School of Dietetics in 1934 (which also admitted non-nursing students), and at the Glasgow and West of Scotland College of Domestic Science.[85] Yet despite the continuation of non-degree students in the dietetics profession in this period, the influence of KCHSS graduates in the early years of the profession was considerable. The British Dietetics Association, finally organised in 1935, had no fewer than six KCHSS graduates (out of eight members) on the first executive committee.[86] KCHSS was therefore able to ensure that science standards in the budding profession were sufficiently high and to maintain its pre-eminence in dietetics education.[87]

CONCLUSION

The dietetics postgraduate diploma, combining theoretical with practical work, marked the apogee of household science's success, but in terms of its original goal – to create a new discipline addressing the domestic sphere as a whole – the household science movement was a failure in Britain. To a large extent its demise can be ascribed to financial constraints, which limited KCHSS's ability to establish a solid interdisciplinary research base and thus a claim to 'academic territory' *vis-à-vis* other disciplines.[88] Yet, apart from purely academic concerns, its demise must also be seen in relation to broader social trends in the inter-war period. The continued concern about the ill health and malnutrition of the working classes, combined with financial retrenchment, heightened the demand for expedient and direct solutions to social ills. Contemporary opinion was divided between those who attributed nutritional deficiencies chiefly to poverty and those who blamed the ignorance of the working-class housewife, but for both groups the remedies were essentially pragmatic – either family allowances, free school milk and meals, or domestic science classes and child-care clinics.[89] There was thus little support for the indirect, academic solutions to social reform embodied in the household science movement.

At the same time, specialisation within the constituent disciplines of household science fragmented the original unifying element of the course, which had been based on an increasingly irrelevant conception of women's roles in social welfare. At the time of the founding of the household science course in 1908, women's 'domestic' roles were seen to embrace a broad spectrum of activities such as child-care, nutrition and hygiene, which extended beyond the walls of the home to the broader community. This 'municipal housekeeping' concept of women's roles and responsibilities was initially used to justify middle-class women's involvement in voluntary work, but inevitably also their entry into paid professional work.[90] For the women of the household science movement, the educated woman's duty to reconstruct 'the home' through the application of science was thus a natural extension of these 'domestic' responsibilities. Yet the desire for a scientific understanding of 'home life' – food, economics, hygiene and sociology – paradoxically served to sever their connection with the domestic sphere. Thus the 'municipal housekeeping' concept was quickly eroded in the inter-war period as women's social welfare roles such as health visiting and sanitary inspection were professionalised and removed from the home. Moreover, the advancing medicalisation of health care in the early twentieth century also served to heighten the role of the medical or scientific 'expert'. Perry Williams's analysis of nineteenth-century women sanitary reformers points out that the advance of medical science eroded a Victorian concept of sanitary reform which was predicated on the principle that 'good health was a product of good housekeeping' and which included considerations of air, diet, clothing and even emotional states.[91] Household science had sought to work within modern scientific paradigms and to develop a new type of scientific expert, yet its interdisciplinary approach to social problems, based on a similar holistic notion of women's domestic roles, was equally subject to displacement by specialist experts as the twentieth century progressed.

KCHSS had prevented the medicalisation of dietetics, yet the emergence of dietetics was itself a product of the drive towards specialisation. KCHSS's increasing emphasis on the scientific aspects of food, which had played such a crucial factor in its success in dietetics, ultimately led to rejection of the household science approach to the study of food in all its aspects (chemical, social, economic) in favour of the more specialised 'pure' discipline of nutrition, as is seen in the post-1939 developments. The college had originally considered creating a four-year dietetics degree based upon the existing household science curriculum in the early 1940s, but this model was eventually rejected as too 'diffuse' and 'superficial' and the B.Sc. in nutrition was instituted instead.[92] The inclusion of cookery in the new degree was a legacy of the household science movement; however, the euphemistic labelling of cookery as 'the preparation of food for human consumption', in the nutrition curriculum, together with the renaming of the college as 'Queen Elizabeth College' in 1953 – when men were admitted for the first time – marked the final rejection of the household science movement's attempt to create a broader intellectual foundation for nutrition and other socially relevant subjects.[93] The household science course deteriorated rapidly thereafter, attracting on average only six students a year. It was discontinued in 1967, when the Department of Household Science was renamed the 'Department of Food and Management Science'; this department merged with the Nutrition Department in the 1970s to become the 'Department of Food Science and Nutrition'.[94] The last remnants of the household science legacy were eliminated with the dismantling of QEC's Food Science Department in the late 1980s.[95] The dietetics diploma continued to be offered in the post-war period, but its status, like that of household science, quickly faded as QEC evolved a more general 'pure' science profile.[96] KCHSS's expertise in dietetics was thus ceded to the domestic science colleges and the polytechnics where more practically oriented dietetics courses continue to flourish.[97]

NOTES

The archives of KCW and KCHSS are held at King's College London, Strand. The following abbreviations are used in conjunction with KCHSS references: AB/ABM = Academic Board/Academic Board Minutes; EC/ECM = Executive Committee/Executive Committee Minutes. Material referred to as PJF comes from the collection of a former KCHSS student, Patty Jarvis Fisher, which was subsequently destroyed after her death in 1991; copies of the letters cited here are in the author's possession. RCP refers to the archives of the Royal College of Physicians. CMAC refers to the Contemporary Medical Archives Centre of the Wellcome Institute for the History of Medicine, London. I am grateful to the above institutions for permission to cite from their archives. I am also grateful to Elspeth M. Averill (née Marshall), who gave much valuable information about KCHSS and the early dietetics profession, and to Martin Mottram, who provided insights into the motivations of his father, V. H. Mottram.

1 This chapter is developed from N. L. Blakestad, 'King's College of Household and Social Science and the Household Science Movement in English Higher Education, c. 1908–1939', unpublished D.Phil. thesis, Oxford University, 1994. For an overview of the college's history see N. Marsh, *The History of Queen Elizabeth College. One Hundred Years of University Education in Kensington*, London, 1986. See also J. Yudkin,

'Degrees in Nutrition at London University', *BNF Nutrition Bulletin*, 1990, vol. 15, pp. 191–5.

2 The exception is D. F. Smith, 'Nutrition in Britain in the Twentieth Century', unpublished Ph.D. thesis, University of Edinburgh, 1986.

3 The course was originally 'home science', then 'home science and economics' and finally 'household and social science'. Blakestad, 1994, op. cit., pp. 143 f.

4 *Syllabus of Lectures, King's College for Women*, KCHSS: KCW/SYL16, 1908–9.

5 *Syllabus of Classes, Household & Social Science Department, Session 1915–16*, KCHSS: QEPH/SYL/3, pp. 14–17.

6 See Marsh, 1986, op. cit., pp. 46–57.

7 Queen Elizabeth College was amalgamated with Chelsea College and King's College (Strand) in 1985.

8 For numbers of students see Blakestad, 1994, op. cit., Appendix C, p. 405.

9 C. F. Langworthy, 'Department of Agriculture and Home Economics', *Lake Placid Conference on Home Economics. Proceedings of the Seventh Annual Conference, June 26–July 1 1905*, Lake Placid, NY, 1906, p. 150.

10 A. Chown, 'Courses in home economics for colleges and universities', *Lake Placid Conference on Home Economics. Proceedings of the First, Second and Third Conferences*, Lake Placid, NY, 1901, pp. 79, 107–9.

11 E. S. Eppright and E. S. Ferguson, *A Century of Home Economics at Iowa State University. A Proud Past, a Lively Present, a Future Promise*, Ames, IA, 1971, pp. 3–9.

12 A. P. Norton, 'Reports from colleges which have introduced home economics', *Proceedings from the Sixth Lake Placid Conference*, Lake Placid, NY, 1904, p. 40; E. Fitzpatrick, *Endless Crusade. Women Social Scientists and Progressive Reform*, New York, 1990, pp. 81–7.

13 M. Rossiter, *Women Scientists in America. Struggles and Strategies to 1940*, Baltimore, MD, 1982, pp. 64–5; P. M. Glazer and M. Slater, *Unequal Colleagues. The Entrance of Women into the Professions, 1890–1940*, New Brunswick, NY, 1987, p. 145.

14 A. Ravenhill, *Memoirs of an Educational Pioneer*, Toronto, 1951.

15 A. Ravenhill, 'School training for the home duties of women', I, 'The teaching of "Domestic Science" in the United States of America', *Special Reports on Educational Subjects*, PP xxvi, 1905.

16 Ravenhill, 1951, op. cit., p. 123.

17 Lady Rücker was a member of Annan's 'intellectual aristocracy'. N. G. Annan, 'The intellectual aristocracy', *Studies in Social History. A Tribute to G. M. Trevelyan*, London, 1955, p. 269.

18 M.R.T. [M. R. Taylor], 'The day of small things', *The Magazine of the Household & Social Science Department*, KCHSS: Q /SER5/1, May 1920, pp. 32–3; A. Smithells, 'School training for home duties of women', *Report of the Seventy-sixth Meeting of the British Association for the Advancement of Science, York, August 1906*, London, 1907, pp. 781–4.

19 G. Sutherland, 'The movement for the higher education of women: its social and intellectual context in England, *c.* 1840–80', in P. J. Waller

(ed.), *Politics and Social Change in Modern Britain. Essays Presented to A. F. Thompson*, Brighton, 1987, p. 43.

20 L. M. Faithfull, *In the House of My Pilgrimage*, London, 1924, pp. 121–2.

21 H. D. Oakeley, *My Adventures in Education*, London, 1939, pp. 111–12, 116–17; R. Wein, 'Women's colleges and domesticity, 1875–1918', *History of Education Quarterly*, Spring 1974, pp. 35–9.

22 'University standard in home science', *Education*, vol. xvi, No. 312, 1 July 1910, p. 9.

23 M. Atkinson, 'The economic relations of the household', in A. Ravenhill and C. Schiff (eds), *Household Administration. Its Place in the Higher Education of Women*, New York, 1911, pp. 174–5.

24 Faithfull, 1924, op. cit., p. 122.

25 Atkinson, 1911, op. cit., pp. 174–5.

26 'ATDS annual meeting: May 8, 1908', *Education*, vol. xi, No. 282, 22 May 1908, p. 379.

27 'Hostel and laboratories for home science', *Education*, vol. xxiv, No. 601, 3 July 1914, p. 14.

28 A. Smithells, 'The university and women's work', in *From a Modern University. Some Aims and Aspirations of Science*, London, 1921, pp. 68–9.

29 Smithells to Lady Rücker, 27 June 1907, KCHSS: QA/CC/70.

30 I. Goodson, 'Becoming a school subject', in *The Making of Curriculum. Collected Essays*, London, 1988, pp. 166–72.

31 G. Newman, *Infant Mortality. A Social Problem*, London, 1906.

32 'Science of the home: Mrs. Lyttleton's amusing plea for training', *Daily News*, 5 May 1909, p. 6, col. g.

33 'Home economics as a career for women', *The Times*, 4 May 1909, p. 14, col. c.

34 'Women for the hearth', *Lady's Pictorial*, vol. lv, No. 1405, 1 February 1908, p. 148.

35 J. Harris, *Private Lives, Public Spirit. A Social History of Britain, 1870–1914*, Oxford, 1993, p. 95.

36 J. Lewis, *Women and Social Action in Victorian and Edwardian England*, Aldershot, 1991, pp. 7, 11–12.

37 'The disintegration of family life', *The Times Woman's Supplement* 14, 31 December 1910, p. 109.

38 C. Dyhouse, *Feminism and the Family, 1880–1939*, Oxford, 1989, pp. 111–14, 117; C. P. Gilman, *The Home. Its Work and Influences*, London, 1903; P. W. Allen, *Building Domestic Liberty. Charlotte Perkins Gilman's Architectural Feminism*, Amherst, MA, 1988, pp. 45–7; L. F. Pearson, *The Architectural and Social History of Cooperative Living*, Basingstoke, 1988, p. 69.

39 Pearson, 1988, op. cit., pp. 69, 119–22.

40 Dyhouse, 1989, op. cit., pp. 117–18, 123; H. G. Wells, *A Modern Utopia*, London, 1905, pp. 216–17.

41 A. Ravenhill, 'Hygiene and household economics', in S. Wilkinson (ed.), *The Nation's Need. Chapters on Education*, London [1903], pp. 91–2; M. Atkinson, 'Science in the home: the complete housewife in the making', *Daily News*, 1 June 1909, p. 4, col. e.

42 A. Ravenhill, 'The claims of home science on professional women', *Education*, vol. xvi, No. 370, 12 August 1910, p. 98.

43 Ravenhill, 1903, op. cit., p. 91.

44 'Home economics as a career . . .', op. cit., p. 14, col. c.

45 'Women and household economics', *Education*, vol. xi, No. 266, 31 January 1908, p. 82.

46 Ravenhill, 1951, op. cit., p. 127.

47 Blakestad, 1994, op. cit., pp. 190 f.

48 Mottram had been a member of the Society for the Promotion of University Settlements at Cambridge. V. H. Mottram, unpublished autobiography, CMAC, GC/151/7/2, p. 10; interview with Martin Mottram, Salisbury, 7 December 1993; P. Fisher, 'Vernon Henry Mottram', in *Dictionary of National Biography, 1971–1980*, Oxford, 1986, pp. 604–5; 'There lived a Prof.', *K.C.W. Magazine*, KCHSS: Q /SER5/2, March 1928, p. 14.

49 D. F. Smith, 'The social construction of dietary standards: the British Medical Association–Ministry of Health Advisory Committee on Nutrition Report of 1934', in D. Maurer and J. Sobal (eds), *Food, Eating, and Nutrition as Social Problems. Constructivist Perspectives*, New York, 1995, pp. 279–303.

50 V. H. Mottram, *Food and the Family*, London, 1925; V. H. and E. C. Mottram, *Sound Catering for Hard Times*, London, 1932; V. H. Mottram and J. Lindsay, *Manual of Modern Cookery*, third and revised edition, London, 1936.

51 Mottram had been working as a lecturer at Toronto and Montreal in 1914–15. Mottram to P. J. Fisher, 24 March 1954, PJF; Fisher, 1986, op. cit., pp. 604–5; V. H. Mottram, unpublished autobiography, op. cit., p. 15, col. a.

52 ECM, KCHSS: QA/C/M4, 15 May 1928, pp. 298–300; 'Needs of the College', October 1929, ECM: QA/C/M5, 5 November 1929, append. p. 29; Mottram to P. Fisher, 24 March 1954, PJF.

53 'Dr Janet Lane-Claypon's Report', KCHSS: Q /PP1/Pt.1, 14 February 1913, p. 4.

54 See Marsh, 1986, op. cit., pp. 79–95, for an overview of the financial difficulties during this period; see also Blakestad, 1994, op. cit., pp. 301 f.

55 E. Miller, *Century of Change. The Queen's College, Glasgow*, Glasgow, n.d. [c. 1975], p. 48; A. Buchan, 'The growth and development of the Dietetic Department' 4, 'The Royal Infirmary, Edinburgh', *Nutrition* vol. 7, No. 2, Summer 1954, p. 73; 'Rose Simmonds, 1886–1951', *Nutrition*, Winter 1951, p. 274.

56 Mottram and Enid' Hutchinson both note that Abrahams studied at KCHSS but she does not appear in college degree records; it is possible she took KCHSS's one-year Applied Science course. E. Hutchinson, *A History of the British Dietetic Association*, London, 1961, p. 8; Mottram to Fisher, 24 March 1954, PJF.

57 Hutchinson, 1961, op. cit., p. 10.

58 R. D. Apple, 'Science gendered: nutrition in the United States,

1840–1940', in H. Kamminga and A. Cunningham (eds), *The Science and Culture of Nutrition, 1840–1940*, Amsterdam, 1995, p. 149; H. T. Craig, *The History of Home Economics*, New York, 1945, p. 30.

59 Mottram to Fisher, 24 March 1954, p. 2, PJF.

60 Hutchinson, 1961, op. cit., p. 9.

61 Interview with Elspeth M. Averill (*née* Marshall), Oxford, 2 June 1994.

62 ABM, KCHSS: QA/AB/M3, 24 March 1930, append. pp. 354–6; ECM, KCHSS: QA/C/M5, 11 March 1930, p. 106.

63 Hutchinson, 1961, op. cit., pp. 35, 11.

64 M. Andross, 'The growth and development of the Dietetic Department' 2, 'Glasgow & W. Scotland College of Domestic Science', *Nutrition*, vol. 7, No. 4, winter 1953, p. 177; Hutchinson, 1961, op. cit., p. 35; D. M. Northcroft, 'Openings other than teaching for holders of Domestic Subjects diploma', *Housecraft*, vol. iii, No. 3, March 1930, p. 61.

65 S. H. Belfrage, 'What is a dietitian? Scientific study of nutrition develops a new profession', *Journal of Careers*, vol. xiv, No. 158, December 1935, p. 672.

66 'Dietetics as a career', *New Health*, vol. xiii, February 1938, p. 11; interview with E. M. Averill, Oxford, 25 January 1993; ECM, KCHSS: QA/C/M5, 4 October 1932, p. 520; QA/C/M6, 1 November 1932, pp. 14–16; AB, 'Arrangements for proposed course in dietetics', KCHSS: QA/C/M6, 10 January 1933, append. p. 49.

67 Hutchinson, 1961, op. cit., p. 10; R. Strachey, 'Women's Employment Federation', KCHSS: QAP/GPF7/34 (May 1935).

68 Hutchinson, 1961, op. cit., pp. 10–12.

69 Bertrand Edward, Viscount Dawson of Penn (1864–1945). Dawson served as personal physician to Edward VII and George V. Ibid., p. 12.

70 Interview with Averill, Oxford, 25 January 1993.

71 'Dietetics Annals' [n.d.], RCP: uncatalogued papers, 'Dietetics Cttee 1933–35' (hereafter: 'Box 1933–35'), p. 1.

72 Interview with Averill, Oxford, 2 June 1994.

73 'Memo. for Lord Dawson: Points discussed . . . at the Langham Hotel, 27 March 1933' (28 March 1933), RCP: uncatalogued papers, 'Dietetics Cttee 1933–34, 35' (hereafter: 'Box 1933–34, 35'); Helene Reynard to Lord Dawson, 22 November 1933, RCP: Box 1933–34, 35; interview with Averill, Oxford, 2 June 1994.

74 Interview with Averill, Oxford, 5 June 1994.

75 'Memo for Lord Dawson', 9 October 1933, RCP: Box 1933–34, 35.

76 H. Reynard to Sir J. Atkins, 15 July 1934, KCHSS: Q /PP1/Pt.1, p. 1.

77 'Meeting of the Sub-committee on Curriculum . . . April 24th. 1934', RCP: Box 1933–34, 35, p. 2; see also H. Reynard to C. E. Newman, 31 May 1934, RCP: Box 1933–34, 35.

78 'Memo. for Lord Dawson . . . Langham Hotel', op. cit., pp. 1–2.

79 Dawson to Reynard, 10 February 1934, and 'Note made by Lord Dawson, 3 Feb. 1934', RCP: Box 1933–34, 35.

80 ABM, KCHSS: QA/AB/M4 (13 March 1934), p. 306; Minutes of Council Meeting, KCHSS: QAP/GPF2/9; Hutchinson, 1961, op. cit., p. 13; *Course for the University of London Academic Postgraduate Diploma*, KCHSS: QEPH/SYL17a, n.d. [*c.* 1936], p. 2.

81 [Dawson] to Atkins, 10 August 1934, and Atkins to Dawson, 30 August 1934, both in RCP: Box 1933–34, 35.

82 Atkins to Dawson, 30 August 1934; 'Interview with Miss Reynard December 8th 1934', RCP: Box 1933–35; Dawson to Charles E. Newman, 28 May 1934, RCP: Box 1933–34, 35.

83 'Report from Joint Committee on Dietetics', 11 April 1935, RCP: Box 1933–35, p. 1; Hutchinson, 1961, op. cit., p. 13; Dawson to Reynard, 10 May 1936, KCHSS: QA/C/M6, 9 June 1936, append. p. 471.

84 'University of London: Regulations for Academic Post-graduate Diploma in Dietetics', KCHSS: QA/GPF2/9, June 1936; *Annual Report 1935–36*, KCHSS: QEPH/RPT13, p. 8; *Course for the University of London Academic Post-graduate Diploma in Dietetics*, KCHSS: QEPH/SYL11 [*c.* 1936–53], p. 2; Hutchinson, 1961, op. cit., p. 13.

85 Buchan, 1954, op.cit., pp. 75–6; 'The British Dietetics Association: dietetics as a career', *Nutrition*, vol. ii, No. 4 (Winter 1953), pp. 182–3.

86 Hutchinson, 1961, op. cit., p. 14.

87 This course was dropped in 1936, largely because nurses could not afford it. ABM, KCHSS: QA/AB/M5 (13 October 1936), pp. 94–6; see also unsigned letter to Reynard, 10 February 1934, RCP: Box 1933–34, 35; 'Note made by Lord Dawson Feb. 3rd 1934', op. cit.; 'Meeting of the Sub-committee ... University College Hospital ... (30 Jan. 1934)', RCP: Box 1933–35, p. 1; ABM, KCHSS: QA/AB/M5, 13 October 1936, pp. 94–6, 10 November 1936, p. 108; Reynard, 'Notes regarding Dawson's Committee', KCHSS: Q /PP1/Pt.3, n.d. [*c.* 1936], p. 1.

88 See Blakestad, 1994, op. cit., pp. 285–335; R. E. Kohler, *From Medical Chemistry to Biochemistry. The Making of a Biomedical Discipline*, Cambridge, 1982, pp. 4–5.

89 D. F. Smith and M. Nicolson, 'Health and ignorance: past and present', in S. Platt, H. Thomas, S. Scott and G. Williams (eds), *Locating Health. Sociological and Historical Explorations*, Aldershot, 1993, pp. 228–32; V. Berridge, 'Health and medicine', in F. M. L. Thompson (ed.), *The Cambridge Social History of Britain 1750–1950*, vol. 3, *Social Agencies and Institutions*, Cambridge, 1990, pp. 232–3.

90 J. Lewis, 1991, op. cit., p. 1.

91 P. Williams, 'The laws of health: women, medicine and sanitary reform, 1850–1890', in M. Benjamin (ed.), *Science and Sensibility. Gender and Scientific Enquiry, 1780–1945*, Oxford, 1991, pp. 60–88.

92 Marsh, 1986, op. cit., pp. 105–6.

93 Yudkin, 1990, op. cit., pp. 192–4.

94 The original 'Household and Social Science' course was renamed 'Household Science' in 1953 and the remnants of social science were eliminated from the curriculum. Marsh, 1986, op. cit., pp. 232, 245–6.

95 Queen Elizabeth (Kensington) Branch, King's College Old Students' Association, 'The demise of Food Science', *Envoy*, 1991, pp. 3–6.

96 Marsh, 1986, op. cit., p. 233 ff.

97 Hutchinson, 1961, op. cit., pp. 75–6, note 11.

5

RELIEF AND RESEARCH

The nutrition work of the National Birthday Trust Fund, 1935–9

A. Susan Williams

Between 1935 and 1939 the National Birthday Trust Fund (NBTF) distributed supplementary food – mostly Marmite and dried milk foods – to nearly 26,000 undernourished pregnant women. These women lived in regions of England and Wales that were suffering very high rates of unemployment and had been selected by the Special Areas Act of 1934 for government aid to promote regional development. The NBTF project began simply as a means of providing relief, but quickly developed into a combination of relief and research. The experimental side arose out of negotiations for funding with the Commissioner for the Special Areas of England and Wales, whose remit did not include 'poor relief' but did allow for research that was designed to promote social improvement. In order that the relief programme should qualify for funding, therefore, it was converted into an experiment to test whether or not the NBTF foods (especially Marmite, which is rich in B vitamins) reduced the risk of maternal death.

Viscountess Astor, a Conservative MP who was interested in women's welfare, regarded the research side of the work as unimportant in the light of its value as relief. In 1938 she asked the Minister of Health in the House of Commons, 'Will the Right Hon. Gentleman ask expectant mothers what *they* think about it, and then they *need not bother about having any experimental stage?*'[1] Social critics like Richard Titmuss and campaigning organisations like the Committee against Malnutrition were very impressed by the NBTF research, regarding it as self-evident that malnourished women were more vulnerable to maternal death than well-fed women.[2] This positive view of the NBTF nutrition work has dominated references to it by post-war historians. One such historian, for example, in an article published in 1985, referred to the NBTF programme as 'one of the most convincing pieces of evidence for the fact that some women were actually dying of malnutrition in Britain in the 1930s'.[3]

What has become obscured, though, is the verdict of ministerial advisers (medical and scientific) and independent scientists. A minute in the Ministry of Labour reported in 1939 that 'The statistics with which we have been supplied in justification of the benefits derived from the scheme seem entirely misleading and calculations appear to have been based on such an inadequate selection of cases as to render them practically worthless'.[4] John Boyd Orr, author of the report *Food, Health and Income. A Survey of the Adequacy of Diet in Relation to Income* (1936), eventually concluded that the NBTF's results were 'statistically such that no definite conclusions could be drawn'.[5] Some of the Medical Officers of Health (MOHs) participating in the NBTF scheme shared this view, although they were grateful for the extra food. Dr T. Islwyn Evans, the Medical Officer of Health (MOH) for Llantrisant and Llantwit Fardre in South Wales, objected that the study did not take into consideration the general health of the mother or the fact that his mothers received foods at the clinic that were similar to the NBTF foods. 'I beg to point out these,' he wrote to the NBTF, 'as *only a few* of the difficulties I find in getting at a true estimate of the value of the experiment'.[6]

This chapter traces the development of the NBTF nutrition work, uncovering the contradictions that developed from the combining of relief and research. It also identifies some of the difficulties generated from organising food aid in such a way as to satisfy the requirements of funders. Further, it examines the meaning of philanthropy in a situation where the money used to pay for charitable aid had not been raised privately, but was supplied by a government body.

THE NATIONAL BIRTHDAY TRUST FUND

The NBTF was set up as a voluntary organisation in 1928 (becoming a trust in 1930) in order to help reduce the high rate of maternal mortality, which in that year in England and Wales was over four per thousand births and appeared to be steadily rising.[7] Its founder was Ina, Lady George Cholmondeley, who was assisted in this task by the Marchioness of Londonderry, renowned for her wealth and power, and Lucy Baldwin, the wife of the Conservative Prime

Minister. They were soon joined by other prominent members – mostly women – of the social and political elite.[8] The name of the organisation derived from an initial plan to collect at least 1s (that is, 5p, not allowing for inflation) from every member of the British public on their birthday, in the (vain) hope of raising 42 million shillings (£2.1 million) by these means.

The NBTF aimed to appear apolitical, but the dominant members of the committee were either directly involved in, or supporters of, the Conservative Party. Like the National Governments of the inter-war period, therefore, the NBTF was Conservative in all but name. Lucy Baldwin drew public attention to this connection in 1929 and 1935, when she broadcast a fund-raising appeal for the NBTF from Chequers, the Prime Minister's country residence. This association was useful to the Conservative Party, since politics now had to appeal to all women as well as all men. The female electorate had been much enlarged by an Act passed in 1928 (the same year in which the NBTF was created), which granted women the right to vote on an equal basis with men; this was an extension of the provision made in 1918, which had enfranchised women aged 30 and over. Documents in a file at the Public Record Office, labelled *Brief to Counter Labour Party's Campaign*,[9] refer to the efforts of the Labour Party to address women-related issues, particularly maternal mortality; a memorandum in 1934 reported, 'I understand that the [Conservative Party] Central Office will prepare counter propaganda . . .'.[10] Since the Conservatives were eager to find opportunities 'of countering the very persistent socialist propaganda against us on the subject of Nutrition',[11] the food programme of the NBTF was a valuable tool. At one stroke, it demonstrated that the Conservative Party was engaged in two key electoral issues – maternal death and the hunger of the poor.

The NBTF was just one of several voluntary organisations concerned about maternal death, all of which were run by women but which reflected various class interests. The Maternal Mortality Committee, which was created in 1927, was representative of all shades of opinion – key members included Gertrude Tuckwell, a trade unionist and activist in the labour movement, and Lady Iveagh, chairman of the Conservative Party. It assumed the role of a lobbying group, urging local authorities to provide better maternity services. Another organisation that tackled the issue of mothers' health was the Women's Co-operative Guild (WCG), which had been founded in 1883 and was composed entirely of working-class women.

The NBTF sought to reduce maternal death in a variety of ways. Through the Joint Council of Midwifery, an offshoot organisation, it was responsible for a report that led directly to the 1936 Midwives Act, which established a national service of salaried midwives. The NBTF raised the status of midwifery further by establishing a national headquarters for midwives in London. Many inter-war projects initiated by the NBTF aimed 'to secure for the poorer mother the same relief from suffering as is invariably offered to her well-to-do sister'.[12] This concern for poor women underpinned not only the nutrition scheme, but also the NBTF's pioneering role in the development of pain relief for mothers giving birth at home and in the foundation of the first human milk bank in Britain. After the Second World War, the NBTF maintained its interest in the health of pregnant women and babies, but shifted away from policy-making and philanthropy to a full commitment to research. To do this effectively, it developed a set of alliances with medical institutions that replaced its earlier link with the social elite. It has mounted national surveys of various aspects of the maternity services, including the influential perinatal mortality survey of 1958. Where cohort studies have developed from these surveys, it has provided funds and support for such research.

THE NUTRITION WORK OF THE NBTF

The nutrition project began in the Rhondda Valley, a coal-mining area of South Wales that had been hit hard by the Depression and became one of the Special Areas. It was the idea of Lady Juliet Rhys Williams,[13] a leading member of the NBTF, who lived south of the Rhondda at Miskin Manor in Pontyclun. She was appalled by the maternal death rate in the region, which in 1933 was almost seven per thousand and higher than the overall rate of England and Wales, which was nearly five.[14] On behalf of the NBTF, in 1934 she arranged to co-operate with the MOH of the Rhondda Urban District Council in his efforts to reduce maternal mortality. There was no talk of distributing food to mothers at this stage; instead, the NBTF supplied additional maternity services to the region, on the grounds that deficiencies in maternity care were responsible for mothers' deaths. But despite this intervention the rate of maternal death at the end of 1934 jumped even higher, to over eleven per thousand births.[15] This figure was especially shocking when compared with the national rate for England and Wales, which had barely risen at all.[16]

At this point, midwives working in the Rhondda for the NBTF drew its attention to the undernourishment of many women, which was 'so striking', they suggested, as to explain the high maternal death rate.[17] This idea was consistent with growing speculation that an inadequate diet undermined the health of mothers. In 1932, Dame Janet Campbell, the Senior Medical Officer for Maternity and Child Welfare at the Ministry of Health, suggested in *High Maternal Mortality in Certain Areas* that nutrition played a more important part in maternal illness than was generally realised.[18] The Children's Minimum Council, which was created by Eleanor Rathbone in 1934 (and of which Dame Janet was one of the vice-presidents), argued that, from the nutritional point of view, the needs of mothers and children should claim priority.[19] The Trades Union Congress General Council passed a resolution stressing the need for better provision of meals for expectant and nursing mothers and in 1934 sent a copy to the Minister of Health.[20]

The hunger of miners and their families was evident throughout South Wales. Already weakened by the hardships of more than a decade of coal strikes and the General Strike of 1926, they were now impoverished by unemployment and had to rely on the relief provided by the Public Assistance Committees and the Unemployment Assistance Board (UAB), which meant there was scant money available for food.[21] Women ate even less nourishing food than their husbands and children, because of the uneven distribution of resources within households. *Working-Class Wives*, Margery Spring Rice's account of working women's lives in the 1930s, observed that women were almost always going without food, in order to feed their husband and children. 'In an undernourished family,' she observed, 'she is certainly the worst sufferer'.[22] The maternity and child welfare authorities were supposed to ensure that expectant and nursing mothers and young children received the nourishment they needed, but in 1935 food was provided by only 235 out of 316 local education authorities, many of which gave as little as possible.[23] The Rhondda Urban District Council was one of the few authorities to take this responsibility seriously: it had distributed milk to malnourished mothers since 1919, greatly increasing provision during the 1926 General Strike and the years of the Depression.[24]

The NBTF decided to enlarge its maternity scheme in the Rhondda by distributing extra food to hungry mothers. During 1935 3,776 4 oz jars of Marmite (a yeast extract), 3,053 8 oz jars of Brandox Essence of Beef, 2,510 9 oz tins of Ovaltine (a milk food), twenty 1 lb packets of Natyo (a composition of herb and mineral remedies), and 121 1 lb packets of Dorsella Milk Foods were given to over 1,000 undernourished women who were pregnant.[25] When the maternal death rate fell in 1935 to just under five per thousand,[26] Lady Rhys Williams triumphantly attributed the reduction to the NBTF's supplementary food.[27]

THE NBTF EMBARKS ON RESEARCH

Determined to save the lives of as many pregnant women as possible, Lady Rhys Williams led the NBTF on a nutrition crusade. In November 1935 she applied to the Commission for the Special Areas of England and Wales for funding to extend the Rhondda scheme to other Special Areas. At first the commissioner rejected the request, pointing out that the commission had been set up to promote regional development, not to serve a Poor Law function.[28] However, he was put under pressure to reconsider by the highest levels of government, because of the NBTF's connections with Lucy Baldwin, who had sent a letter – from 10 Downing Street – to the Minister of Health, pleading with him to support the application.[29] There was also a fear that turning down an opportunity to feed hungry women would not be good publicity for the government. After lengthy consultations, the commissioner thought up a way of funding the NBTF without appearing to depart from his mission. He proposed that, instead of simply distributing food, they should conduct an 'experiment with different types of foods'; in that way, he said, the scheme would no longer count as relief but would qualify as research.[30] The NBTF willingly agreed. This was the start of funding support from the commission that reached a total of £15,900 (£626,778 at 1996 prices, allowing for inflation) before the NBTF nutrition programme came to an end in 1939. However, the commissioner was 'never . . . enamoured of the scheme'.[31]

In 1936–7 the Special Areas Commission funded the provision of extra nutrition in South Shields, Sunderland, Gateshead, Merthyr Tydfil and parts of Monmouthshire, all of which were suffering from severe economic depression; the distribution of food in the Rhondda was continued by the NBTF with financial help from Lord Bute and Sir Rhys Rhys Williams. Approximately 9,000 women received the foods, which were the same as those distributed the year before, apart from the substitution of milk for Brandox Essence of Beef on the advice of the Ministry of Health.[32] Since the nutrition programme had now become an experiment, it was necessary to have a control group. To create this, the 'fed' cases were subtracted from the total figures of the areas involved and the remainder was used to provide a basis for comparison. In other words, the control group comprised the pregnant women in the selected areas who did not receive special foods.

The results of this phase of the nutrition scheme seemed to be as impressive as those of 1935. Taking together the figures for 1 January 1935 to 30 June 1937, Lady Rhys Williams reported in a letter to *Public Health* that the puerperal death rate per thousand births for the 10,384 women who received extra nutrition was 1.64; among other cases, she said, the death rate was 6.15.[33] She also identified a 50 per cent reduction in stillbirth and the neonatal death rate (that is, in infant death within the first four weeks of life).[34] These figures were greeted with suspicion by the Ministry of Health, however. A. J. Machlachlan, Assistant Secretary in the Ministry, told the Special Areas Commission that 'we retain the view that this scheme has no value as scientific investigation'.[35] There was good reason to question the methodology of the experiment. For one thing, the 'fed' group and the 'control' group were not strictly comparable, since the women receiving supplements all attended antenatal clinics, while the majority of the other group did not. Also, deaths from abortion were automatically excluded from the 'fed' category, owing to the fact that foods were given during the last three months of pregnancy; but these deaths were included in the area figures, which gave no indication of the period of pregnancy at which the death occurred. Other factors, too, biased the experiment. In some areas, women in the control group received extra nourishment from their local authority. In Sunderland, for example, necessitous mothers received milk and fresh butter with bread or biscuits daily.[36] On top of this, disinfectant and packages of sterilised dressings[37] were issued by the NBTF to the women receiving the food, which are likely to have reduced the risk of puerperal infection; the company Reckitt & Sons wrote to object that Lady Rhys Williams did not give Dettol 'its due share of the credit'.[38]

THE NBTF FOODS

The NBTF parcels 'were an exceedingly popular gift', noted two scientists in the course of an independent study,[39] and were welcomed by many MOHs in the Special Areas. The foods have 'done a tremendous amount of good work in my area', enthused the MOH for Caerphilly, Dr W. R. Nash. 'The women attending my Ante-Natal Centres are in the main so poor', he explained, 'that it is necessary to supplement and adjust the diet in almost every case'.[40] Dr J. H. Rankin, the MOH for Gellygaer, thanked the NBTF 'for all you are doing for this district'.[41] The MOH for Gateshead, Dr James Grant, remarked that he 'personally would not know how to meet the situation were the distribution of foodstuffs to be withdrawn'.[42] In his district, he said, 'the women call the Birthday Trust children "Ovaltine Babies"'.[43] Relative to the very low incomes in the area, the NBTF foods were luxury items (and did not, as Lady Rhys Williams herself pointed out, contain enough actual food to diminish hunger[44]). In Cardiff and the Rhondda, the average income per head, exclusive of rent and rates, was estimated to range from 4s 9d (24p) for the unemployed, to 10s 6d (53p) for the employed. This weekly sum, which had to cover clothes, heating and lighting, as well as food,[45] would not have stretched to pay for a 4 oz jar of Marmite (which cost 1s 6d, or 8p, in the shops), an 8 oz jar of Brandox (which cost 3s 4d, or 17p), or an 8 oz tin of Ovaltine (1s 10d, or 9p).[46]

The Birthday Trust foods were not popular with everyone. According to Miss Riddick, the secretary of the Joint Council of Midwifery and Lady Rhys Williams's right-hand person, some husbands fed the milk foods in the NBTF parcels to their whippet dogs (which apparently always won their races).[47] In some regions, Marmite was disliked intensely. One MOH complained in early 1939 that the most outstanding feature of the experiment was the difficulty of persuading patients to take Marmite; about 50 per cent of his mothers, he said, took the first ¼ lb and then flatly refused to continue.[48] The Special Areas Commissioner objected to the NBTF's choice of foods on the grounds that they were 'largely proprietary articles'.[49] Edward Mellanby, Secretary of the Medical Research Council (MRC), also 'severely criticised' Lady Rhys Williams for 'handing out proprietary preparations in her well-meant efforts'.[50] The commissioner and Mellanby objected particularly to Marmite, because they regarded it as a vitamin supplement; milk and other 'natural' foods, they maintained, were a better form of nourishment. Milk was highly recommended by the Ministry of Health's Advisory Committee on Nutrition: 'From the health standpoint there is no other single measure which would do more to improve the health, development and resistance to disease of the rising generation than a largely increased consumption of safe milk by mothers, children and adolescents'.[51] At about 3½d (1½p) a pint,[52] it was also much cheaper than Marmite, Brandox or Ovaltine.

The NBTF foods had been recommended to Lady Rhys Williams by Professor F. J. Browne, a prominent obstetrician at University College Hospital, whom she thanked later for 'your advice in the choice of foods (particularly Marmite)'.[53] The views of Dame Janet Campbell, which informed much of the inter-war work of the NBTF, are also likely to have influenced the selection of foods. In 1932 she wrote that vitamin deficiency was the most obvious defect to remedy in the prevention of maternal death. It was worth considering, Dame Janet added, whether some of the money spent by the local authorities on dried milk could not be spent to better advantage on giving irradiated ergosterol or some vitamin-containing preparation.[54] Lady Rhys Williams must have read this document, since she referred to it on several occasions.

THE BIG EXPERIMENT OF 1937–9

In 1937, the Commissioner for the Special Areas agreed to fund a larger experiment throughout the Special Areas of England and Wales. Despite his reservations about the research, he hoped that it would produce conclusive evidence on the value to mothers of the extra food. To increase the chances of a successful outcome, he asked the NBTF to create a committee of experts to supervise the work. The NBTF referred this task to the Joint Council of Midwifery, which on 28 April 1937 set up a research committee that was chaired by the obstetrician Louis Rivett. Also on the committee were Lady Rhys Williams, who was honorary secretary, James Young, a Professor of Obstetrics, and Dr Margaret Balfour, who had conducted research into maternal nutrition while Chief Medical Officer to the Women's Medical Service in India,[55] and had directed an investigation by the Children's Minimum Council into the supply of subsidised milk to mothers and children. Dr R. A. McCance, secretary of the MRC Nutrition Committee, and his colleague Dr E. M. Widdowson (both of whom were shortly to become distinguished and canonical figures in nutrition[56]) were brought on to the committee as scientific experts, on the advice of Mellanby, who was concerned that the funding 'should not be frittered away'.[57]

McCance and Widdowson were initially very interested in the project. McCance wrote to Mellanby:

> When Lady Rhys Williams came to us at your suggestion our reactions to these results of hers were: 1. They ring true. 2. What should now be done? We set out to plan the work with the feeling that – (a) her results should be checked up again this year, (b) if they are true, Marmite is probably the active agent, (c) we must not assume Marmite to be the active agent until it has been proved.[58]

Widdowson has since recalled, 'We felt our job was to look at the nutrition work of the NBTF objectively, put it to a scientific test. The results were so striking . . . and they'd been published and publicised. So it was only right that we should look into it further'.[59] However, it was not McCance and Widdowson but Rhys Williams and Balfour who directed the experiment and the data analysis, ignoring or overriding many of the scientists' suggestions. There was 'no properly designed scientific study', recalls Dr Widdowson, 'because they couldn't understand what we were trying to do'.[60]

The research committee proposed a massive scheme to test the value of the different constituents of the diet so far supplied, paying special attention to Marmite.[61] This phase of the nutrition programme lasted from April 1937 to June 1939, distributing food to over 15,000 women in 10 areas in the north of England and 18 areas in South Wales (see Table 5.1).[62] The food was given during the three months before confinement or for nine weeks before delivery and three weeks after. Every fortnight the women participating in the experiment were given 1 lb of Ostermilk and ½ lb of Ovaltine or Colact (all milk foods, of which Colact was flavoured with chocolate powder), in addition to either a 4 oz carton of Marmite or an 8 oz bottle of Minadex (Table 5.2). Sterile dressings and Dettol were supplied, as before.

Minadex, a preparation containing vitamins A and D, calcium, phosphorus and iron, was introduced by McCance and Widdowson as a control on the yeast extract, because it has no B vitamins in it. However, it did not develop into the useful control they hoped for; instead, the mothers taking Minadex ended up simply as a com-

Table 5.1 Areas participating in the NBTF nutrition scheme,
April 1937–June 1939

England	*Wales*
Newcastle-upon-Tyne	Aberdare
Gateshead	Bridgend
Sunderland	Caerphilly
South Shields	Cardiff Rural Area
Tynemouth	Gellygaer
Wallsend	Glynmorryg
Hartlepool	Cowbridge
West Hartlepool	Neath
Jarrow	Merthyr Tydfil
County Durham	Maesteg
	Llantrisant
	Mountain Ash
	Monmouthshire
	Penybont
	Pontypridd
	Pembroke Dock
	Port Talbot
	Ogmore

Source M. I. Balfour, 'Supplementary feeding in pregnancy', *The Lancet*, 12 February 1944, p. 208.

Table 5.2 Total supplies of food, April 1937–June 1939

Minadex	16,821 6 oz bottles
Ostermilk	111,446 1 lb tins
Colact	32,737 1 lb tins
Marmite or similar yeast extract	254,679 oz in 8 oz and 4 oz cartons

Source: NBTF/R27

ponent of the overall 'fed' group. The group that was used as a comprised women who were not receiving special foods, as before, with the difference this time that, like the 'fed' mothers, they attended ante-natal clinics. To create this group, 'The MOHs were ... asked to give figures for the women who attended antenatal clinics but did not receive Birthday Trust foods and these figures were used as controls'.[63] All cases of abortion and miscarriage were excluded from both the 'fed' and the 'control' group.

Balfour took responsibility for analysing the data that were collected. This proved difficult, since many of the problems that had plagued the nutrition scheme in its earlier stages had still not been sorted out, despite the efforts of McCance and Widdowson to introduce a rigorous approach to the work. It was impossible, for example, to know whether or not the women actually ate the foods. Some may have given them to their children: one woman whose mother received the extra nourishment recalls that 'My Mam didn't use it all for herself. She used it for us three children, as my Dad was a 1914 wounded soldier and we had very little to live on'.[64] There was evidence, too, that some women were not actually getting the supplement they were supposed to receive. 'I find that a small number of mothers who had previously received Marmite under the original scheme have recently inadvertently been given Minadex since the supply of Marmite has been exhausted', confessed one MOH in August 1937.[65] Some MOHs were doubtful, in any case, about official figures for puerperal sepsis. In the Rhondda, only one case of sepsis had been notified during a half-year, which the MOH for the region thought was most unlikely.[66]

Several MOHs did not keep proper records for the NBTF. 'Dr Taylor of Glyncorrwg does not appear to have a great deal of knowledge or control of the scheme', complained Miss Riddick.[67] Dr J. Jamieson of Northumberland County wrote to say that he was finding the task rather difficult, 'as we were some time in getting distribution started and many of the mothers ceased attendance before the distribution was completed'.[68] Dr Edith Williamson of County Durham, whose terse letters indicate growing impatience with the scheme, briskly advised the trust that she could not collect the information 'with any degree of accuracy'.[69] The submitted records were often confused and unreliable. In the returns from Cymmer there are cases of duplicated healthy births in the 'fed' group: one mother who received a tin of Ostermilk and a carton of Marmite appears to have given birth to three children within seven months.[70] Moreover, as the statistician A. Bradford Hill later pointed out to Lady Rhys Williams, the 'fed' group and the control group were still not strictly comparable regarding age, parity, and duration and amount of antenatal care.[71] 'It is very difficult', she admitted, 'to get such an experiment as this carried out as scientifically and accurately as we should like'.[72]

In July 1939, she reported in a letter to *Public Health* on the preliminary results of the experiment. The maternal death rate of the 'fed' group, she said, was 3.72 per thousand, while the rate for the control group of 'unfed' mothers was 5.42. The stillbirth and the neonatal death rates for the 'fed' group were 34 and 25, respectively; and the rates for the control group were 46 and 38.[73] These figures were less impressive than the results of the earlier phases of the nutrition scheme. This was due, explained Lady Rhys Williams, to the reduction in the number of deaths from sepsis that had occurred throughout the country as a result of the intro- duction of sulphonamides, especially Prontosil.[74] Other factors, too, contributed to the nationwide fall in maternal death, including the reforms of the 1936 Midwives Act and a decline in the virulence of puerperal fever.[75]

FAILURE TO EXTEND THE SCHEME

Convinced of the value of the nutrition scheme, Lady Rhys Williams dreaded the consequences of bringing it to an end – 'women and babies will die if we do, who could otherwise be safe'.[76] She proposed extending the scheme, which prompted Dr McCance and Dr Widdowson to advise that, if further work were to be done, the groups of mothers should be strictly comparable. 'We suggest', wrote McCance,

> that the general plan should be to have two groups, one having yeast or Minadex or both, and the other group having a preparation made to look and taste like Minadex but to contain no minerals or vitamins. The Medical Officers should not be told that any group is being used as a control. . . . Further, the results would carry more weight if you yourself did not know which areas were receiving the active and which the inactive preparation.[77]

This plan to use a placebo qualifies this experiment as a double blind 'randomised controlled trial', eight years before this method was developed by the Medical Research Council in connection with its studies of the effect of streptomycin on tuberculosis.[78]

The idea of giving a placebo to malnourished pregnant women was greeted with horror by Lady Rhys Williams, who cried out, 'These are women, not rats!'[79] Whereas the scientists regarded the work as a research project, Lady Rhys Williams was primarily motivated by a desire to feed hungry women. In later discussions about the NBTF nutrition scheme, Dr Widdowson has remarked that:

You've always got to differentiate between relief and research. We faced this in Germany after the war. We were there to study the effects of undernutrition on men, women and children. There were other organizations concerned with relief. You have to keep them separate, because the objectives are different. Lady Rhys Williams was concerned with relief, saving women's lives. We were concerned with research.[80]

Lady Rhys Williams was not alone, though, in her objection to the idea of deliberately withholding food from hungry people. At the time, when 50 per cent of the nation had been described as underfed by John Boyd Orr, director of the Rowett Research Institute in Aberdeen, such a principle was abhorrent to many people. Dr T. Islwyn Evans, a MOH in South Wales, for example, said that he was unwilling actually to withhold food in order to create a control group – 'as things are at present it is quite impossible for me to withhold foodstuffs from a sufficient number of people to form a control'.[81] A minute in the Ministry of Labour asked, 'Will anybody deliberately select a "control group" and watch them do without extra nutrition which might save their lives?'[82]

Lady Rhys Williams consulted Boyd Orr on a plan to extend the nutrition scheme to the Special Areas of Scotland. At first he was fired with enthusiasm.[83] But a year later the department of the Commissioner for the Special Areas of Scotland wrote to say that the Scientific Advisory Committee of the Scottish Board of Health had decided against the scheme.[84] An explanatory letter from Boyd Orr was evasive,[85] but the full story behind the decision finally emerged from R. W. Johnstone, chairman of the Central Midwives Board for Scotland. He wrote 'confidentially' to Lady Rhys Williams to say that the Scientific Advisory Committee and Sir John Boyd Orr had expressed lack of confidence in any of the NBTF results.[86] Earlier doubts about the value of the NBTF work appear to have developed into a complete loss of faith. A minute in the Ministry of Labour commented in the spring of 1939 that 'it was often suspected there might be a "snag" in the extraordinary results claimed by Lady Williams'.[87] The Nutrition Committee of the Medical Research Council produced a scathing report on the research, claiming that its results could not be ascribed to any single factor, such as improved nutrition.[88]

The NBTF failed to obtain any further funding from the Special Areas Commission of England and Wales.[89] Although the Ministry of Health 'reluctantly and grudgingly' supported the NBTF's application in 1939 to the commission, because it did not wish to appear unwilling to provide extra food to pregnant women, the Treasury opposed the plan.[90] In any case, the commissioner was determined not to 're-enter a field that we had no reluctance in leaving'.[91] Then, when Britain declared war on Germany on 3 September, all negotiations were brought to a sudden end.

WRITING UP THE RESEARCH RESULTS

While the armed forces went to war, Dr Balfour soldiered on with her analysis of the records for the 1937–9 nutrition experiment. Although 15,333 mothers had received supplementary foods,[92] the cards for only 14,181 women were submitted, and many of them had to be discarded because they were not properly filled in. In the end the cards for only 11,618 women were used to evaluate the experiment,[93] which represents a loss of 24 per cent altogether. On the basis of these data, Dr Balfour produced a draft report in July 1942. It claimed that, in the 'fed' group, there was a reduction in neonatal stillbirth mortality that was 'statistically significant', as well as a reduction in the maternal mortality rate that was 'very sugges- tive but not quite statistically significant'.[94] To reach this conclu- sion, Balfour had compared the 'fed' group, which included all those women who had received special foods, including Minadex, with a group of mothers who had not received any extra food.

Dr McCance and Dr Widdowson were not impressed. Having devoted considerable time to reading the report, they said, they were 'unhappy about the whole thing'. Complaining in particular that the Marmite and Minadex data had not even been separated, Dr McCance told Dr Balfour:

> You have written the whole paper on the assumption that the supplementary feeding does produce a real difference in maternal and infant mortality. When the results support your beliefs you make a lot of them, when they do not you tend to gloss them over. You have not convinced us that the supple- mentary feeding has had the beneficial effect that you attri- bute to it.[95]

Lady Rhys Williams was outraged. 'I was horrified', she wrote to Balfour, 'at the childishly worded letter of Dr McCance'. She added, 'He accuses you of exactly what he seems to me to be practising himself, namely, bias in favour of the results whereas he is against them.' She attributed the scientists' criticism not to a difference in opinion over methods, but to personal animosity. 'If you think that his opposition is due to your kind remarks about me at the beginning', she told Balfour, 'please omit them. I am inclined to think that this may be part of the trouble ... go on keeping your end up'.[96] Miss Riddick was equally indignant:

> I especially liked his remark that you had written the whole paper on the assumption that the feeding did produce a real difference in maternal mortality and infant mortality ... one, I should think, usually wrote a paper with some belief as the basis, or why write at all![97]

Balfour produced another draft of the report, which met some of the criticisms put forward by McCance and Widdowson. This time, she made no claims for any effect on maternal mortality, explaining instead how difficult it was to assess this when there were so few maternal deaths in the limited series studied. She gave the stillbirth and neonatal figures with more confidence, on the basis of the Marmite data – 'feeding with Marmite, or a similar yeast extract, during pregnancy, results in a statistically significant reduction in the stillbirth rate and neonatal mortality'.[98] The Marmite group was compared not with the Minadex group but with a group of women who had not received any special foods; the number of women taking Minadex was explained as being too small to draw any conclusions. Balfour referred for confirmation of her conclusions to two contemporary studies: one conducted by a group of scientists at the University of Toronto in Canada[99] and another carried out by the People's League of Health, in co-operation with ten London hospitals.[100] Like the NBTF study, these trials claimed that supplementary feeding during pregnancy improved the health of mother and child; Vitamin B played an important role in these studies (although they did not use Marmite or a yeast food), and they were controlled trials, without the benefit of random allocation. But whereas the NBTF had studied women who gave birth at home, the other studies were conducted in a hospital context, and the Canadian study had used a placebo.

The *British Medical Journal* refused to publish Balfour's findings, on the grounds that they were 'open to criticism on statistical and other grounds'.[101] She had more success with *The Lancet*, which agreed to publish her report on condition that some alterations were made. The editor was puzzled to find under the heading 'Deaths: number', such figures as 127.6 and 243.6. '[H]ow did fractions of babies manage to die?' he asked, adding, 'It makes me think of the harassed food controller who told the farmer that he mustn't kill a whole pig at once.'[102] At last, on 12 February 1944, the results of the experiment appeared in *The Lancet*. Yet again, Balfour's overall conclusions were based on combining the Marmite and the Minadex data into one single 'fed' group, which was compared with a group of 'unfed' mothers:

> In a feeding experiment covering 10 areas in the North of England and 18 in South Wales, 11,618 pregnant women received food supplements consisting mainly of vitamins A, D and B-complex, and calcium, phosphorus and iron. They were compared with 8095 pregnant women who received no such supplements. Both classes were getting extra milk in some form.
>
> There was a significant reduction in the stillbirth and neonatal mortality rates of the fed group as compared with the controls.[103]

CONCLUSION

On the surface, the NBTF nutrition scheme had all the trappings of traditional philanthropy. The labels on the food parcels – bearing messages like 'With Best Wishes from the National Birthday Trust Fund' and 'A Gift from the National Birthday Trust Fund' – signified benevolence.[104] This spirit dominated a lavish affair at the Guildhall in London on 28 March 1939, which was organised by the NBTF in the name of Safer Motherhood. It was supposed to raise money for the cause, but was more successful as a social occasion than as a fund-raising exercise. It was attended by Queen Elizabeth, the Lord Chamberlain, and many of the British and European nobility. Lady Londonderry organised a guard of honour, a group of debutantes between the ages of 17 and 23.

Two hundred of the recipients of NBTF food were invited to this occasion, with all their expenses paid (including a dry shampoo). One was a woman in New Tredegar, South Wales, who had seven children between the ages of 16 years and 5 months; her husband 'wasn't working. He couldn't get a job ... He collapsed in the pit. He had dust. But they wouldn't certify him.' Her daughter recalls:

> I don't know how my mother was chosen, but they thought she was the best one to send, I suppose. She was a perfect mother. They used to say, it was like Dr Barnardo's homes, our house ... my mother used to take in washing, and she used to have 3s a week for taking in this washing. She used to save that, and that was our outings. Because this came up, we used to have little meetings, with our aunts, and we all decided that Mam should have the money to buy the clothes to go. I can remember the hat![105]

These women looked very different from their rich sisters, to judge by photographs that were taken of the event and a report in the *Daily Mail*:

> Debutantes in fluffy white frocks, carrying fresh-flower posies and silk cushions, were shoo-ed away at the Guildhall ... to make way for working-class mothers to form a guard of honour for the Queen ... Two hundred mothers gave their Sunday best an extra ironing, had a dry shampoo overnight, and polished their least-worn shoes.[106]

They were also treated differently. Whereas the ladies with tickets enjoyed a splendid meal, the working-class mothers had to make do with a cold snack in the corridor. It was found 'impossible to give the 200 mothers a meal in the Guildhall after the Reception, so it has been decided to give them *a nice packet of food each*'.[107] These packets of food, which were the cheapest 'Standard Picnic Luncheon Box' available from J. Lyons at a cost of 9d (4p) each, contained '1 Beef Sandwich; 1 Small Pork Pie; 1 Junior Swiss Roll; 1 Dessert Fruit; 1 1d Bar Chocolate'.[108]

The event at the Guildhall recalls the philanthropy of earlier times, when vast social inequalities were accepted and the very rich dispensed alms to the poor.[109] But the NBTF nutrition scheme was *not* philanthropy in that sense, because (apart from small contributions from Lord Bute and Sir Rhys Rhys Williams) it was not actually funded and administered by the very rich. It was paid for almost entirely by the Commission for the Special Areas (therefore the tax-paying public), and most of the data were collected by Medical Officers of Health, who were servants of the state.

If the Commissioner for the Special Areas had been free to make his own decisions, either he would not have funded the NBTF scheme at all or he would have insisted that milk should replace Marmite. It is arguable that, in a period of very great suffering from hunger, the latter would have been a better use of government money. But the persistent faith of Lady Rhys Williams and Dr Balfour in Marmite is not surprising, given the prevalence, during the 1930s and 1940s, of ideas ascribing a wide variety of conditions to poor diet. The notion that 'sub-clinical' vitamin deficiencies could result in poor health and increased susceptibility to infections, without any signs of frank deficiency, was not uncommon. Such a position was shared by Boyd Orr and Mellanby and underlay the official nutritional supplement schemes that were established around the time when Dr Balfour was completing her analysis of the NBTF data.[110]

The NBTF experiments were muddled and inconclusive. However, Lady Rhys Williams and Balfour would have been gratified by later research findings which have demonstrated the value of vitamin B to the health of pregnant women and their infants.[111] Since 1992, the Department of Health has been advising pregnant women to increase their intake of yeast extracts, as a good source of folic acid, which is one of the B vitamins and which reduces the risk of certain defects in newborn babies. The story of the NBTF food programme indicates the complexity of nutrition research, especially when that research is also intended as relief.

NOTES

I wish to thank Dr E. M. Widdowson for giving me important insights in a long interview and also for her valuable comments on drafts of this chapter. I am grateful, too, to David Smith and Bernard Harris for their helpful editorial suggestions and to members of the NBTF History Steering Group for their continued advice and critical support. However, the opinions expressed in this chapter are entirely my own and I take responsibility for them. The research upon which the chapter is based was funded by the National Birthday Trust Fund.

1 *Hansard*, 24 March 1938, col. 1373; emphasis added.
2 R. M. Titmuss, *Poverty and Population*, London, 1938, pp. 153–4; *The Bulletin of the Committee against Malnutrition*, London, January 1938.
3 Margaret Mitchell, 'The effects of unemployment on the social conditions of women and children in the 1930s', *History Workshop*, spring 1985, No. 19, p. 115. See also John Burnett, *Plenty and Want*, London, 1989, third edition ('In 1934 experiments by Lady Williams in the depressed Rhondda Valley showed that no improvement in

ante-natal service reduced the high maternal mortality rate until food was distributed to expectant mothers – when this was done, it fell by 75 per cent', p. 271); and K. Laybourn, *Britain on the Breadline*, Gloucester, 1990, p. 63.

4 Minute by A. W. Holloway, 15 March 1939; handwritten note, 16 March 1939, Public Record Office (hereafter PRO) LAB 23/93.

5 R. W. Johnstone to Lady Williams, 25 May 1939, National Birthday Trust Fund archives held by the Contemporary Medical Archives Centre at the Wellcome Institute for the History of Medicine in London (hereafter NBTF)/T6/2; emphasis added.

6 T. Islwyn Evans, MOH for Llantrisant and Llantwit Fardre, 26 May 1938, NBTF/T8/2/2; emphasis added.

7 These figures are based on the classification in use from 1911 onwards and do not include associated causes. A. Macfarlane and M. Mugford, *Birth Counts*, London, 1984, p. 271.

8 A full history of the organisation is given in *Women and Childbirth in the 20th Century. A History of the National Birthday Trust Fund, 1928–1993*, by A. Susan Williams, Gloucester, forthcoming.

9 PRO MH 55/265.

10 Memorandum to Sir Arthur Robinson, 15 November 1934, PRO MH 55/265.

11 Sir Joseph Ball to N. Chamberlain, 1937, Conservative Party Archives, held by the Bodleian Library at the University of Oxford (hereafter CPA)/CRD 1/24/3.

12 'Safer Motherhood', NBTF/G4/(1).

13 She was Lady Williams until 1938, when her husband, Sir Rhys Williams, changed his name by deed poll to Sir Rhys Rhys Williams; this made her Lady Rhys Williams. For the sake of consistency, she is referred to as Lady Rhys Williams throughout this chapter.

14 Rhondda Urban District Council (RUDC), *Report of the Medical Officer of Health [MOH] for 1933*, p. 38; Macfarlane and Mugford, 1984, op. cit., p. 271.

15 RUDC, *Report of the MOH for 1934*, p. 13.

16 Macfarlane and Mugford, 1984, op. cit., p. 271.

17 Lady Juliet Williams, 'Malnutrition as a cause of maternal mortality', *Public Health*, October 1936, p. 11.

18 Dame Janet Campbell, Isabella D. Cameron and Dilys M. Jones, *High Maternal Mortality in Certain Areas*, London, 1932.

19 Children's Minimum Council, 'An Appeal for the Improvement of Child Nutrition', n.d., CPA/CRD/ 1/60/7.

20 TUC General Council to Sir Hilton Young, 30 November 1934, PRO MH 55/217.

21 *Unemployment and the Housewife*, a report of a public meeting held on 10 November 1936 at the Essex Hall, Strand, London (issued by the Committee against Malnutrition), p. 3.

22 Margery Spring Rice, *Working-Class Wives*, 1939; reprinted London, 1989, p. 170.

23 For a discussion of this see C. Webster, 'The health of the school child

during the Depression', in N. Parry and D. McNair (eds), *The Fitness of the Nation. Physical and Health Education in the Nineteenth and Twentieth Centuries. Proceedings of the 1982 Annual Conference of the History of Education Society of Great Britain*, History of Education Society, 1983, p. 71.

24 In 1934, it spent £16,829 16s 5d on its Milk Assistance Scheme. RUDC, *Report of the MOH for 1934*, p. 35.

25 RUDC, *Report of the MOH for 1935*, pp. 38–46.

26 RUDC, *Report of the MOH for 1935*, p. 13.

27 Lady Juliet Williams, October 1936, op. cit., p. 11.

28 Minute by Tribe, 3 December 1935, PRO LAB 23/92.

29 Mrs Stanley Baldwin to Kingsley Wood, Minister of Health, 27 November 1935, PRO LAB 23/92.

30 M. Stewart (Commissioner) to Mrs Baldwin, 3 January 1935, PRO LAB 23/92.

31 M. Stewart to Irene Ward, 16 June 1936, PRO LAB 23/92.

32 Miss Meyer to L. J. Picton, 7 April 1936, NBTF/T1.

33 Lady Juliet Williams to the editor of *Public Health*, November 1937.

34 Ibid.

35 A. J. Machlachlan to Tribe, 23 November 1936, PRO LAB 23/92.

36 County Borough of Sunderland, *Report of the MOH for 1936*, pp. 115–16.

37 Llantrisant and Llantwit Fardre Rural District Council, *Report of the MOH for 1936*, p. 9.

38 F. Langthorpe, Reckitt & Sons, to Lady Williams, 11 March 1937, NBTF/S2/2(1).

39 This was an observation on the distribution of foodstuffs in Gateshead. R. A. McCance, E. M. Widdowson and C. M. Verdon-Roe, 'A study of English diets by the individual method' III, 'Pregnant women at different economic levels', *Journal of Hygiene*, 1938, vol. 38, p. 616.

40 Dr W. R. Nash to Lady Williams, 4 November 1938, NBTF/T8/2/3.

41 Dr Rankin to Lady Rhys Williams, 13 May 1938, NBTF/T8/2/3.

42 James Grant to Lady Williams, 2 March 1938, NBTF/T8/1/1(1).

43 'Report by Dr M. Balfour on her Tour of the North of England', July 1937, NBTF/T15.

44 Lady Williams, 'Results of experimental schemes . . .', *Public Health*, April 1937.

45 'Memo from Lady Williams with regard to Advisory Leaflets', 1936, NBTF/F2/5/2(4).

46 These prices were obtained from NBTF/F2/5/2(3).

47 Information supplied in a letter from Mrs M. Wynn to A.S.W., February 1992.

48 John Rennie to Lady Williams, 17 February 1939, NBTF/T10/3/1.

49 M. Stewart to Irene Ward, MP, 16 June 1936, PRO LAB 23/92.

50 Minutes by A.J.M., n.d., PRO LAB 23/92.

51 Ministry of Health, *Advisory Committee on Nutrition. First Report*, London, 1937, p. 13, PRO RG 26/72.

52 Price given in 'Report re Adequate Dietaries for Pregnant Women at Certain Income Levels' by British College of Obstetricians and Gynaecologists [1936], PRO MH 55/642.

53 Lady Williams to Professor F. J. Browne, 9 December 1937, NBTF/S7/2/1.
54 Campbell, Cameron and Jones, 1932, op. cit.
55 In a dietetic study in Bombay in 1932, Balfour and S. K. Talpade showed that women on diets containing whole wheat or millet (both, like yeast, good sources of the vitamin B complex) had fewer premature infants than women whose diet consisted largely of polished rice. *Indian Medical Gazette*, 1932, vol. 67, p. 601.
56 For a comprehensive account of their work see M. Ashwell (ed.), *McCance and Widdowson. A Scientific Partnership of 60 Years*, London, 1993.
57 Minute by A.J.M., 19 March 1937, PRO LAB 23/93.
58 R. A. McCance to E. Mellanby, 28 April 1937, NBTF/T2(2).
59 Interview with Dr E. M. Widdowson by A.S.W., 9 August 1991.
60 Ibid.
61 'Report of the National Birthday Trust Fund Nutrition Scheme for Expectant Mothers (for the information of the Commissioner for Special Areas)', September 1937, NBTF/T1.
62 These figures were taken from 'Malnutrition and maternal mortality', *Mother and Child*, September 1939, vol. x, No. 6, p. 248.
63 Margaret I. Balfour, 'Supplementary feeding in pregnancy', *The Lancet*, 12 February 1944, p. 209.
64 Mrs P.H. of Sunderland to A.S.W. [October 1991].
65 W. Campbell Lyons to Lady Williams, 26 August 1937, NBTF/T8/1/1(1).
66 This MOH believed that the puerperal sepsis figures were explicable if the expectant mothers were buying Marmite, but he did not see how this could be found out ('Report by Dr M. Balfour on the Tour of the South Wales Areas', September 1937, NBTF/T15). He appears to have been convinced of the value of Marmite in the prevention of maternal death.
67 'Report by Dr M. Balfour on the Tour of South Wales Areas', September 1937, NBTF/T15.
68 Dr J. Jamieson to Miss Riddick, 2 December 1938, NBTF/T8/2/2(1).
69 Dr Edith S. Williamson, Welfare Medical Officer for Durham County, to Miss Riddick, 24 October 1938, NBTF/T8/2/2(2). Dr Williamson may well have disapproved of the NBTF, because of its Londonderry connection. Lord Londonderry was a major coalowner in the Durham area and had a reputation for showing little interest in the welfare of his miners and treating them very badly.
70 Returns from Health Visitor, E.R., Cymmer, near Port Talbot, sent to NBTF on 25 April 1940, NBTF/T13/8.
71 A. Bradford Hill to Lady Rhys Williams, 5 January 1938, NBTF/T6/1.
72 Lady Williams to W. Campbell Lyons, 1 September 1937, NBTF/T8/1/1(1).
73 Letter from Juliet Rhys Williams, *Public Health*, July 1939.
74 Ibid.

75 See chapter 15 of Irvine Loudon, *Death in Childbirth*, Oxford, 1992, pp. 254–73.
76 Lady Rhys Williams to E. Mellanby, 22 February 1939, NBTF/T3.
77 McCance to Lady Rhys Williams, 14 December 1938, NBTF/T2(2).
78 For a full discussion of this, see A. Oakley, 'Who's afraid of the randomised controlled trial? Some dilemmas of the scientific method and "good" research practice', *Women and Health*, 1989, vol. 15, p. 26.
79 Reported by L.S.G. in telephone interview with A.S.W., 29 October 1991.
80 Interview with Dr E. M. Widdowson by A.S.W., 9 August 1991.
81 T. Islwyn Evans to Lady Williams, 26 May 1938, NBTF/T8/2/2.
82 Minute, 19 May 1938, PRO LAB 23/93.
83 John Boyd Orr to Lady Williams, 27 May 1938, NBTF/T5/2.
84 This information is contained in a letter from Lady Rhys Williams to Dr McKinlay, 24 May 1939, NBTF/T5/2.
85 John Boyd Orr to Lady Rhys Williams, 27 May 1939, NBTF/T5/2.
86 R. W. Johnstone to Lady Rhys Williams, 25 May 1939, NBTF/T6/2; emphasis added.
87 Minute by A. W. Holloway, 15 March 1939, PRO LAB 23/93.
88 MRC Nutrition Committee, 'Report of the Nutrition Committee . . . on the Administration of Supplementary Foods . . . by the Joint Council of Midwifery', 13 February 1939. An account of this report is given in a Ministry of Health minute to de Montmorency, 4 August 1939, PRO LAB 23/94.
89 Commissioner for the Special Areas (England and Wales) to Lady Rhys Williams, 24 May 1939, NBTF/T3(2).
90 Minute to Dalton, 9 September 1939, Minute from Dalton, 3 October 1939, PRO LAB 23/94.
91 Minute signed I.D.C., 5 August 1939, PRO LAB 23/94.
92 Letter from Lady Rhys Williams, *Public Health*, July 1939.
93 M. I. Balfour, 'Supplementary feeding in pregnancy', *The Lancet*, 12 February 1944, pp. 208 ff.
94 M. I. Balfour, 'Supplementary feeding in pregnancy', first draft, 1942, p. 11, NBTF/T17/3/2.
95 McCance to Balfour, 19 August 1942, NBTF/T17/3/2.
96 Lady Rhys Williams to Balfour, 19 August 1942, NBTF/T17/3/2.
97 Miss Riddick to Balfour, 19 August 1942, NBTF/T17/3/2.
98 M. I. Balfour, 'Supplementary feeding in pregnancy', second draft, NBTF/T17/3/1.
99 J. H. Ebbs, F. F. Tisdall and W. A. Scott, 'The influence of prenatal diet on the mother and child', *Journal of Nutrition*, 1941, vol. 22, pp. 515–26.
100 'Nutrition of expectant and nursing mothers', *The Lancet*, 4 July 1942, pp. 10–12; see also *British Medical Journal*, 18 July 1942.
101 Quoted in a letter from N. Gerald Horner to Balfour, 25 May 1943, NBTF/T17/3/1.
102 M. N. Jackson to Balfour, 26 May 1943, NBTF/T17/3/1.
103 Balfour, 1944, op. cit, p. 19.
104 These labels are held in the NBTF archives, NBTF/T18.
105 Interview with Mrs G.J., Phillipstown, New Tredegar, by A.S.W., 1 August 1991.

106 *Daily Mail,* 30 March 1939.

107 NBTF to Mrs Woolf, East Islington Mothers' and Babies' Clinic, February 1939, NBTF/G7/9/3.

108 Miss Riddick to J. Lyons & Co., 24 March 1939, NBTF/G7/9/2.

109 David Cantor has described this kind of charity as 'the benevolent means by which elites tried to maintain social order'. His argument, which is presented in 'The aches of industry: philanthropy and rheumatism in inter-war Britain', in J. Barry and C. Jones (eds), *Medicine and Charity before the Welfare State,* London, 1991, pp. 238 ff., can usefully be applied to the work of the NBTF between the wars, since its members were very rich and some relied on labour in the Special Areas to create their wealth. For example, the Rhys Williams family owned coalfields in South Wales and the Londonderry family were coalowners in Durham. This may explain why the NBTF nutrition scheme began in South Wales, where there was repeated social disturbance in the 1920s and 1930s. In the very month of 1928 in which the National Birthday Fund was inaugurated, the Minister of Labour was warned that the situation in South Wales 'is becoming dangerous ... the screw may ... have been turned too tight'. W.A.R. to Minister of Labour, 1 November 1928, PRO LAB 23/93.

110 See F. C. Kelly, 'Fifty years of nutritional science', *Medical Officer,* 1935, vol. 53, pp. 65–6, for an illustration of the contemporary argument about 'sub-clinical malnutrition'. The quest for biochemical tests of malnutrition was linked with the idea of partial vitamin deficiencies. See Chapter 2, p. 47, and Chapter 7, p. 159.

111 See, for example, A. H. A. Wynn, M. A. Crawford, W. Doyle and S. W. Wynn, 'Nutrition of women in anticipation of pregnancy', *Nutrition and Health,* 1991, vol. 7, pp. 69–88, especially figure 6, p. 83.

6

THE POPULARISATION OF MILK AS A BEVERAGE DURING THE 1930s

Francis McKee

THE TARNISHED IMAGE OF MILK

Today we tend to take milk's status as a beverage for granted and we are surprised that milk only attained this distinction in the 1930s. Our culture associates milk with purity, health and goodness – deep associations rooted, no doubt, in milk's whiteness and the childhood bond of breast-feeding. These associations have mythic status in northern Europe and in North American society, where milk is an important element in national diets. In Britain, at the turn of the century, however, milk was regarded with suspicion and distaste. Its popularisation as a beverage in the 1930s was partly based on the rehabilitation of its mythic status in the eyes of the public, and in order to understand why milk's image had become so tarnished it is useful to consider its early history.

First, it must be remembered that 'milk' could as easily refer to ewe's milk or goat's milk until the mid-eighteenth century. These types of milk were eventually eclipsed by the popularity of cow's milk, which was considered the most tasty and, possibly, because cattle proved more profitable to keep. Although cow's milk super-seded the others in southern England, it took much longer for Scotland, northern England and Wales to follow suit.[1] Second, by the late seventeenth century a division had sprung up between milk supplies for the growing towns and the availability of milk in the countryside. Enclosure of grazing land reduced the number of milch cows kept by country labourers, who increasingly turned to ale as a beverage and tasted dairy products only in the form of butter and cheese. In the towns and cities, which were now too large for the inhabitants to walk out to the surrounding countryside for milk, dairy shops and town dairies were set up. A dairy shop would supply milk and dairy products on the premises while also sending milkmaids through the streets with pails slung on yokes. Town dairies housed cattle close to the town centres where conditions were usually cramped and unhygienic. The cows were generally confined and fed on brewer's grains, cabbage and bean shells. Milkmen in the towns were frequently accused of watering the product and the milk carried through the streets in open pails inevitably absorbed the filth of the towns. To counter this, cows were often driven through the streets and milk could be bought direct from the udder – in London, a herd grazed in St James's Park for this purpose. By the late nineteenth century, the railways enabled farmers to transport their milk to the cities, and closed milk churns on perambulators were used to deliver the milk to the customer's door.[2] However, the poor conditions of town dairies and the lack of hygiene control on rural farms still meant a persistently dirty supply of milk, which often carried disease – tuberculosis, in particular. Clean, fresh milk remained a relative luxury in the towns at this time. The poor either went without or, towards the end of the century, substituted the cheaper canned, condensed milk which was increasingly available.[3]

Pasteur's work in the 1850s had revealed the dangers of disease which could be transmitted through small amounts of dirt in milk. The process of pasteurisation, however, was used in the dairy industry only from around 1890 onwards. Even then, farmers were more impressed by the power of the process to kill germs and prolong the travelling life of milk than by its public health aspects. It took almost another decade before that dimension was appreciated.

Pasteurisation, however, was still not universally accepted in Britain at the time and, indeed, was still regarded with distrust in many quarters. Some opponents of the process thought that it was simply a means of making dirty milk saleable and maximising the farmers' profits.[4] This at least was a rational argument, but other objections were deeply rooted in superstitions surrounding the life-giving force of milk. These objections are probably found in their most extreme form in the work of Harlow Davis, an American health guru at the beginning of the twentieth century. Davis declared mother's milk essential to the physiological and psychological development of a child, and claimed that its potency was rooted in the fact that milk was a living ferment. 'It is', he declared, 'the presence of this occult influence in the mother's Milk which makes any adequate substitute for it impossible.' He went on to celebrate the value of cow's milk for consumptive patients, saying the milk should be drunk before the magnetic warmth of the cow had left it. He stated:

> Herein lies the great secret which, strange to say, has been overlooked, not only by the laity, but also by most medical men. Every glass of Milk which is drunk by the patient while it is yet warm from the cow, is equivalent in nourishing and stimulating qualities to a glass of blood ... Once more I will emphasize the fact that there is a vast difference between the Milk warm from the cow and Milk when artificially heated. One glass of the naturally warm Milk will give more vitality than a quart or more of milk which has lost its natural warmth. This is owing to Milk straight from the udder teeming with electricity, or animal magnetism, which is in reality a form of liquid life; and all of such life-element is lost by evaporation after the milk has cooled.[5]

Davis's rhetoric is the more extreme form of a generally held suspicion at the time. Many perceived pasteurisation as unwelcome tampering with nature, and this perception was exacerbated by the consumers' suspicion of farmers and milkmen, who had for so long presented them with watered and contaminated versions of milk. The ideal of milk as a good, pure and life-giving beverage was under assault, but a recent survey has shown that children's books published at the turn of the century found bread and milk constantly used as a reward for the good and the pure, suggesting that belief in the natural goodness of milk still survived.[6]

SCIENTIFIC GROUNDWORK FOR THE REHABILITATION OF MILK

In the early decades of this century a combination of social and scientific forces was to restore the reputation of milk and elevate it to the status of a staple of the nation. Central to this change was the work of nutritionists. One of the first blows in the campaign was the publication in July 1928 of a report by John Boyd Orr of the Rowett Research Institute in Aberdeen on experiments involving the supply of milk to schoolchildren.[7] Orr was continuing the work of Dr Corry Mann, whose Medical Research Council study had shown that extra milk had been of benefit to boys in a children's home, who received the milk in addition to a good diet.[8] Mann's research raised the questions of which constituents of milk produced the increase in weight and height of the boys, and whether similar results could be achieved by increasing the milk consumption of children living in the community.

Funded by the Empire Marketing Board, Orr carried out a series of experiments to test the nutritive value of whole milk, separated milk and a control food of equal calorific value. Using schools in seven cities and towns in Scotland and Belfast, and approximately 1,400 children aged from 5 to 14, Orr found that there was a clear correlation between an added milk diet and extra growth of the children. The experiments allowed him to formulate three conclusions. First, he claimed that the increase in the height and weight of children who received an added milk diet was 20 per cent greater than that of children who received no extra milk. Second, this gain was accompanied by a general improvement in the children's condition. Third, separated milk was as capable of producing these results as whole milk.[9] Although his report made a significant contribution to milk's reputation as a necessary part of the human diet, it could have a sustained impact only if the issue of dairy hygiene was resolved. Orr suggested that this could be done by improving the condition of dairy herds and the conditions in which the milk was collected. This improvement was to be allied to an effective policy of pasteurisation. A new ideal was thus articulated – 'clean milk from healthy, tested herds'.

During the same year, steps were taken to tackle the question of the quality of milk when the Hannah Dairy Research Institute was founded. The institute was to be sited at Auchincruive, near Ayr, on the estate of J. M. Hannah of Girvan Mains. This estate was also to be the home of the dairy school and experimental farm of the West of Scotland Agricultural College. The Hannah Institute was funded by a combination of public and private grants, determined by the Development Commission's policy, which stated that one-third of the institute's maintenance was to be provided by a non-government source.[10] The Highland and Agricultural Society voted a sum of £250 per annum towards this cost and announced that the new institute would first enquire into the occurrence of tuberculosis in dairy herds. This investigation was to assess the scale of the problem and the value of tuberculin tests on the herds.[11]

Although the institute did not actually open on site in Ayr until 1931, work began immediately. The institute's first bulletin, *Surplus Milk and Milk Residues*, by Arthur MacNeilage, appeared in 1929. MacNeilage summarised work carried out in 1926 for the Scottish National Milk and Health Association, pointing out that, in cheese and butter manufacture, almost 25 per cent of the separated milk and 75 per cent of the whey produced as by-products were currently running to waste. E. P. Cathcart, Regius Professor of Physiology at Glasgow University and interim director of the institute, summed up the situation in his preface to the report, commenting: 'If these residues were devoid of food value there would be little object in effecting their recovery. But each of these residues has a considerable value as a food'.[12] Cathcart went on to stress the commercial potential of separated milk, pointing out that £3 million worth of condensed, separated milk was being imported annually into Britain at that time. Scotland's wasted milk, he argued, would be sufficient to provide the whole of Scotland's imported condensed milk.

In 1929, Dr Norman Wright became assistant director of the Hannah Institute, and in 1930 he was appointed director. In 1929 he published an article in the *British Medical Journal* which complemented the findings of Orr and MacNeilage. He reported that Glasgow corporation's hospitals had been using milk supplied only from tuberculin-tested herds of cattle for a period of two years. Within that time not one sample out of 550 examined had been found to be infected. In the previous years, 1921–6, the hospitals had used herds which were not tuberculin-tested and out of 923 samples twenty-eight had been found to be infected. The implications for the public were worrying. Wright acknowledged that pasteurisation would reduce the risk of tubercle-infected milk but he pointed out that at that time in Glasgow, for instance, only 30 per cent of the public's milk supply was pasteurised.[13]

Taken together, the findings of Orr, MacNeilage and Wright gave a clear indication of the future of milk as a national beverage. Orr's experiments demonstrated the physical benefits of milk as a central element of the diet. MacNeilage's work underlined the commercial possibilities of the milk supply and Wright's investigations proved that a reliable, clean supply of milk could be created. The combination of these arguments made milk a vital issue in national food production.

The battle to establish milk as a national beverage, however, had only begun. While it was one thing to point out the nutritional advantages of the increased consumption of clean milk, it was another to actually achieve this increase and ensure the cleanliness of the milk. One of the greatest obstacles was economic. MacNeilage had struck a nerve with his evidence of large-scale wastage and lost profits from separated milk. His results were seen as 'a serious charge against the traditional thriftiness of the average Scots farmer', and accounts of his report were often prefaced by head-lines such as 'Curds and Whey are Wasted in Thrifty Scotia'.[14]

AMBIVALENT FARMERS; GOVERNMENT SCHEMES

Attempts to rectify the situation and to capitalise on the potential of separated milk were slower to materialise. The cost for farmers at the time may have been prohibitive and the technology may also have been too experimental – a research factory for transforming whey into powder was still at an early stage in Bladen, Dorset, in 1930.[15] More important, perhaps, was the question of the pricing of milk and the cost to farmers of pasteurisation. On the latter issue, farmers were unwilling to invest quickly in new technology until pasteurisation was proved to be beneficial beyond any shadow of a doubt. The smaller, casual producer–retailers of milk, in particular, were worried that they would be squeezed out of business. Wright argued that in North America the compulsory pasteurisation of milk had greatly lessened public fears of infection and provided the farmer with a stable market for his product. In addition, he noted the survival of many small dealers who adapted by either installing small-scale plants, co-operating with larger plants or buying from larger businesses.[16]

Farmers, however, argued that compulsory pasteurisation was unnecessarily expensive, as there was not sufficient consumer demand for it. This point was constantly made whenever farmers replied to accusations that they were contributing to tuberculosis in children. In 1932, for instance, Scottish farmers issued a state-ment on this subject, asserting: 'The public are to blame to the extent of refusing to buy specially purified and tested grades of milk, which are, of course, dearer than raw milk'.[17] The farmers went on to claim that the real problem was not the adulteration of milk but the adulteration of language used in the pasteurisation controversy. This was not a completely facetious argument. The Scottish Milk Marketing Scheme graded milk as 'Certified', 'Tuberculin Tested', or 'TT', and 'Grade A'. 'Grade A' was untested milk and thus the highest-risk product of the three, but its name, suggesting excellence, caused much confusion. The question of price, however, was the more sensitive issue. The Scottish Milk Marketing Board, and a Milk Marketing Board for England and Wales, were established after the Agricultural Marketing Acts of 1931 and 1933, to bring more stability to the price of liquid milk.

In order to provide cheaper milk for children various schemes were introduced to supply milk in schools.[18] The National Milk Publicity Council began to develop the sale of milk in 1929 when they offered ⅓ pint bottles of milk to schools in the London metropolitan area at a cost of 1d per bottle or free to 'necessitous children'. By 1931 this scheme had grown to provide milk for over 500,000 children and the council was beginning to think of extending it to factories. This scheme had the advantage of addressing the issues raised by Boyd Orr's 1928 report on the nutritional potential of milk for children while also distributing surplus milk supplies. The publicity value of the scheme was also significant in such a time of recession. In the long term, however, the advantages to the dairy industry were immense. By providing milk for schoolchildren, the council was nurturing a generation who would grow up to think of milk-drinking as a nutritious and commonplace habit. In 1934 these schemes were superseded when the Milk Act was introduced, making milk available to children at a price subsidised by the government and the Milk Marketing Boards.[19]

Despite the progress of the Milk Marketing Boards and the school milk schemes, the controversy over pasteurisation continued throughout the 1930s. The argument that milk lost some of its natural qualities when pasteurised remained a strong weapon. In addition, reference was frequently made to an incident in Montreal in 1927 when 450–500 people died in an epidemic of typhoid fever which was traced to milk supplied from a dairy which practised pasteurisation.[20] Farmers also referred to medical authorities who claimed that the population was immunised from tuberculosis through limited exposure to the bacillus in the milk supply. It was claimed that, by supplying tubercle-free milk to children, the government was rearing a new generation that would be highly vulnerable to tuberculosis from other sources. Many of the arguments against pasteurisation functioned more at the level of fear and superstition than of reason and were therefore all the harder to dislodge.[21]

A NEW MYTHOLOGY OF MILK

Proving scientifically that tuberculin-tested herds and pasteurisation ensured clean, reliable milk was not enough by itself to persuade the public to enshrine milk in the ranks of national beverages. And while the school milk schemes and the Milk Act were sowing seeds among future generations, more was needed to convince the adult population. One of the most successful steps in the promotion of milk was the alliance of its traditional, mythic associations of purity and goodness with the futuristic, clinical domain of the scientific laboratory. This alliance both assuaged public fears over contamination and rehabilitated the image of milk. For example, in 1932, in the *Aberdeen Press and Journal*, the head of the dairy department of the Duthie experimental stock farm of the Rowett Institute described dairy byres as follows:

The floors, walls, and roofs . . . are kept thoroughly clean. The cows are fed at least half an hour before milking and groomed an hour before milking in order that the air may become freed from the dust stirred up by these operations. To ensure efficient grooming the long hairs on tails and udders are clipped. Before milking the udders and teats of every cow are thoroughly cleansed with a clean damp cloth . . .

All persons employed in or about a dairy keep their clothing at all times in a thoroughly clean condition and wear clean overalls and caps during the milking of the cows . . . the hands and forearms of the milkers are thoroughly cleansed and dried before milking is begun, and are kept clean throughout milking.

All utensils and vessels used for the reception of milk are thoroughly washed and scalded with boiling water or steam after use and are stored mouth-downwards in a place free from dust . . .[22]

The key word here is 'thoroughly', repeated constantly to emphasise the purging of dirt. The strenuous efforts to banish dust recall the laboratory and the operating theatre. Milk is elevated from the muck of the Victorian byre to the world of twentieth-century science. Another newspaper report linked milk, in the reader's mind, with the periodic table of the elements, and through association lifted milk from the stink of the farm to the realm of science and technology:

> Seven surprising elements have been found in cow's milk. They are substances never before identified in the lacteal fluid.
>
> One of them is strontium, which is the base of the red fire of . . . [fireworks]. Another is titanium, an element that supplied the smoke screens of the World War. Vanadium, well known in building and commerce; lithium, which has lent its name to some kinds of springs, and silicon, one of the main constituents of the earth's crust, are among the finds.
>
> The others are rubidium, which makes silvery coatings on the inside of radio tubes, where it absorbs gas, thereby preserving the vacuum and the service of the tube: and boron, which is exhaled by volcanoes as boric acid.
>
> . . . The milk was dried, burned to ashes and sufficient electric current applied to the ash to convert it into luminescent vapor. By this light, photographic plates registered the spectra, the lines of which revealed the presence of the elements.[23]

This final passage of the article, while describing an actual scientific process, presents a striking image of milk's demise and its phoenix-like revival from the ashes as a pure, scientific subject. Such articles severed milk's long-standing association with impurities and helped to reactivate its primitive image of vitality.

These kinds of comparison were not limited to the dairy industry alone and must be seen within a wider context of the transformation of the kitchen and the public's concept of diet.

By the end of the nineteenth century, science had permeated into the domestic sphere, partly through nutritional science and its association with home economics. In a recent article, 'Science gendered: nutrition in the United States, 1840–1940', Rima Apple has argued that the new role of science in the home was quickly reflected in the food industry's advertising campaigns:

By the end of the century, advice to women on the importance of nutritional scientific information in their everyday life could be found in women's magazines, on the lecture circuit and in texts written for home use. Manufacturers also emphasised the necessity of scientific knowledge, or at least the need for an appreciation of scientific knowledge, to ensure the healthy feeding of the family. Sometimes it was enough merely to mention an illustrious scientist . . . Many other advertisers designed promotions based on contemporary chemical and physiological data to persuade women to purchase their products. . . Obviously advertisers were convinced that a successful marketing campaign needed to address the nutritional bases of their products and inform the consumer in scientific terms why she should buy the advertised item. It was necessary to present the image of a product that was manufactured in accordance with contemporary nutritional knowledge. Furthermore, such advertisements gave added credibility to the image of scientific motherhood by implying, if not baldly stating, that women needed science to carry out their domestic duties successfully.[24]

When 'scientific motherhood' involved the substitution of bottle milk for breast-feeding, there were potentially harmful consequences, particularly prior to the widespread introduction of pasteurisation. P. J. Atkins has argued recently that infected milk was

strongly linked at least to diarrhoeal deaths, which accounted for 10–20 per cent of infant mortality throughout the period 1871–1920. . . The switch to a greater consumption of fresh cows' milk and condensed milk at the end of the nineteenth century meant a greater convenience for working mothers, but their offspring may have suffered. The death rate among weaned infants was high, at least double that of those at the breast. Of deaths before the age of one, about half were of babies fully on artificial food, or 57 per cent for deaths from infant diarrhoea . . . probably caused by a group of microorganisms . . . which may be transmitted to the milk in dirt and dust.[25]

However, according to Atkins, medical opinion, in general, 'supported the technical innovation of feeding bottles, the commercial introduction of proprietary farinaceous baby foods, and the increasing retail availability of relatively cheap cow's milk', and the medical profession therefore gave its approval to the massive advertising campaigns which were mounted to 'make mothers aware of alternatives to breast-feeding and give the impression that artificial foods were superior'.[26]

It is difficult today to comprehend fully the excitement with which scientific innovations were greeted by some enthusiasts, but it can be sensed in an extreme example of the rise of 'domestic science', found in the cookery book written by the Italian Futurist artist, Filippo Tommaso Marinetti, in 1930. Intoxicated by the technological achievements of the early twentieth century, Marinetti and other Futurists attempted to extend the machine age to diet and cookery. Their greatest enemies were the stodgy, calorie-laden recipes of nineteenth-century cooking. Marinetti suggested that in all social classes 'meals will be less frequent but perfect in their daily provision of equivalent nutrients'. He went on to argue that to revolutionise the kitchen and create the perfect meal a 'battery of scientific instruments' should be installed:

> ozonizers to give liquids and foods the perfume of ozone, ultra-violet ray lamps (since many foods when irradiated with ultra-violet rays acquire active properties, become more assimilable, preventing rickets in young children, etc.), electrolyzers to decompose juices and extracts, etc. in such a way as to obtain from a known product a new product with new properties, colloidal mills to pulverize flours, dried fruits, drugs, etc.; atmospheric and vacuum stills, centrifugal autoclaves, dialyzers. The use of these appliances will have to be scientific, avoiding the typical error of cooking foods under steam pressure, which provokes the destruction of active substances (vitamins, etc.) because of the high temperatures.[27]

Obviously the *Futurist Cookbook* was not entirely serious and its readership would have been limited to a small avant-garde clique. It is clear from the passage, however, that Marinetti was combining food and technology in the light of nutrition science. He was, in fact, absorbing the nutritionist into his pantheon of new gods of the machine age. While it would be foolish to make any claims for Marinetti's *Cookbook* as a direct influence on the popularisation of milk as a beverage in Britain, he does provide a background for other design elements which played a significant role in the story: in particular, the development of the ice-cream parlour, the café and the milk bar.

ICE-CREAM AND MILK SHAKES

In 1929, at the annual meeting of the Scottish National Milk and Health Association, a resolution was passed calling for the introduction of a statutory standard for ice-cream. The Association argued that:

> One of the most important things they had to do if they were to get people to eat ice-cream, was for the Government to fix a standard for ice-cream the same as they had for milk. Then the public would have faith in their ice-cream and know that it contained a valuable food and nothing else.[28]

This was a significant step forward for ice-cream in Scotland. The resolution of the Milk and Health Association was not simply a call for a standard ice-cream, it was also, finally, a recognition of ice-cream as a respectable commodity. During the 1900s ice-cream had been closely linked with the story of Italian immigration into Britain and, in particular, into Scotland. One of the ways in which Italians made a living in Glasgow in the late nineteenth century was through the street vending of ice-cream. By the 1900s the vendors had graduated to small ice-cream and aerated water shops – sweetshops, as they would be known today. The rapid spread of these shops met with severe opposition from the authorities and they gained a notoriety in the press which was fuelled by a whisky trade already fearful that the temperance movement could harm their business.[29]

Riding on a wave of temperance reform at the time, the enterprising Kate Cranston had opened a series of tea rooms in Glasgow, providing an elegant alternative to pubs for the middle classes. The tea rooms offered not only an alternative to beer and spirits, but also a new entertainment option for middle-class women, eager to escape their houses and mix in public, yet proper, spaces. The pseudo-Japanese refinement of Rennie Mackintosh's designs created such spaces, the best remaining example being the Willow Tea Rooms in Sauchiehall Street. Even in the details of his furniture, such as his characteristic high-backed chair, he provided discretion in the public arena.

Mackintosh provided the city with a series of café interiors that transformed the notion of public eating in Glasgow. Tea and other refreshments were no longer to be taken only on a functional level in dull, unimaginative surroundings. In Miss Cranston's rooms, public eating had become an adventure. Glasgow, a city which had for so long accepted the constraints of Presbyterianism, was beginning to enjoy itself. As the old moral codes loosened and new concepts of leisure were introduced, the city's prosperous middle classes and its large work force alike began seeking new entertainments: cinemas were opened, while music halls and dance halls flourished. For the working class and the young, ice-cream parlours and, later, Italian cafés would provide a cheaper and less formal equivalent of Cranston's tea rooms. Moreover, they would provide a place for younger girls to congregate.[30]

It was in this context that the Italians brought ice-cream shops to the attention of the Glasgow public. The immigrant owners of the shops must have been surprised by the hostility they faced in the early years of ice-cream in the city. The conservative forces that controlled the city were already made anxious by the growing entertainment industry in Glasgow. For them, the Italian ice-cream shops epitomised the evil of luxury being smuggled into the souls of Glaswegians. The Italians were very obviously Roman Catholics, 'aliens' or foreigners, and Sunday traders. When all these attributes were linked with the sale of something so obviously luxurious, unnecessary, insanitary and ephemeral as ice-cream the forces of conservatism had found the embodiment of all they feared.[31]

Throughout the 1900s the press constantly reported on the evils of these 'Ice Cream Hells' and the police, after several nation-wide conferences on the subject, led a series of prosecutions against the Italian shopkeepers for late opening, Sunday trading, shebeening and gambling. The *Glasgow Herald*'s account of one of these prosecutions reveals the image of ice-cream which was being created at the time as it records the evidence given by the policemen involved in the case:

Sergeant Spence, of the Northern District, speaking of the behaviour of the boys and girls who frequented the ice-cream shops, stated that they were in the habit of smoking cigarettes and dancing to music supplied by a mouth organ, while the language was more forcible than polite . . . witness added that he had seen the boys and girls kissing and smoking and cuddling away at each other . . . Detective Young, Northern Division, stated that he had known many little girls . . . about twelve or thirteen years of age who had since been before the Magistrates, and were now prostitutes. The boys who had accompanied them as girls were now living off them, and were going out acting as their bullies at night. [The judge asks] Do you ask us to believe that the downfall of these women was due to ice-cream shops? [Answer] I believe it is.[32]

The luxurious attributions of ice-cream were here being linked with a grim image of shops that acted as universities of crime. The shopkeepers attempted to fight the smear by founding their own society which developed close ties with the temperance movement. They brought their complaints to the House of Lords, without success. Throughout Scotland the reputation and image of ice-cream remained tainted and the prosecutions continued.[33]

The resolution of the Milk and Health Association was therefore aimed, partly, at rehabilitating ice-cream in the eyes of the public. Their further efforts were accompanied by a gradual change in the design of the buildings in which ice-cream was sold. The cafés and ice-cream parlours became futurist temples of cleanliness, with bright stainless steel, polished marble, glass and myriad reflecting surfaces. Nardini's, in Largs, remains as testimony to this day. The ice-cream itself was served in more elaborate forms such as tall-glass sundaes or in a variety of cones and wafers.

The other related phenomenon is the rise of the milk bar in the 1930s. At a meeting of the League of Nations Mixed Committee on Nutrition in 1937, Lord Astor claimed that while milk bars were unknown in England only a few years before, over 600 had sprung up during the previous twelve months.[34] These establishments were also gleaming, reflective temples of health. Their popularity seemed to demonstrate the success of the campaigns to encourage the recognition of milk as an enjoyable beverage in its own right. Part of the appeal of the milk bars was their American style, and running through all the milk campaigners' rhetoric is the image of America as the model for British milk consumption. The fresh, hearty image of the New World could be used to offer a precedent for a healthier life style which would encourage adults embarrassed to be seen consuming a drink previously thought to be for children. A *Sunday Post* article, for instance, used this ploy to promote milk as a temperance beverage:

I went into a cafeteria in Washington one day, and saw a man drinking a rather attractive-looking cocktail. I had never seen one quite like it, and, being curious, I called over the waitress and told her to bring me one. When she brought it there was a ghost of a smile on her face. I lifted the glass and took a good pull at it. It was milk. The Americans are great milk drinkers. They average a quart a day. The men will go into a bar and order a glass of milk without a blush, drink it, and walk out again with their heads held high.[35]

The milk bar was sanctioned by the example of America and all the New World's vigour, drive and wealth. If American men could drink it without shame, then it must be a manly enough drink for the British, or so the argument ran. The problem for advocates of milk was its age-old associations with mother's milk, children and the sick. In a leader column devoted to milk bars in 1936, *The Times* confronted this problem, pointing out first that the new establishments were termed 'bars' to make them sound as manly as pubs. The editor wrote:

'Parlour' springs to the mind, a suggestive word. But a new venture could hardly prosper under a device with fusty and effeminate associations. The first men who stood at milk bars to consume one of the fifty varieties of non-alcoholic shakes were already victims of taunts from the public house, where 'milksop' has naturally revived as a term of abuse.[36]

The milk bars employed two other techniques to simulate the public-house experience. Drinks were ordered from a barmaid behind a counter as they were in a pub and the customer paid for the drink as soon as it arrived, a feature which caused much comment at the time. Second, the drinks were given exotic names, just like the fashionable alcoholic cocktails of the inter-war period. Customers could buy a 'Bootlegger's Punch', a 'Goddess Dream' or a 'Blackberry Cocktail', all made with milk and costing 4*d* each.[37]

The bars were almost all built by one syndicate working from London with the intention of opening 500 such establishments across Britain. Known as 'Black and White Milk Bars' because of their decor, the first was opened in July 1935 at 68 Fleet Street by a clergyman, Canon Sheppard. *The Times* noted:

The new bar is attractively decorated and equipped. A painted landscape covers one wall while the others have a black and white colour scheme. Chromium fittings of various kinds surround the inside of a bar which occupies three sides of a large room. It is intended to serve about 50 different non-alcoholic drinks with milk as a basis . . . the best to be tried ranged from plain Guernsey milk to caramel milk shakes. There were malted milk drinks, yeast milk drinks, lemon and strawberry phosphates, various milk shakes, a milk cocktail, and ice-cream drinks. Milk could be had iced or hot. A special notice informed the company that the glass and silver utensils served had been automatically and thoroughly washed and sterilized.[38]

By April 1936 there were ten milk bars in London and the first had just been opened in Glasgow by the chairman of the Scottish Milk Marketing Board, who declared:

After the issue of peace and war there was no more important issue before the nation at the moment than that of better nutrition, and research had brought the absolute necessity of greater consumption of liquid milk into the forefront of British public affairs.[39]

He went on to promise that a further ten milk bars would be opened in Glasgow and that the Scottish Milk Marketing Board would prepare a milk shake recipe book for household use, that shakers would be available at the cost of 1s, and that he would like to see a milk bar opened in every school in the city.

The milk bar, however, had little time to take root in the public's imagination before the Second World War brought new priorities, but the milk shake survived the war to reappear in the flourishing café scene of the 1950s and 1960s. Furthermore, publicity for milk and ice-cream after the war was able to build on the efforts of the 1930s, which had established milk as a respectable and enjoyable alternative to alcohol.

CONCLUSION

In conclusion, it may be argued that that the popularisation of milk in the 1930s depended heavily on the rehabilitation of milk's image in the public domain. At the beginning of the century people were put off drinking more milk due to factors such as cost, contamination and dilution. The work of scientists at the Hannah Dairy

Research Institute the Rowett Institute, and elsewhere allayed public fears of contamination. Nutritional research also succeeded in renewing milk's mythic powers by grafting them on to evolving myths of the high-tech laboratory and the scientist as visionary. It was not just that these scientists and organisations were actively engaged in improving the quality of milk but the way in which this work was presented to the public that helped to establish milk as a popular drink. By restoring confidence in the product and attempting to regulate its price, nutritional research and government milk schemes persuaded customers that milk was again safe and worthwhile. It may, however, have been the cafés, milk bars and ice-cream shops that made milk enjoyable again. The editorial in *The Times* summed up the milk bar phenomenon as follows:

> Now the more subtle-minded servants of the public ... have taken the dullness out of milk. The commonplaces of centuries are given a new radiance. Milk makes you sleep o' nights, gives you a milky complexion, makes muscle, gives you a healthy old age, and makes the toddler king of the castle. What more can men and women want?[40]

NOTES

I am grateful to David Smith for making available to me a file of photocopied press cuttings on the subject of milk and dairy farming in Scotland. They were collected by him during visits to the Hannah Research Institute (HRI), the Rowett Research Institute (RRI) and the Queen's College, Glasgow (QCG), during the late 1970s. Full references to many of these newspaper articles have been provided, but this did not prove possible in all cases. Where a full reference is lacking, the location of the cutting has been cited.

1 C. A. Wilson, *Food and Drink in Britain*, London, 1973, pp. 136–50.
2 Ibid., p. 152.
3 J. C. Drummond and A. Wilbraham, *The Englishman's Food. A History of Five Centuries of English Diet*, London, 1991 (orig. 1939), pp. 193–5, 299–303.
4 M. Pyke, *Food and Society*, London, 1968, pp. 77–80.
5 A. Davidson, *On Fasting and Feasting*, London, 1988, p. 186.
6 D. Hayman and B. Sobey, 'Bread and milk', *Petits Propos Culinaires*, 1991, vol. 37, pp. 21–6.
7 J. B. Orr, 'Milk consumption and the growth of school children', *The Lancet*, 1928, vol. 1, pp. 203–3.
8 H. C. Corry Mann, 'Diets for boys during school age', *Medical Research Council Special Report Series*, 1926, No. 105.
9 Orr, op. cit.

10 J. A. B. Smith, *A Brief History of the Hannah Research Institute*, Ayr, 1978.

11 'Dairy research: new institute's first move', *Glasgow Herald*, 8 November 1928, p. 3, col. b.

12 E. P. Cathcart, 'Preface' in A. MacNeilage, *Surplus Milk and Milk Residues*, Glasgow, 1929.

13 N. C. Wright, 'The incidence of tuberculosis infection in the milk of Scottish cities', *The Lancet*, 1929, vol. 2, pp. 452–4. See also 'Surplus milk', *Glasgow Herald*, 12 March 1929, p. 2, col. c.

14 'Curds and whey are wasted in thrifty Scotia', *Evening Tribune*, Winnepeg, Canada, 14 September 1929 (HRI); 'Tubercle-free milk: Glasgow's experience', *Glasgow Herald*, 24 September 1929, p. 8, col. e.

15 'The waste tap: millions of gallons of whey. Can we turn it off?', *Glasgow Herald*, 13 August 1930, p. 12, col. b.

16 Ibid.

17 'Surplus milk: the condensing outlet', *Glasgow Herald*, 25 May 1932, p. 4, col. d.

18 Harris suggests that the earliest attempts to develop a 'milk-in-schools scheme' date back to 1923. See B. Harris, *The Health of the Schoolchild. A History of the School Medical Service in England and Wales*, Buckingham, p. 124.

19 Drummond and Wilbraham, op. cit., pp. 447–8.

20 *Glasgow Herald*, 24 September 1929, op. cit.

21 Pyke, op. cit., pp. 29–30; *Glasgow Herald*, 25 May 1932, op. cit.

22 *Aberdeen Press and Journal*, 11 January 1932 (RRI).

23 'Fireworks, zinc in milk; cow versatile', *Ithaca Journal*, New York, c. 1930 (HRI).

24 R. D. Apple, 'Science gendered: nutrition in the United States, 1840–1940', in H. Kamminga and A. Cunningham (eds), *The Science and Culture of Nutrition, 1840–1940*, Amsterdam, 1995, pp. 129–54.

25 P. J. Atkins, 'White poison? The social consequences of milk consumption, 1850–1930', *Social History of Medicine*, 1992, vol 5, pp. 207–27.

26 Ibid.

27 F. T. Marinetti, *The Futurist Cookbook*, London, 1990 (orig. Rome, 1930).

28 'Food value of milk', *The Scotsman*, 23 February 1929 (RRI).

29 M. Rodgers, 'Italiani in Scozzi: the story of the Scots Italians', in *Odyssey. Voices from Scotland's Recent Past*, Edinburgh, 1982, pp. 14–16; B. Sereni, *They Took the Low Road*, Barga, 1974, pp. 3–24.

30 F. McKee, 'Ice-cream and empires', in *Bellgrove*, Glasgow, 1991, pp. 2–4.

31 Ibid.

32 'Ice-cream hells', *Glasgow Herald*, 7 June 1906, p. 11, col. f.

33 F. McKee, 'Ice cream and immorality', in *Oxford Symposium on Food and Cookery. Public Eating*, London, 1992, pp. 199–205.

34 'Nutrition conference in Geneva: England's 600 milk bars', *The Times*, 25 February 1937, p. 13, col. b.

35 *Sunday Post*, 7 February 1935 (QCG).

36 'Milk bars', *The Times*, 4 September 1936, p. 13, col. d.

37 Ibid.

38 'London "milk bar": new premises open in Fleet Street', *The Times*, 2 August 1935, p. 9, col. f.

39 'Milk bar opened at Paramount Theatre,' *Glasgow Herald*, 14 April 1936, p. 5, col. c.
40 *The Times*, 4 September 1936, op. cit.

7

NUTRITION SCIENCE AND THE TWO WORLD WARS

David F. Smith

Several of the chapters in this volume have shown that throughout the twentieth century individuals and groups such as Horace Fletcher, the National Birthday Trust and the London Food Commission have sought the application of nutritional knowledge by government. Such individuals and groups have attempted to enrol the scientific community, but scientists themselves have also frequently harboured ambitions to influence government food policies, and the two World Wars presented special opportunities to pursue such ambitions. By comparing the involvement of nutrition scientists in government during the two wars, this chapter will illustrate some features of the institutional, professional and scientific development of nutrition in Britain during the first half of the twentieth century.

THE FIRST WORLD WAR

Before 1914, state support for science was limited, although funding for agricultural and biomedical research was undergoing expansion through the activities of the Development Commission and the Medical Research Committee, (later Medical Research Council, MRC).[1] However, there was little involvement of scientists in government, and for decades scientists had contributed to the 'body of rhetoric, argument and polemic' of 'public science' which supposed that the potential of science was being neglected, particularly in view of the perceived threat from Germany.[2] The outbreak of the war provided British scientists with an opportunity to display the importance and value of science. Initially they concentrated on questions directly connected with waging war, such as the design of munitions and defence systems, military medicine, and the problems of war-related industries. However, as the nature of the conflict became clear, serious attention began to be paid to civilian problems.

With regard to military diets, Margaret Barnett has pointed out that the world-wide controversy about energy requirements during the first decade of the century led to various experiments which aimed to assess the appropriate level of army rations. However, the conclusion of the British study was that reductions in the customary high-energy, high-protein rations would be inadvisable. The level of rations for active service was subsequently relatively uncontroversial, although there were occasions when it was necessary for the authorities to seek advice and commission research. The alleged over-generosity of the rations for home forces resulted in a calorimetric study of the energy expenditure of troops in training, conducted by E. P. Cathcart and J. B. Orr.[3] Cathcart, former Lecturer in Physiological Chemistry at Glasgow, had become Professor of Physiology at the London Hospital and a member of the staff of the Director General of Army Medical Services during the war. Orr, Cathcart's former student, had been appointed in 1914 to a new Development Commission-funded post of researcher in animal nutrition in Aberdeen, but had spent the war as a medical officer in the army and navy, before being seconded to work with Cathcart.

The adequacy of diets was, however, no longer entirely a question of energy and protein. In 1912 F. G. Hopkins introduced the notion of 'accessory food factors', and Casimir Funk put forward the alternative term 'vitamine', suggesting that beri-beri, scurvy, pellagra and rickets were probably due to vitamine deficiencies.[4] But in August 1914, when war was declared, British military-medical authorities were far from universally convinced as to the importance of what would become known as the 'newer knowledge of nutrition'.[5] Colonel F. Smith, writing from experience in India, argued that beri-beri should be regarded as 'a disease which may be carried . . . by infected individuals' and that those favouring a dietary theory were 'flogging a dead horse'. In contrast, W. W. O. Beveridge, Professor of Hygiene at the Royal Army Medical College, stated that rations should contain such 'articles as tend to ensure immunity from . . . "deficiency diseases"'.[6] There were some significant outbreaks of scurvy and beri-beri, particularly on the Gallipoli peninsula and among Indian troops in Mesopotamia. Harriette

Chick of the Lister Institute became involved in experiments and advice which aimed to alleviate these problems.[7]

Regarding civilian feeding, the Royal Society eventually took the lead in agitating for scientific policies. In November 1914 the society formed a committee to 'organise assistance to the Government in conducting or suggesting scientific investigations in relation to the war',[8] and sub-committees dealing with communiations technology and physics, chemistry and engineering. The following June Sectional War Committees were established for chemistry, hysics, engineering and physiology. E. H. Starling, Jodrell Professor of Physiology at University College London, was appointed chairman of the Physiology Committee, Walter Fletcher, secretary of the MRC, became secretary, and Hopkins, now Professor of Biochemistry at Cambridge, was made one of the members.

The Physiology Committee became heavily involved with chemical warfare and members were invited to serve on official committees concerned with this matter.[9] During 1915, the committee also began to take an interest in food,[10] initially considering the food supply of the enemy, and producing, in August 1915, *The Food Supply of the German Empire*,[11] an analysis of a German publication. In February 1916 the committee began to turn to the British situation, and issued a memorandum on 'The Restriction of the Importation of Fruit':

> The decision of the Board of Trade to restrict the importation of fruit . . . appears to have been taken on the supposition that such a restriction would merely diminish the consumption of a luxury . . . Physiological evidence, however, shows conclusively that a healthy diet must always contain a proportion of natural foods that have undergone no artificial treatment, and uncooked fruit plays an important part in this connexion.[12]

The argument was illustrated by 'recent experience at one of the larger public schools' where the diet supplied 'neither salads nor uncooked fruit . . . There was widespread ill health, which wholly disappeared when a supply of apples was provided'. The allusions to the importance of vitamins clearly indicate the influence of Hopkins but this is the only memorandum issued during the war which based its arguments so strongly upon the vitamin theory. A passage containing much the same message was also included in a pamphlet by Hopkins and T. B. Wood, Professor of Agriculture at Cambridge, entitled *Food Economy in Wartime*.[13]

In March 1916, the Physiology Committee decided to take up the topic of Wood and Hopkins's pamphlet, when Hopkins, Wood and two others were appointed to a sub-committee to consider 'the question of the advisability of issuing to the press a report on food economy in wartime'.[14] W. B. Hardy, Biological Secretary of the Royal Society, took the initiative in co-ordinating this sub-committee. The original group was soon joined by W. H. Thompson, Professor of Physiology at Trinity College Dublin, and D. N. Paton, Regius Professor of Physiology at Glasgow.

Hardy had heard that the Cabinet would be interested in 'what food reserves there are in the country, and what food would be needed . . . if food supplies were cut off '.[15] Recently, in the Cabinet War Committee, there had been inconclusive discussions of means of stimulating agricultural production. David Lloyd George, Minister of Munitions, took the problem most seriously.[16] Hardy arranged a preliminary meeting of the Royal Society group and told Starling they had concluded:

> An enquiry . . . should not be initiated in a hole in a corner way, but should come as a definite request from the Cabinet or from some responsible Minister, because it can only be carried through with the cordial co-operation of the Board of Agriculture and the Board of Trade.[17]

Hardy arranged a meeting with Mr Runciman, President of the Board of Trade, and informed an official that if the appropriate statistics were provided, the sub-committee would convert them to 'true food values' which could be 'compared with quantities calculated from the dietary requirements of the population'. Hardy mentioned that the sub-committee had considered 'the possibility of effecting a saving in food . . . by publishing advice as to the . . . purchase of materials for the household', and explained that a similar scheme was operated by the Board of Agriculture:

> The officials . . . collect statistics of supplies available and prices . . . The figures are put into the hands of Professor Wood, who applies the necessary physiological corrections, and then draws up definite advice to farmers . . . This is embodied in leaflets which are distributed monthly . . .[18]

The sub-committee 'would be willing to attempt to formulate a similar scheme for human food'. Hardy successfully engineered an official request, as a report was issued nine months later entitled *The Food Supply of the United Kingdom. A Report Drawn up by a Committee of the Royal Society at the Request of the President of the Board of Trade.*

Hardy sought to expand the influence of the sub-committee at every opportunity. In mid-1916, Asquith's government stood accused of failing to prevent food price rises and the formation of a committee to investigate the problem was announced. Hardy immediately proposed that the new committee should include a scientist, suggesting Paton.[19] Hardy was also determined that the report of the sub-committee would make as much impact as possible and became alarmed when a draft contained some contradictory statistics. He told Paton:

> [The] discrepancy ... politically speaking ... very much weakens the document. The Royal Society comes in as a body of specialists to fix the fundamental scientific data. They may be in doubt themselves, but for the benefit of the politician and permanent official, they should have ... drawn up one set of analyses, which in their opinion, was the best ... It is so important that the prestige of the scientific man should not suffer at this juncture in Government circles ...[20]

Hardy's scientistic visions were tempered by some members of the sub-committee who possessed a more sophisticated understanding than Hardy of dietary habits. Paton, for example, who had supervised projects on the diets of the working class in Edinburgh and Glasgow, was certainly aware that the diet of the population could not be manipulated like the rations of livestock. When a new Food Department of the Board of Trade, an increase in the extraction rate of flour, and the imminent appointment of a Food Controller were announced, Paton commented to Hardy: 'I see your friend Runciman has adopted our recommendation about milling. You should persuade him that his controller should have scientific advice ...'[21] But Paton further advised Hardy that the Controller would 'not be able to legislate upon purely scientific lines. He will have to consider the habits and prejudices of various parts of the nation'.[22]

On 6 December 1916 Lloyd George became Prime Minister, an event welcomed by an editorial in *Nature*. At last, it was hoped, scientific experts would be accorded proper respect.[23] Lord Devonport accepted the appointment of Food Controller and a Ministry of Food was created. In order to advise the Ministry, the Royal Society reconstituted the Food Sub-committee as the Food (War) Committee, but its relationship with the Ministry was tense from the start. A memorandum passed at the first meeting set the tone. The idea of introducing a 'meatless day' had been mooted. The committee warned that this would either be without effect, as people would increase their meat consumption on other days, or counter-productive; to allow animal feed to be diverted to humans there was a need to slaughter animals, not to conserve them. The document discussed measures to increase the food supply, emphasising the complexity and dangers of each, and the necessity of appointing 'a man of science to . . . the Food Controller's establishment . . . who must be placed in such a position that all the proposals . . . come before him at an early stage'.[24] Such a man would have the Food (War) Committee at his disposal, and would be able to transmit suggestions from the committee to the Controller. T. B. Wood was appointed Scientific Adviser to the Ministry, but the Committee soon became disappointed with the role and status assigned to both Wood and themselves. Hardy complained that during the first four months the Ministry never used Wood as a channel of communication 'except with regard to minor technical points' and that 'save for one case when his advice was asked and ignored', Wood 'was not accorded an opportunity of expressing his views . . . '.[25]

During its early deliberations the committee established a position, expressed in a memorandum on 'The Primary Importance of Breadstuffs', which it subsequently maintained. This memorandum noted that 'no other food . . . will enable a man to do as much work for the money he spends on food as bread' and argued that it would be impossible to ration bread 'without the gravest danger to the health and efficiency of the poorest element of the population'.[26] The committee also produced a memorandum on the voluntary rationing scheme which had been announced, arguing that

the request that the manual labouring classes should reduce their normal consumption of flour by 1 lb per week . . . would have serious consequences . . . With such a limitation . . . it would become practically impossible for the classes in question to get the supply of energy in their food which is required for their work . . . [27]

The committee became increasingly disaffected with the Ministry at a time when the Cabinet was showing intense interest in food, following Germany's resumption of unrestrained submarine warfare in February 1917. The committee's criticisms were brought to the attention of the Cabinet by Professor W. G. S. Adams, fellow of All Souls College, Oxford, and a member of Lloyd George's secretariat. A memorandum prepared in April complained that 'elementary and fundamental physiological and economic considerations' had been disregarded, the main point being that the Food Controller did not appreciate that 'the efficiency of the manual worker depends as directly upon his food supply as does the mileage of a motor car upon its petrol'.[28]

In its public statements, the committee became concerned almost exclusively with energy. In direct contradiction to the earlier memorandum on the importation of fruit, the committee resolved in March 1917 that 'unless there are grave counterconsiderations, the prohibition of the import of fruit . . . should be strictly maintained since, bulk for bulk, its nutritive value is far below that of wheat'. This position was confirmed a week later when Miss Chick was present for a discussion on antiscorbutics: 'No motion was made, it being felt that the prospect was satisfactory'.[29] Contrary to the impression given recently by Mikuláš Teich,[30] recommendations by the Royal Society were not heavily influenced by the vitamin theory. And even Hopkins, when speaking on 'The Choice of Food in War Time' in March 1917, made only faint allusions to vitamins and concentrated upon the effects of the food choices of the rich upon the availability of cheap energy foods for the poor.[31] In the speeches of other members of the Royal Society committee, for example one by Paton in July 1917, messages based upon vitamins were entirely absent.[32] The emphasis on educating politicians and officials on the basic thermodynamic aspects of nutrition continued throughout the war. The committee rarely considered protein or vitamins in their statements,[33] and serious attention was given to one deficiency disease, scurvy, only after the armistice, when it was agreed that a memorandum by Chick should be circulated.[34]

Following the resignation of Devonport at the end of May 1917, and his replacement by Lord Rhondda, the relationship between the committee and the Ministry improved, with the Food Controller regularly requesting reports. Nevertheless, the expansion of government intervention proved problematic. Towards the end of 1917, as queues for groceries lengthened, and to the dismay of the committee, the Ministry revived the voluntary rationing scheme. Rhondda was promptly informed:

> The Food (War) Committee ... learn from the public press that an official scale of voluntary food rations is to be announced ... and that this scale has 'been carefully considered by scientific people and food experts'. The Committee beg to point out that they have not been consulted ... and cannot accept any responsibility ...[35]

This brought a fulsome apology, and the Food (War) Committee was invited to nominate a representative to join a committee preparing a scheme of compulsory rationing. Paton was nominated,[36] and the Food (War) Committee was regularly consulted on the progress of the Rationing Committee's deliberations. However, constant vigilance was necessary to ensure that its advice was incorporated into official policy.[37]

The First World War proved to be an opportunity to press the case for greater involvement of scientists in the formulation of food policies, and the strategy adopted by the Food (War) Committee depended upon the unity of the experts on a small number of fundamental messages concerning the energy content of the diet. In the field of chemical warfare, once its representatives had been invited to join official committees, the Royal Society became inactive, satisfied that the scientific point of view was now receiving sufficient attention. In the case of food, however, the need for prolonged agitation and constant vigilance indicates the relatively small degree of success, and the high degree of frustration experienced.

THE INTER-WAR PERIOD

On several occasions the Royal Society committees prepared memoranda on the organisation of nutrition research, and shortly after the armistice the Food (War) Committee discussed a plan for a 'National Laboratory for Research in Nutrition'. A paper by Starling referred to difficulties arising from the 'absence of exact knowledge' of nutrition and continued:

> nutrition from a national standpoint is practically a new science and therefore requires researches instituted with the

direct object of solving new problems which arise. These researches can only be carried out in an institute properly equipped for the purpose and provided with funds sufficient to carry out experiments on a large scale and to maintain an effective staff.[38]

Hardy argued for the establishment of a calorimetric laboratory like that of the Carnegie Institution in Boston. The war, he claimed, had 'thrown important light upon the physiological basis of national efficiency, political unrest and of social security'. So that the 'imperfect nutrition of the working classes' might no longer be 'a hindrance and danger to the state' it was necessary to establish the 'physiological minimum necessary for bodily efficiency ... a fundamental datum in fixing a minimum wage'.[39]

A sub-committee prepared a report which argued that nutrition research could not only assist 'the assessment of the minimum wage' but would also be 'of immense value in dealing with the labour problem in tropical and sub-tropical climates' and would even 'assist the solution of the vexed question of equal pay for equal work irrespective of sex'. It was proposed that a 'Nutrition Research Board' should be formed consisting of 'experts in the science of nutrition' with representatives of government departments, and funding from the MRC, the Department of Scientific and Industrial Research (DSIR) and the Development Commission.[40] The DSIR, established in 1916, began to support food research from 1917, with the close involvement of Hardy.[41] The report was endorsed by the council of the Royal Society, leading to a conference of the Development Commission, the DSIR and the MRC, and the establishment of a further committee convened by Starling. After a meeting in July 1919, a memorandum was prepared proposing a

Central Authority charged with the duty of providing a complete survey of the position, able to further [enquiries] by expert advice and pecuniary assistance ... and ... to make suggestions as to the permanent form a State Department of Human Nutrition might assume.[42]

Starling called no further meetings, but Paton attempted to revive the scheme in April 1920 when he suggested that a board should be formed with Cathcart as director.[43] By this time Cathcart was Professor of Physiological Chemistry in Glasgow. Paton and Sir Thomas Middleton of the Board of Agriculture and

Fisheries prepared a further memorandum arguing for an 'Inter-Departmental Council ... on which ... scientific bodies ... would be represented' which would survey research, advise on the distribution of grants, and promote a better understanding of nutrition among the public.[44] However, only one, lukewarm, reply to this memorandum was received.[45] By 1921, in which year the Ministry of Food was dismantled, support for the establishment of a nutrition research organisation had evaporated. The momentary sense of common purpose which appeared to exist among the senior scientists just after the end of the war did not return during the inter-war period.

There are several reasons for this disarray. First, even Paton and Middleton's scaled down proposal cut across the interests of several new institutions which were attempting to define their roles, in what had become very difficult economic circumstances. Second, the shift from wartime ambitions to peacetime science led many of those who had acted as nutrition experts during the war to revert to other, less political, fields. Starling, for example, developed his pre-war interests with studies of the regulation of circulation.[46] Third, a bitter controversy erupted over the aetiology of rickets involving key members of the Food (War) Committee, Hopkins and Paton, on opposite sides.

Hopkins's former pupil, Edward Mellanby, viewed rickets as a vitamin deficiency, while Paton and Leonard Findlay, lecturer and later Professor of Paediatrics in Glasgow, argued that the disease was due to lack of fresh air and exercise. In support of their position, Paton and Findlay attempted to mobilise the medical profession's suspicions of laboratory science, and fears that vitamins were about to become the latest of a long series of dietetic fads.[47] For example, in the context of the rickets controversy, Robert Hutchison, Physician at the London Hospital, expressed reservations about claims as to the importance of vitamins, although, as Teich has pointed out, he had previously seemed ready to assimilate this new dimension to nutrition.[48] Others who joined the sceptics included Boyd Orr and Cathcart. As first director of the Rowett Research Institute in Aberdeen, Orr began to argue that, compared with vitamins, minerals were of far greater practical importance.[49] Cathcart wrote in 1919 that '"accessory substances" ... play a very great part in keeping the body in a perfect state of health',[50] but in 1921 commented that 'attempts are being made to convert a valuable and interesting field [vitamins] into a happy hunting ground for the charlatan and manufacturer of proprietary remedies'.[51] Cathcart, who succeeded Paton as Regius Professor of Physiology in Glasgow in 1928, became well known for scepticism regarding vitamins.[52] Hopkins, meanwhile, began to speak and write unapologetically of the importance of vitamins in medicine and public health. He asserted the importance of fresh fruit in exactly the same terms as had appeared in the February 1916 Royal Society memorandum.[53]

By the mid-1920s the rickets controversy was generally considered to have been resolved in Mellanby's favour. By that time Mellanby was Professor of Pharmacology at Sheffield and in 1933 he succeeded Fletcher as Secretary of the MRC. The division of nutrition scientists into vitamin enthusiasts and vitamin sceptics was partially institutionalised by the existence of two MRC committees concerned with different aspects of nutrition: the Committee on Quantitative Problems in Human Nutrition, chaired by Cathcart, and the Accessory Food Factors Committee, chaired by Hopkins (and later by Mellanby). And Orr's research on minerals was supported by the Research Grants Committee of the Empire Marketing Board, chaired by Orr's friend and ally, the Glasgow medical graduate Walter Elliot, MP. These divisions over the importance of vitamins were overlain with divisions as to the extent, causes of, and solutions to nutritional problems.

Cathcart tended to regard nutritional problems as relatively uncommon, caused by the ignorance of mothers, and best tackled by education, carried out by voluntary organisations.[54] He supervised dietary surveys for the MRC which aimed to provide estimates of calorie requirements, and to correlate the nutrition of children with 'maternal efficiency' or 'parental efficiency'.[55] Mellanby, in contrast, regarded nutritional problems as widespread, and argued for greater involvement of the state in ensuring the application of the 'newer knowledge of nutrition'.[56] In 1931, the Ministry of Health appointed an Advisory Committee on Nutrition, and Mellanby, Hopkins and Cathcart all became members. When the committee was asked to report on an accusation that the Ministry had been laggardly in applying the findings of MRC nutrition research, and a memorandum on this was discussed, Cathcart objected to a statement that evidence linking rickets and dental disease with vitamin D was 'cogent'.[57] When a memorandum for the public was suggested Mellanby expressed his frustration: '. . . it seems . . . hopeless to expect unanimity on a memorandum of wider scope ... unless, of course, it is meant to consist of harmless generalisations'.[58] During the First World War Hardy had attempted to enhance the power of his committee by masking differences between the members. With the foundation of the Advisory Committee on Nutrition the tables were turned. A committee was appointed which was unable to reach any conclusions which would challenge the Ministry of Health and government.

From the early 1930s, Orr began to take a less sceptical position regarding vitamins.[59] His views on the extent, causes and solution of nutritional problems also began to diverge from those of his former teacher in Glasgow. Orr began to support the view that comparing the results of dietary and economic surveys with estimates of nutrient requirements, and the cost of an adequate diet, showed that a large proportion of the population was suffering less than optimal nutrition. This position was most famously expressed in *Food, Health and Income*, first published in 1936.[60] Orr called for measures which could solve the problems of both nutritional underconsumption and chronic agricultural over-production, and became closely associated with the international movement for the 'marriage of health and agriculture'.[61]

The notion that a large proportion of the population were inadequately fed was vigorously opposed by the government. It was argued that statistics compiled from the returns of school medical officers showed that schoolchildren had suffered little from the unemployment of the early 1930s.[62] Since before the First World War, school medical officers had been assessing the 'state of nutrition' of schoolchildren by clinical inspection, an arrangement which continued, with little modification, throughout the inter-war period.[63]

The Advisory Committee on Nutrition became embroiled in controversy in 1933–4, when a committee of the British Medical Association published a report on the minimum cost of an adequate diet, using dietary standards which were more generous than those previously employed by the Advisory Committee.[64] The committee was reconstituted in 1935 and Orr became a member, but it remained relatively ineffective. *Food, Health and Income* was referred to the committee and an investigation was started to test the validity of its conclusions. This was still on-going at the beginning of the Second World War and was never completed.[65]

This very brief account of developments during the inter-war period has presented a picture of nutrition as a field riven with controversy. It has not, however, indicated the growth of the field. Besides the establishment of the Dunn Nutritional Laboratory, discussed by Mark Weatherall in the present volume, and the Rowett Research Institute, concentrations of scientists interested in nutrition existed at various other new institutes such as the National Institute for Research into Dairying at Reading and the Hannah Dairy Research Institute near Ayr. As Sally Horrocks has shown, an increasing number of scientists in the food and pharmaceutical industries took an interest in nutrition, and the profession of dietetics was founded, as discussed by Nancy Blakestad. Finally, the National Birthday Trust, discussed by Susan Williams, was just one of a wide range of voluntary bodies which engaged in nutrition-related activities, ranging from relief of poverty and popular education to research and political campaigning.

By 1939, a few senior scientists had made some inroads into the machinery of government, but the ambitions of some of them to formulate and oversee a scientific food policy remained largely frustrated. However, in the coming war, not only this small group but many of the larger group of more junior scientists would also look for opportunities to advance their ambitions.

THE SECOND WORLD WAR

The war was declared on 3 September 1939, on the 9th a Ministry of Food was re-established, and on the 11th Orr wrote to Mellanby suggesting that a small committee of 'nutritional and agricultural experts' should be formed to advise the new Ministry.[66] Mellanby's reply was stand-offish: 'there is nothing wrong with the initiative in this office [MRC head office] . . . I spend a good deal of my time barging into these people and telling them what they ought to do . . .'[67] As far as finding a place for himself in the wartime food system was concerned, it seemed that Orr could expect little help from Mellanby. Orr continued his public campaign for a food and agricultural policy based on nutritional needs, in much the same way as before the war. He became honorary president of the Glasgow and Aberdeen branches of the Children's Nutrition Council,[68] a group formed by the merger of the two main 1930s nutrition pressure groups, the Committee against Malnutrition and the Children's Minimum Council. He produced a succession of books and pamphlets, including a Fabian Tract issued in 1940, and wrote the preface to J. R. Marrack's *Food and Planning*, published in 1942 by the left-wing publishers Gollancz. He was increasingly involved with campaigning for a post-war food system which would meet nutritional needs, regenerate the world economy, and form a firm foundation for peace.[69]

The Advisory Committee on Nutrition did not meet after the outbreak of the war, but in mid-October 1939, in order to help Walter Elliot, now the Minister of Health, to comment on the proposed food policy, Hopkins, Mellanby, Cathcart and Orr were invited to an informal meeting. Despite previous disagreements, it was recorded that the 'body of physiologists' unanimously recommended that economic use should be made of all animal fats, that the price of milk should be decreased, and the extraction rate of flour raised.[70] When the physiologists were called together again in December they seemed equally united and were reported to have agreed that 'a change in diet of the people is highly desirable, and the war presented an opportunity, which should be taken to bring about a change'.[71] It was also agreed that the MRC would set up a Committee on Special Diets to consider the question of special diets for invalids. This meeting, and Orr's involvement in it, was referred to in Parliament as a means of reassuring the public about the food situation.

Jack Drummond, Professor of Biochemistry at University College, London, became the Ministry of Food's 'Chief Adviser on Food Contamination' in October 1939 and 'Chief Scientific Adviser' in February 1940. In the past Drummond had been closely associated with the MRC, and, like Mellanby, was an original member of the Accessory Food Factors Committee. However, Drummond had resigned in 1932 following a row in which he was accused of not having given sufficient credit to other workers in a publication on cod liver oil.[72] Drummond subsequently became interested in food history, publishing *The Englishman's Food* just before the war.[73] In June 1940 a Scientific Food Committee was appointed to advise the War Cabinet's Food Policy Committee. Sir William Bragg, President of the Royal Society, became chairman, B. S. Platt, who assisted Mellanby on nutritional matters, became one of the secretaries, and Mellanby, Cathcart and Orr were among the members.[74]

During the war Mellanby continued to address himself largely to the Ministry of Health as he had done during the inter-war period. However, he now enjoyed considerable more success. The formation of the Special Diets Committee was just the beginning of his enhanced influence. On Christmas Eve 1940, Wilson Jameson, the Chief Medical Officer, informed Mellanby that he had concluded that it would be best for the Food Section of the Ministry to 'rely on the . . . Medical Research Council for scientific advice on nutrition . . .'.[75] Mellanby replied that this task would be best accomplished by a group consisting of himself, Platt and S. J. Cowell. Cowell, Professor of Dietetics at University College Medical School, had been Mellanby's assistant in Sheffield.[76] In January 1941 this group was consulted on a question concerning the supply of fish oils. But Mellanby wanted the Ministry to be concerned with more than welfare foods. He told Jameson that the question in hand

> . . . raises fundamental issues which concern the whole attitude of the Ministry of Health towards the feeding of the population. . . it should be one of the important functions of the Ministry . . . to give direction to the appropriate Government Departments concerning the amount and kinds of foods to be produced . . .[77]

Mellanby declared that the 'present situation is most unsatisfactory . . . and, if things go on as at present, I can see not only inefficiency but something of a scandal arising'.[78] In May 1941 Jameson established an 'informal Standing Committee . . . to discuss with officers of the Ministry of Food medical and nutritional problems arising out of the war'.[79] Jameson invited Mellanby to become a member and requested his opinion on some papers submitted by Drummond. Mellanby objected to a proposed 5 per cent cull of the dairy herd:

> This would be . . . a calamity but I think that it would be even more tragic if it happened without the Ministry of Health making some kind of effort and protest to stop the rot . . . it is time the Ministry . . . took their coats off and made their voices heard.[80]

In December 1941 Jameson's committee was expanded and reconstituted on a more formal basis. By this time the Scientific Food Committee had become inactive and so the Jameson committee became the main source of nutritional advice to the government. This strengthened bureaucratic control and marginalised relative outsiders such as Orr.

To a large extent, Mellanby achieved his long-sought ambition of becoming central to the provision of nutrition advice to government departments, but the process of generating that advice was often fraught with difficulties. To take one example, in April 1941 Mellanby received a request from the Ministry of Food for the Accessory Food Factors Committee to produce a new, comprehensive set of food composition tables for planning purposes.[81] Hugh Magee, Senior Medical Officer of the Ministry of Health, was asked to act as convenor of a sub-committee to carry out the task. After a few weeks of exchanges about procedures and who was going to do the work, the members of the sub-committee proceeded to argue about whether carbohydrates should be expressed as sugar or starch, what conversion factors should be used for calculating the energy content of foods, and what figures should be used for flours of different extraction rates. Magee found himself taking on the role of referee, a task he was still performing over two years later.[82]

THE NUTRITION SOCIETY

While Mellanby and other senior scientists were conducting their wartime manoeuvres, many junior scientists felt that their expertise was inadequately deployed. From October 1940, on the initiative of S. K. Kon, of the National Institute for Research into Dairying, a series of 'Informal Conferences of Nutrition Workers' prepared recommendations which were sent to government departments. The fourth, for example, discussed skimmed milk:

> In Australia and New Zealand the buttermaking season is at its peak. Unless a decision is sent to these countries soon, much skim milk will not be dried ... The British Government is fighting an enemy who is doing his best to starve us out. To waste a ... first class and ... cheap foodstuff ... is assisting the enemy.[83]

It was reported at the following meeting that Drummond was 'very pleased to have the support of the conference in this matter',[84] but it also emerged that Mellanby had barred MRC-supported workers from attending the conferences. He had told them:

> one of the official duties of the MRC is to assist other Government Departments by supplying technical advice and undertaking necessary investigations. Any attempt on the part

of an outside body to fulfil this same responsibility ... can only lead to confusion.[85]

Mellanby's actions were unpopular, but provided an opportunity for Orr. Orr suggested to Kon that a properly constituted society should be formed.[86] A sequence of events followed, leading to the first Nutrition Society conference in October 1941. Orr became chairman and Leslie Harris, Director of the Dunn Nutrition Laboratory, honorary secretary.

All the early meetings of the Nutrition Society had a fairly practical orientation but it was soon apparent that the programme did not meet with universal approval. Harris received a letter from N. W. Pirie and F. Yates, of Rothamsted Experimental Station, and F. le Gros Clark, suggesting that papers should be pre-circulated, and that reports should be drawn up after each conference. Clark was secretary of the Children's Nutrition Council, and formerly secretary and founder member of the left-wing Committee against Malnutrition. Pirie, Yates and Clark argued:

> ... the only justification for setting up a society ... is that its deliberations are ... of ... practical importance ... If ... [the Nutrition Society conferences] are being held, no effort should be spared to make them as productive and conclusive as possible.[87]

However, while Pirie, Yates and Clark wanted the society to be more closely involved in policy-making, others did not. Harris received a number of letters complaining about the May 1942 meeting on 'Collective Feeding'. The opening address was given by the Minister of Food and the morning session chaired by Dowager Lady Reading, chairman of the Women's Voluntary Service. Platt complained: 'I think that the programme ... looks more like a bill for a variety show than the notice of a meeting of a scientific society!!'[88] Magee wrote, '... my fear is the introduction of politics into the Society ... having had a politician to open a meeting ... you have opened the door to the introduction of political discussions'.[89] In these circumstances the proposals of Pirie and his colleagues made little impact.

In 1943, following further representations from members, a questionnaire about the desirability of starting a 'Technical Section' to hold meetings of a more scientific nature was circulated. Of the 489 members, 216 voted, and of those 109 were prepared to pay for additional technical meetings. But Harris claimed that there was overwhelming approval of 'meetings of the kind so far organised' and observed that criticisms tended to 'cancel each other out'.[90] For example, while one respondent complained that the existing meetings were 'a playground for social workers' another wanted 'discussions which would point the way to world policy'.[91] The character of Nutrition Society conferences consequently remained essentially unchanged during the war. Each concerned a particular, usually practical, and sometimes policy-oriented, theme, but there was never any attempt to reach a Nutrition Society 'line'. Activists who wanted to engage more directly in the making and application of nutrition policy had to be content with independent activities or working through groups such as the Children's Nutrition Council.

However, the Nutrition Society did become involved in some advisory and co-ordinating activities, the main example being its 'Bureau of Nutrition Surveys'. The origins of this organisation may be traced to an article written anonymously by John Yudkin,[92] published in *The Times* in August 1942. Yudkin, then based at the Dunn Nutritional Laboratory, argued that methods for the 'detection of very early signs of nutritional deficiency' such as 'disability to see in the dark' for vitamin A, and 'blood and urine analyses' for vitamins B_1 and C, made it possible to 'diagnose deficiency which may not lead to any obvious symptoms but impairs efficiency and lowers resistance . . . [and to] advise the authorities . . . on the relative merits of food policies . . .'. Research into biochemical and other tests for malnutrition had been conducted at the Dunn since the 1930s. Yudkin complained that 'there . . . still is no systematic survey of selected groups at regular intervals . . .' and suggested that the main reason was the large number of organisations concerned with nutrition. He asserted:

> What is needed is a Nutrition Council, composed of clinicians, laboratory workers, and Medical Officers of Health . . . It would draw up a plan for periodical nutrition surveys . . . [and would] work in close collaboration with the Ministry of Food so that food policy could be co-ordinated with nutritional policy . . . [93]

The need for, remit and organisation of a Nutrition Council were debated in the letters page of *The Times* and soon afterwards Jameson called a meeting of people involved in nutrition surveys. Later he told Harris that he had formed the view that the Nutrition

Society 'must be the essential element ...' in any machinery established for the co-ordination of nutrition surveys.[94] The society established a Bureau of Nutrition Surveys with a part-time director assisted by an advisory committee. Activities to improve communications between research groups, and to standardise methods of survey, were organised. But some members supported the Bureau only reluctantly. Immediately after the end of the war in Europe, R. A. McCance, one of the most outspoken members of the 'scientific' tendency in the society, took the opportunity of resigning from the advisory committee: 'I am not really in sympathy with the objects of the committee, for I rather disapprove of all this co-ordination, and I am not getting enough time to attend to my own work'.[95] But the main reason why the bureau was wound up in 1946 was that its grant from a charitable trust was discontinued, and the government failed to provide alternative funding. After the war the Nutrition Society soon took on more of the attributes of a conventional scientific society – it started holding 'Open Scientific Meetings' for short communications, and began to accept original articles for publication in its journal. Most of the conferences also became much more esoteric.[96]

CONCLUSIONS

The Second World War, like the first, proved to be a great opportunity for some scientific experts in nutrition to realise long-held ambitions to become involved in the formulation and implementation of a scientific food policy. By 1939 there were a number of senior scientists who had made some inroads into the apparatus of the state, and who were poised to take advantage of wartime opportunities. Edward Mellanby was particularly well placed as secretary of the Medical Research Council, and, through careful manoeuvring, he achieved a position in which he could regard his ambition to become 'Government Nutrition Adviser' as at least partially realised. He subsequently jealously defended the position.

By that time, however, there was also a large group of more junior scientists who wanted to apply their work to the war effort and to be involved in policy-making. Their attempt at self-organisation, and the responses of more senior scientists, led to the establishment of a new society. The wartime development of the Nutrition Society was marked by tensions between those who wished it to be policy-oriented and those who wished it to develop more in the direction of a conventional scientific society. After the war the latter tendency swiftly prevailed.

During the Second World War the influence of nutrition science upon government policy was unprecedented. The period is often thought of by nutrition scientists as a golden age, when the government was receptive to their views because controversy abated, nutrition scientists worked together, and agreement on policies was easily achieved. However, the archival evidence suggests that such a view places excessive emphasis on the role of co-operation and consensus. The wartime influence upon government policy was not the product of consensus, but was achieved in spite of substantial disagreements within the scientific community.

NOTES

The author wishes to record his gratitude to Bernard Harris, Andrew Hull, Malcolm Nicolson, Derek Oddy, Hamish Maxwell-Stewart and two anonymous referees, for their valuable comments. Thanks are also due to the Wellcome Trust for their financial support of the author during the preparation of this chapter.

1 R. Oldby, 'Social imperialism and state support for agricultural research in Edwardian Britain', *Annals of Science*, 1991, vol. 48, pp. 509–26; A. L. Thomson, *Half a Century of Medical Research*, vol. I, *Origins and Policy of the Medical Research Council (UK)*, London, 1973.

2 F. M. Turner, 'Public science in Britain, 1880–1918', *ISIS*, 1980, vol. 71, pp. 589–608.

3 E. P. Cathcart and J. B. Orr, *Energy Expenditure of the Infantry Recruit in Training*, London, 1919.

4 F. G. Hopkins, 'Feeding experiments illustrating the importance of accessory food factors in normal dietaries', *Journal of Physiology*, 1912, vol. 44, pp. 425–60; C. Funk, 'The etiology of the deficiency diseases', *Journal of State Medicine*, 1912, vol. 20, pp. 341–68.

5 E. V. McCollum, *The Newer Knowledge of Nutrition*, New York, 1918.

6 F. Smith, 'Beriberi or polyneuritis among British troops in India', *Journal of the Royal Army Medical Corps*, 1914, vol. 23, pp. 64–6; W. W. O. Beveridge, 'Some essential factors in the construction of field service and expeditionary rations', ibid., pp. 376–96.

7 M. Harrison, 'Crossing the "danger line": diet, disease and morale in Mesopotamia', in P. Liddle and H. Cecil (eds), *Facing Armageddon. The First World War Experienced*, London, 1996; W. H. Horrocks, 'Prevention of food deficency diseases', in W. G. Macpherson, W. H. Horrocks and W. W. O. Beveridge (eds), *Medical Services Hygiene of the War*, vol. II (Official History of the War), London, 1923, pp. 83–107.

8 Meeting, 5 November 1914, Royal Society Archives (hereafter RS), Council Minutes, 1908–14, vol. 10, p. 475.

9 Physiology (War) Committee, 'First Interim Report', 23 January 1918, RS MS 505, file 'Royal Society (War) Committee'.

10 For accounts of the work of the Royal Society in the area of food during the First World War see: J. G. Stark, 'British Food Policy and Diet in World War One', unpublished Ph.D. thesis, London School of Economics, 1985, chap. 4; A. Hull, 'Passwords to Power. A Public Rationale c. 1900–1925', unpublished Ph.D. thesis, Glasgow University, 1994, chap. 4, and M. Teich, 'Science and food during the Great War: Britain and Germany', in H. Kamminga and A. Cunningham, *The Science and Culture of Nutrition, 1840–1940*, Amsterdam, 1995, pp. 213–34.

11 Physiology (War) Committee, '*First Report. The Food Supply of the German Empire*', 15 August 1915, RS Food (War) Committee (hereafter FWC), Reports and Memoranda.

12 Physiology (War) Committee, 'Memorandum on the Importation of Fruit', 22 February 1916, ibid.

13 T. B. Wood and F. G. Hopkins, *Food Economy in Wartime*, Cambridge, 1915.

14 W. B. Hardy to A. D. Hall, 10 March 1916, RS MS 505, file 'C–M'.

15 W. B. Hardy to E. H. Starling, 27 March 1916, RS MS 505, file 'R–T'.

16 Minutes of the 79th Meeting of the War Committee, 23 March 1916, Public Record Office (hereafter PRO) CAB 22/14.

17 W. B. Hardy to E. H. Starling, 29 March 1916, RS MS 505, file 'R–T'.

18 Memorandum with W. B. Hardy to Mr Eddison, Board of Trade, 29 March 1916, RS MS 505, file 'Board of Trade'.

19 W. B. Hardy to J. Thomson, 19 June 1916, RS MS 505, file 'R–T'.

20 W. B. Hardy to D. N. Paton, 10 August 1916, RS MS 505, file 'Paton, D. N.'.

21 D. N. Paton to W. B. Hardy, 19 November 1916, ibid.

22 D. N. Paton to W. B. Hardy, 3 December 1916, ibid.

23 Editorial, 'At last!', *Nature*, 1916, vol. 98, pp. 285–6.

24 Food (War) Committee, 'Memorandum presented to HM Minister for Food Control', 18 December 1916, RS FWC Reports and Memoranda.

25 W. B. Hardy to R. H. Rew, 24 April 1917, RS FWC Minutes.

26 Food (War) Committee, 'The National Food Supply. The Primary Importance of Breadstuffs', 2 February 1917, RS FWC Reports and Memoranda.

27 Meeting, 10 February 1917, RS FWC Minutes.

28 Meeting, 24 April 1917, ibid.

29 Meetings, 16 and 23 March 1917, ibid.

30 Teich, 1995, op. cit.

31 F. G. Hopkins, 'On the choice of food in wartime', *Journal of State Medicine*, 1917, vol. 15, pp. 193–202.

32 D. N. Paton, 'Feeding a nation in peace or war', *Journal of State Medicine*, 1918, vol. 26, pp. 65–76, 111–19.

33 A rare reference to protein occurs in a memorandum passed in December 1917, while a rare reference to 'fat soluble "A" substance' occurs in a memorandum passed in February 1918. Meetings, 10 December 1917 and 14 February 1918, RS FWC Minutes.

34 Meeting, 15 November 1918, ibid.

35 Meeting, 12 November 1917, ibid.

36 Meeting, 20 November 1917, ibid.

37 D. N. Paton to W. B. Hardy, 26 January 1918, RS MS 528.

38 E. H. Starling, 'Note for consideration by the Committee on Friday, November 15th, 1918', ibid.

39 W. B. Hardy, 'Human Nutrition Institute', September 1918, ibid.

40 'Report of the Food (War) Committee upon the Organization of State Research in Human Nutrition', 18 January 1919, ibid.

41 E. Hutchinson, 'A fruitful cooperation between government and academic science: food research in the United Kingdom', *Minerva*, 1972, vol. 10, pp. 19–50.

42 E. H. Starling to W. Fletcher, 1 August 1919, PRO FD 1/174.

43 D. N. Paton, 'Nutrition Research Suggestions April 1920', ibid.

44 T. Middleton and D. N. Paton, 'Memorandum', 4 June 1920, ibid.

45 W. Fletcher to D. N. Paton, 7 March 1921, PRO FD 1/4365; W. B. Hardy to W. Fletcher, 21 June 19, PRO FD 1/174.

46 C. J. Martin, 'Ernest Henry Starling 1866–1927', *Proceedings of the Royal Society*, 1928, series B, vol. 102, pp. xvii–xxvii.

47 D. F. Smith and M. Nicolson, 'The "Glasgow school" of Paton, Findlay and Cathcart: conservative thought in chemical physiology, nutrition and public health', *Social Studies in Science*, 1989, vol. 19, pp. 195–238.

48 M. Teich, 1995, op. cit., p. 231; R. Hutchison, contribution to 'Discussion on the importance of accessory food factors (vitamins) in the feeding of infants', *Proceedings of the Royal Society of Medicine*, 1920, vol. 13, Section for the Study of Diseases of Children, p. 87.

49 D. F. Smith, 'The early institutional and scientific development of the Rowett Research Institute', in A. Adam, D. Smith and F. Watson (eds) *To the Greit Support and Advancement of Helth*, Aberdeen, 1996, pp. 45–53.

50 E. P. Cathcart, *Elementary Physiology in Relation to Hygiene*, London, 1919, p. 13.

51 E. P. Cathcart, *The Physiology of Protein Metabolism*, London, 1921, p. 88.

52 For examples see D. F. Smith, 'Nutrition in Britain in the Twentieth Century', unpublished Ph.D. thesis, University of Edinburgh, 1986, pp. 90–1.

53 See, for example, F. G. Hopkins, 'Recent advances in science in relation to practical medicine and the nutritional requirements of the body', *The Lancet*, 1921, vol. 1, pp. 1–7.

54 For explorations of these themes see D. F. Smith and M. Nicolson, 'Health and ignorance – past and present', in *Locating Health. Sociological and Historical Explorations*, Aldershot, 1993, pp. 221–44, and 'Nutrition, education, ignorance and income: a twentieth century debate', in Kamminga and Cunningham, 1995, op. cit., pp. 288–318.

55 See, for example, E. P. Cathcart and A. M. T. Murray, 'A study in nutrition: 154 St Andrews families', *Medical Research Council Special Report Series*, 1931, No. 151.

56 E. Mellanby, 'Duties of the state in relation to the nation's food supply', *British Medical Journal*, 1927, vol. 2, pp. 633–6.

57 M. Greenwood to H. Young, 27 February 1932, PRO MH 56/45.

58 'Summary of comments on M. Greenwood's circular', 28 March 1933, PRO MH 56/46.

59 See, for example, comments in J. B. Orr and M. L. Clark, 'A dietary survey of 607 families in seven cities and towns in Scotland', *The Lancet*, 1930, vol. 2, pp. 594–9.

60 J. B. Orr, *Food, Health and Income. Report on a Survey of Diet in Relation to Income*, London, 1936.

61 R. Bud, 'The Marriage of Health and Agriculture. A 1930s Vision of Biotechnology', paper presented at the spring meeting of the Society for the Social History of Medicine, Glasgow, 2–3 April 1993.

62 C. Webster, 'Healthy or hungry thirties?', *History Workshop Journal*, 1982, vol. 13, pp. 110–29.

63 B. Harris, *The Health of the Schoolchild. A History of the School Medical Service in England and Wales*, Buckingham, 1995, pp. 130–6.

64 D. F. Smith, 'The social construction of dietary standards: the British Medical Association–Ministry of Health Advisory Committee on Nutrition report of 1934', in D. Maurer and J. Sobal (eds), *Food, Eating, and Nutrition as a Social Problem. Constructivist Perspectives*, New York, 1995, pp. 279–304; M. Mayhew, 'The 1930s nutrition controversy', *Journal of Contemporary History*, 1988, vol. 23, pp. 445–64.

65 Smith, 1986, op. cit., pp. 168–84.

66 J. B. Orr to E. Mellanby, 11 September 1939, PRO FD 1/4371.

67 E. Mellanby to J. B. Orr, 18 September 1939, ibid.

68 See Children's Nutrition Council, 'The wage-earner's diet: risk of malnutrition' (letter), *British Medical Journal*, 1940, vol. 2, p. 29.

69 Orr also used film in his campaign. See Chapter 8 in this volume.

70 H. E. Magee, 'Wartime Food Policy. Notes on the Views Expressed by an Informal Meeting of Physiologists Who are Members of the Advisory Committee on Nutrition Set up by the Ministry of Health and the Secretary of State for Scotland Held on 18th October 1939', PRO MH 79/374.

71 'Note on an Informal Conference Called by the Minister and the Secretary of State for Scotland and Held on the 19th December 1939', ibid.

72 For details of this affair see CMAC, PP/MEL/B5, 'Controversy with Drummond, MRC, over c.l.o., 1931'.

73 J. C. Drummond and A. Wilbraham, *The Englishman's Food. A History of Five Centuries of English Diet*, London, 1939.

74 R. J. Hammond, *Food*, vol. I, *The Growth of Policy*, London, 1951, pp. 58–9, 93–4, 220.

75 W. Jameson to E. Mellanby, 24 December 1940, PRO FD 1/2385.

76 E. Mellanby to W. Jameson, 31 December 1940, ibid.

77 Medical Research Council, 'Memorandum on the Supply of Fish Liver Oils to Children in Towns and to People in Shelters', 21 January 1941, ibid.

78 E. Mellanby to W. Jameson, 21 January 1941, ibid.

79 W. Jameson to E. Mellanby, 2 May 1941, ibid.

80 E. Mellanby to W. Jameson, 21 May 1941, ibid.

81 W. A. Lethem to E. Mellanby, 4 April 1941; Minutes of Accessory Food

Factors Committee Meeting, 22 April 1941, PRO FD 1/104. See also 'Diet and Nutrition. MRC Accessory Food Factors Committee Sub-committee on Food Composition', PRO MH 56/233.

82 H. E. Magee to E. Mellanby, 10 June 1942, PRO FD 1/108.

83 H. D. Kay and T. F. Macrae, 'Dried Skim (or Dried Separated) Milk as a Foodstuff in War Time', Rowett Research Institute Archive (here-after RRI).

84 Minutes of the fifth Informal Conference of Nutrition Workers, 15 January 1941, PRO FD 1/4372.

85 E. Mellanby to B. S. Platt, L. J. Harris and E. Hume, 18 February 1941, ibid.

86 J. B. Orr to S. K. Kon, 6 June 1941, Nutrition Society Archive (hereafter NS), Council Minutes, vol. 1, 1941–2.

87 N. W. Pirie, F. le Gros Clark and F. Yates to L. J. Harris, 29 April 1942, NS Committee Minutes, 5 August 1941–19 March 1943.

88 Platt to Harris, n.d., RRI.

89 H. E. Magee to L. J. Harris, 27 June 1942, NS Committee Minutes, 5 August 1941–19 March 1943.

90 Paper referenced 'N.S.C., E.G.6., 21.7.44.', NS file 'General 41–52'.

91 Paper referenced 'N.S.C., E.G.5., 21.7.44.', NS Council Minutes, vol. 2, 1943–7.

92 J. Yudkin, interviewed by D.F.S., November 1979. A transcript of this interview may be consulted at the library of the Wellcome Unit for the History of Medicine, Glasgow University.

93 'Special article: Food and food values. From the scientist to the administrator. Nutrition as an aid to health', The Times, 28 August 1942, p. 5, col. f.

94 W. Jameson to L. J. Harris, 14 December 1942, RRI.

95 R. A. McCance to J. R. Marrack, 12 May 1945, NS Council Minutes 1943–7.

96 Smith, 1986, op. cit., pp. 234–58.

8

AGREEMENT AND DISAGREEMENT IN THE MAKING OF *WORLD OF PLENTY*

Timothy Boon

If . . . we show people by a film that nutritional science can, on the one hand, state what are the minimum requirements of food consumption for a healthy life to be led by the whole community and, on the other hand, state what kinds of food should be grown to meet that need, then the audience is provoked to say: 'Who and what is standing in the way of this common-sense thing being done?'

(Paul Rotha, film-maker)[1]

Throughout this century, the appropriate focus of public health policy has been contested by doctors, politicians and scientists. Many of the arguments, including strong claims for the application of nutrition science, have been staged in public. All media have been used, but by the early 1930s film was seen as the mass medium *par excellence*; in 1934, weekly admissions to the cinema totalled more than 18 million.[2] But cinema was also thought to have powers of persuasion far in excess of other media. An indication of the perceived value of health films is given by the 1939 health education catalogue, which listed over 170 titles produced by thirty-five organisations. It stated that 'the value of the Film as an impressive visual medium of education needs no emphasis'.[3] Those involved in making films did so because they believed them to be significant media of persuasion; for its makers, *World of Plenty* – the subject of this chapter – was a means of making a world in which people would not go hungry.

I have argued elsewhere that it is possible to explain the existence of particular films and how they present their subject by considering them as a product of wider groups than simply those undertaking the technical tasks such as production, camera-operating or direction.[4] I have termed such wider groups 'alliances of interests'. This chapter will illustrate that *World of Plenty* was not in any simple sense made by one group of people, film-makers, about the ideas of others, nutritionists, but was the expression of shared values and beliefs. This essential principle is left largely undiscussed in even the best recent work on documentary film.[5]

Such alliances of interest were held together by various levels of agreement, some of them broad; for example, participants agreed on the importance of scientistic 'planning' solutions to social and public health problems, but others agreed only to offer advice. Some films were also the product of long-term alliances of interest – twenty years, in the case of *World of Plenty*.

WORLD OF PLENTY

It is impossible to convey in writing much of the impact of *World of Plenty*, and my description inevitably concentrates on the commentary. The film's impact comes also from William Alwyn's music, and from the care with which sequences were shot or selected. For example, the convention of movement to the left signifying America, and movement to the right signifying Britain, is rigidly and sometimes playfully sustained. Pearson's account of how the film conveys its account is worth consulting for a more detailed analysis.[6] Were this chapter to be concerned with the film's reception and impact, a primarily verbal account would be a major problem. But, within this argument, which concentrates on the making of the film and the views of people involved, the voice track is in any case paramount. Also, *World of Plenty* does place particular reliance on the script to pursue its arguments. However, whilst it is difficult to convey in print the film's passionate tone, contemporary viewers certainly praised its effectiveness. The *Times* review, for example, stated:

> The audience are left with the impression that they have been treated to a frank, realistic, and pictorially lucid discussion of a complicated problem. It is important to note, however, that the film would not have served this or any other useful purpose if it had not contrived, whilst treating a serious

subject seriously, to keep expectant and amused the spectator's pleasure-loving eye.[7]

The director, Paul Rotha, first suggested a film on food in October 1941, and the resulting film, *World of Plenty*, was first shown publicly at the Hot Springs international food conference in Virginia in late May 1943. It was one of a small genre of films on issues of post-war reconstruction; Rotha's *Land of Promise* and the Cadbury film *When We Build Again* are other examples.[8] As an instance of Rotha's work *World of Plenty* is at the fervent end of a scale on which the majority of his wartime films were less pungently idealistic, for example *Defeat Diphtheria* (1941). For *World of Plenty*, Rotha used the interplay between several voices on the soundtrack to convey the argument of the film, a technique that he first used in *New Worlds for Old* (1938). The first main voice, 'Newsreel', spoken by the Gaumont British News commentator E. V. H. Emmett, was described in the second draft script as follows: 'We've heard him before, on lecture platforms, at election meetings, on the newsreels; the voice of authority, fluent, unhesitant, but so often wrong – before, during, and after the event.' The other main voice, 'Man-in-the-street', spoken by Eric Knight, the script's original author, was 'puzzled, critical, sceptical but eager to know about the chances of a fuller life; perhaps a little slow on the uptake'.[9] An example of their interplay occurs near the beginning, where a series of animated diagrams is used; the script reads:

> *Newsreel* (slowly). On the left are Britain's imports per day in shiploads. On the right you see what she produced for herself. The two added up to her daily consumption of food . . . National food needs thus formed one of the basic elements of a strong flow of healthy world trade.
> *Man-in-the-street* (cynically). Healthy world trade! Yeah, you can prove anything with diagrams. Give me half an hour with Walt Disney and I could pay my Income Tax and never feel it . . .[10]

In addition to these main protagonists, there are two announcers and a handful of other speakers, all unseen. About half the visual content was library footage from over eighty other films. New shooting was undertaken for the animated Isotype diagrams, for a small number of dramatised sequences, and for the contributions of a series of experts.[11]

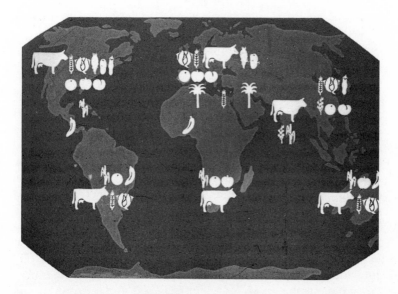

Plate 8.1 Isotype of the world's food-producing areas. Each standard
symbol represents a particular food commodity
Imperial War Museum, courtesy Central Office of Information

World of Plenty sets out to tell the story of food production and
distribution before, during, and after the war. It opens with a
magisterial prologue over shots of grain fields: 'This is a film about
Food. The World Strategy of Food. How it is grown – how it is
harvested – how it is marketed – how it is eaten. In peace or war,
Food is Man's Security Number One'. The argument of 'Part One:
Food – as it was' concentrates on the pre-war problems of food
production and distribution in Britain and America. The state of
the populations of these countries during the Depression is discussed, with the audience being carried by Man-in-the-street to
focus on the injustice of the situation; he says America is 'the
wealthiest nation in the world and a third of it ill-nourished! Laugh
that one off with a diagram, mister!' An American farmer is
introduced to explain how artificially high market prices produced
a glut of farm produce: Newsreel suggests a programme to restrict
the amount of food grown, but is interrupted by a sequence
contrasting food destruction and human needs (quoted below).
This is followed by an explanation of income distribution in
America. There is a comparison with Britain, labouring under

169

similar agricultural policies, partly voiced by L. V. Easterbrook, agricultural correspondent of the *News Chronicle*, and featuring a British counterpart to the American farmer. John Boyd Orr, director of the Rowett Research Institute, interrupts the discussion about whether or not British people look undernourished with a sequence on the newer knowledge of nutrition, British income groups and reductions in the incidence of rickets, and TB. Orr states that at the end of the 1930s 'We were just on the brink of making great progress. We were going to have a world –'. He is interrupted by the sound of shooting, which brings the first part to a conclusion.

'Part Two: Food – as it is' is similar in content, if not in technique, to many wartime food films. It starts with Newsreel, Second Announcer and Man-in-the-street presenting an exposition of increased British food production, and the problems of shipping food in wartime. An excerpt from President Roosevelt's speech of 17 March 1941 introduces Lend–Lease, under which the US government purchased the goods required by Britain from American suppliers; the goods were lent or leased to the British on the understanding that they would be paid for after the war. A dramatised discussion between Man-in-the-street (off-camera) and a 'typical British housewife' explains rationing policy. Man-in-the-street, concerned about the size of the rations, questions Lord Woolton, Minister of Food, who provides further details of food in wartime. An 'Englishwoman' explains how expectant mothers and children are given special supplies. Man-in-the-street wonders 'if all this talk about vitamins is just a fad'; Lord Horder, senior medical figure and one of the King's physicians, explains that the health of Britain is 'remarkably good: better in fact than we expected'. The Englishwoman explains the potential and actual benefits from improved feeding of children and mothers.

'Part Three: Food – as it might be' starts with a moving diagram clarifying the previous sequences:

Second Announcer. We have seen: The State directs food to the Mines and the Factories so that the workers are fit and strong to make the weapons of war ... and to the Fighting Forces so they are fit and strong to use the weapons of war ... To the Youth of the nation to ensure vigorous man-power ... To the Children to ensure vigorous youth ... To the Babies to ensure healthy children ... to the Mothers and Mothers-to-be, to ensure healthy babies ... the circle is complete and

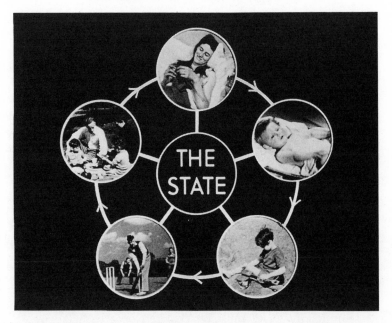

Plate 8.2 How the state should order the distribution of food in the
post-war era
British Film Institute, courtesy Central Office of Information

the relation between the Individual and the State is clear. An
individual's duty to the State is to keep healthy. The State's
duty to the individual is to ensure the *means* to keep healthy.
Newsreel. Except that in the rush hour of war, we've had to
work backwards, from adult to baby. And in the peace to come
it will work forward – healthy mothers – healthier babies –
healthier babies – sturdier children – sturdier children – more
vigorous youth – more vigorous youth – stronger adults.
Stronger and healthier and happier!

This sequence is highly significant for the film's argument because
it not only equates health with good nutrition, but expresses the
problem of malnutrition as subject to a type of contract between
state and citizen, a contract which is presented as the basis of post-
war policy.

After this, Man-in-the-street introduces a sequence about world
food; another American farmer and his family listen to Claude
Wickard, Secretary of the US Department of Agriculture, talking

on the radio about the need for increased production for the Allies. Then comes an exchange featuring American and British farmers. They demand to know whether, in the post-war world, they will be 'left holding the bag' like their fathers were after the last war. A further quotation from Wickard answers the American farmer, and the British farmer is answered by an excerpt of Orr speaking at the British Association's 'Science and World Order' conference in September 1941.[12] Orr claims that wartime need has replaced profit as the motor of agriculture, and mentions the Atlantic Charter, signed by Roosevelt and Churchill in August 1941, which set out the war aims to be pursued if America were to enter the war: 'Freedom from want means food for everybody on the new gold standard of health.' Sir John Russell, director of the Rothamsted Experimental Station, talks of the need to restore food production in enemy-occupied lands. First Announcer states that the Nazis in retreat will 'strip the land bare'; he goes on to state explicitly the scientistic assumption of the film:

> Science has the answer! We know now what can be done! Munition factories must be changed over to make farm machinery. Experts can say what kinds of seeds should be sown; what kinds of fertilizers should be used. And today we have artificial aids for the breeding of animals . . . Our scientists already have the knowledge by which the devastated farmlands can be made productive again.

Orr reiterates the theme of pre-war food production not being geared to the health needs of populations, and First Announcer hammers home the message: 'international trade doesn't make sense unless it is based on supplying human needs by making the resources of the whole world available to all the peoples of the world'. Second Announcer takes up the refrain with talk of the necessity of a world food plan. Newsreel bursts out after this sequence, 'But this is revolutionary!' to which Orr replies 'grimly with great feeling':

> Tell me, what are we fighting for if not for something revolutionary? What do people like you and me hope to get out of this war if not a better world? The empty slogans 'A World Safe for Democracy,' 'A Land Fit for Heroes' – These mean nothing! Plain people know what they want. They want security . . . The Common Man everywhere demands freedom

from want ... We cannot attain freedom from want until every man, woman and child ... shall have enough of the right kind of food to enable them to develop their full and inherited capacity for health and well being.

The film ends with an excerpt from Vice-president Henry Wallace's 'Century of the Common Man' speech, concluding with the statement 'THERE CAN BE NO PRIVILEGED PEOPLE'.

WORLD OF PLENTY: A PRODUCT OF AGREEMENT

World of Plenty was a highly contingent artefact, dependent both on the interests of those closely involved in its production, and on the circumstances under which it was made, particularly the interests of the several Ministries on whose policies it touched. A decade after production started on the film, Rotha maintained that:

Of one thing I am convinced, only four of us – Boyd Orr, Calder Marshall, Knight and I – understood the full scope and scale of the film as it eventually turned out. Officialdom saw it merely as a dull, dreary, non-theatrical picture about food rationing.[13]

Here I am limited by space to a detailed examination of the film as an instance of agreement between the four people centrally involved in its production. The much broader supporting alliance which made the film involved individuals at the Ministry of Information, such as the documentary director Arthur Elton, who favoured documentarists over other film-makers.[14] And the precise levels of agreement with the other people who appear in the film cannot be assessed here.

Whilst each of the four individuals Rotha mentioned brought particular concerns, it is also demonstrable that they shared commitments to several principles which found expression in the film. They shared beliefs in the pressing nature of the social problems of the inter-war years, the relevance of applying scientistic planning solutions to such social problems, the importance of developing an active and engaged citizenry, and the need to educate citizens so that they could act as responsible members of society. Orr and Knight, along with several people in the broader alliance, saw the lack of food as a particularly pressing social problem. While these values were not uncommon during this period, they came together with particular force and influence in the making of *World of Plenty*. Furthermore, commitment to such concerns had brought several of these individuals together in similar projects in the past.

World of Plenty was produced and directed by Paul Rotha, who may be seen, along with John Grierson, as one of the two most significant figures in British documentary. Rotha's pre-war films were often overtly concerned with social issues and their social and historical contexts in a way which distinguishes them from other documentaries of the period. *The Face of Britain* (1935), for example, presents a historical account of the catastrophic effects of industrialisation. The film concluded that such problems could be solved by scientific planning:

> Not only must slums be cleared ... The new communities must be planned in whole and in detail with a full understanding of the cultural and practical needs of a new society ... All the efficiencies and amenities of the twentieth century are ready to be used. New sources of power, new means of communication, new methods and new processes are here for the service of man. This is an age of scientific planning, organisation of co-operation and collective working.

At a conference just before the release of *World of Plenty* Rotha presented his argument for the use of documentary as a tool of citizenship:

> Not only should films about science give facts, but they should present facts in such a way that may well invoke a call to action ... If [they] are going to have real social purpose, they must give people facts and information not drily but dramatically presented. Above all, they must create a desire among the people for science to be used for *all the people*, not for the privileged few alone.[15]

This attitude had underpinned Rotha's letter to the Ministry of Information, proposing a film about food in October 1941. He suggested:

> a film of first-class propaganda value could be a one or two reeler on the strategy of food. You will recall what an important part food resources and conservation played in the

174

BA meeting and how food is tied up in the lease-and-lend agreement? Here, we feel, is a subject of international propaganda value which should be made without delay. We are prepared to start on it at once.[16]

An internal Ministry of Information production meeting on 13 January 1942 agreed that Rotha's friend, Eric Knight, should write a script on 'The Strategy of Food', and that Rotha should produce the film. They both attended a meeting at the Ministry the following day.[17] Rotha's assertion that it was agreed that 'Knight and I should jointly write the script in consultation with Sir John Boyd Orr'[18] does not necessarily contradict the letter of the official record; rather it shows how close was the collaboration on the script.

Knight, a Yorkshireman who had settled in America, was a film critic, novelist and sometime farmer. He is now most often remembered for the book *Lassie Come Home*, a story set in Yorkshire during the Depression. Knight's most significant critical success was *This Above All*, in which he 'tried to raise all the problems concerning war that face the young man of today, brought up on "no more war" and pre-Munich *laissez-faire*'.[19] This can be seen as part of Knight's passionate concern about relations between Britain and America in wartime. He came to London in October 1941 to investigate the state of the British diet under wartime rationing and price controls, with the aim of producing articles and speeches in the interests of Anglo-American understanding. The intended American distribution of 'The Strategy of Food' fitted Knight's interests well.[20] By the time he left for America in early February 1942 he had submitted a script to the Ministry.[21] Knight understood that 'If there are no changes, this will be the first time in the history of film that a script wasn't a matter of discussion, compromise and later rebuilding'.[22] It was intended that Knight should continue to collaborate on the script after his return to America, that he would be in charge of all filming there, and would voice 'Man-in-the-street'. From April 1942 he was working with Frank Capra for the Film Unit of the US Army, on the *Why We Fight* series. He was killed in an air crash in January 1943 – four months before *World of Plenty* was seen in public.[23]

Knight corresponded regularly with Rotha after reading Rotha's book *The Film till Now* in 1932.[24] The subjects of the letters range broadly and indicate close agreement between the two men. Knight's concern for the state of Britain in the 1930s led him to pay a visit at the begnning of 1938, during which he made an extensive tour of the depressed areas, and wrote some journalism. The book *Now Pray We for our Country* (1940) came out of his experiences. His interest was sufficiently detailed that he knew about the British Medical Association's nutrition report.[25] A keen supporter of Roosevelt, Knight advocated active citizenship in a particularly vivid way in a letter written on the eve of war:

> I still believe that kindness and consideration of fellow-men is the only true interpretation of liberalism; that belief in kindness and consideration cannot just come from belonging to a party. It can only come from within each man himself – and it will spring best from him if he is a party of one man. We do not need one big party of ten million men. We need ten million parties of one man each – each one brave enough to convince himself without support.[26]

Knight's letters resound with themes which later featured in *World of Plenty*, including the policy of destroying crops to maintain

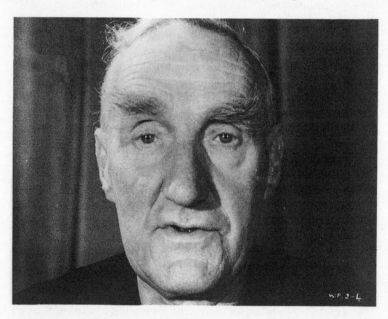

Plate 8.3 'Tell me, what are we fighting for if not for something revolutionary?' – John Boyd Orr, in *World of Plenty*
British Film Institute, *courtesy Central Office of Information*

prices.[27] The film's central theme of fair food distribution is also found in a letter written in August 1941:

> Why should not refrigerator ships carry the fresh vegetables of Florida, the citrus fruits of Texas and Florida, the fruits of Pennsylvania and New Jersey, the enormous glut surpluses that rot here, to the children of the Rhondda Valley and the towns of the Tyneside? Why in the name of God not? If we can do it in war – why shall we not do these things even more so in peace?[28]

Following the first meeting at the Ministry of Information, Arthur Calder Marshall wrote to Knight: 'I am very glad to hear that you are in contact with Sir John Orr and I am sure that he will be of great assistance in this film.' In an internal memorandum he added: 'Knight, Rotha and Sir John Orr are all staying at Clifford's Inn at the present time, and can discuss this film in detail in the evenings'.[29]

Orr had spent the inter-war years building up the Rowett Institute, near Aberdeen. This he achieved using techniques of network-building which would be familiar to any disciple of Bruno Latour.[30] His association with Walter Elliot – a friend since they were undergraduates at Glasgow – was very productive. Elliot was Tory MP for Lanarkshire and a powerful figure at the Empire Marketing Board (EMB), the organisation established by Baldwin's government in 1926 to encourage scientific research into Empire produce and to promote its sale.[31] Until about 1926 he had spent some of the parliamentary recesses at the Rowett undertaking research on animal diets and the mineral content of pastures. When Orr wanted to add a meeting room to the facilities of the Rowett, Elliot

> invited Orr to lunch in London with Lord Strathcona, a man with great interest in Dominion relationships and also blessed with considerable means. As a result, Strathcona offered £5,000, later increased to £8,000 . . . Walter Elliot . . . provided carpets for the public rooms.[32]

The new building was named Strathcona House, and Orr initiated a Founder's Day dinner to which all major financial contributors to the institute were invited, along with influential figures in science and politics.

In this period Orr had been involved with two documentary film projects. The first of these was to have been an EMB film, *Grasslands of the Empire*, which probably came about via his association with Elliot, a key member of both the Research and the Film committees.[33] This film was a particularly striking instance of a project bridging the scientific and public relations functions of the Board. It was reported in July 1929 that 'Mr Grierson [another Glasgow graduate] had already discussed the suggested theme of the film with Dr Orr . . . who was very helpful as to the possibilities and utility of such a film'. Although it was cancelled within six months because 'it had been ascertained that certain elements had not yet been demonstrated on a commercial scale',[34] the grasslands film established relations which were later to bear fruit, for example in the 1936 documentary film *Enough to Eat?* which featured Orr's report *Food, Health and Income.* In this case, not only did the filmmakers go to Aberdeen to film at the Rowett Institute, but Orr was involved during the script-writing stage, making suggestions about how certain themes and individuals might be included.[35] As a sign of continuing close relations between Orr and the documentarists, we may note that Orr later joined the board of Rotha's film company, Films of Fact. They made one final film together, *The World is Rich* in 1946–7.[36] This presented the world food plan which Orr pursued when head of the United Nations Food and Agriculture Organization. Both plan and film are continuations of themes seen in *World of Plenty*.

It is impossible to understand Orr's role in *World of Plenty* without reflecting on his status during the war. He had intended to retire from the Rowett in 1940 at the age of 60, but the coming of war persuaded him not to turn immediately to tending his Angus farm. With the activities at the institute wound down, Orr turned to the task of converting the calls for a scientific food policy with which he had been associated in the 1930s into wartime food policy. He recounts that he persuaded Woolton to establish an expert committee to advise on fluctuating food supplies and their relation to the ration.[37] However, as David Smith has shown, after the demise by 1942 of the War Cabinet's Scientific Food Committee, on which Orr sat, he had little direct access to central governmental decision-making on food or nutrition. Orr was an establishment outsider, lecturing, publishing and pamphleteering, turning his attention increasingly to the subject of post-war food production and distribution.[38] His involvement in *World of Plenty* can be seen as part of this propagandising activity. And the evidence is that he took the task very seriously.

Within a week of the delivery of Knight's first script on 28 January 1942, a meeting was held between Rotha, Knight and Marshall to discuss the script, and soon afterwards Knight returned to America. Before Rotha submitted the first amended version on 20 March, he visited Orr at the Rowett, where they worked together to a sufficient extent for Rotha to budget for a 'typist for Sir John Orr'.[39] Orr continued to contribute throughout the production: Rotha wrote to Marshall in October: 'Since the submission of the budget on 20 April, certain emendations have been made to the script by Sir John Orr and others, that have called for more Isotypes than we at first visualised'.[40] Orr visited Knight twice on his trip to America in November.[41] Rotha was also quick to use Orr's status in promoting the film; for example in January 1943 he wrote:

> Sir John Orr, who plays a *very* important part in the film, has only just come back from Washington, where he has been most operative with regard to potential food rationing plans. I am writing to him by this same mail, asking for any suggestions [on publicity].[42]

At the Hot Springs conference, according to a telegram sent to the Ministry of Information, *World of Plenty* 'was received with prolonged applause and excited much comment and enthusiasm'. This can be seen as a vindication of Orr's investment in the documentary as a form of persuasion, especially as it allowed him to be present by proxy at the culmination of the conference from which he came to think that he had been excluded.[43]

Arthur Calder Marshall was the official at the Ministry of Information who, day-to-day, handled the detailed official side of the film's production. An author and journalist, he provides an example of how liberal-to-left figures were co-opted into government during the war.[44] Earlier, for example, with Lancelot Hogben, H. G. Wells and others, Marshall had been on the editorial panel of *Fact*, a sort of Left Book Club of the month.[45] In the 1930s he had argued that many documentaries were insufficiently critical of their masters. But Rotha also came to make similar criticisms. A sign of how closely Marshall later became attached to the documentarists is visible in his having written the biography of Robert Flaherty, considered a founder of the genre.[46] In an instance which is very suggestive of the workings of the alliances responsible for documentary films, it was Marshall who wrote the script for Rotha and Orr's later film *The World is Rich*.

The production file reveals these four individuals working as a coherent group: Orr seems to have been frequently available to help modify the script; Knight remained committed to the project despite his many movements across America in his last year; Marshall's memoranda reveal him consistently supporting Rotha's view of the film; and Rotha dependably argued on behalf of Orr's and Knight's conceptions of the script.

WORLD OF PLENTY: A PRODUCT OF DISAGREEMENT

If the film can be seen to occupy the common ground of these people's interests, above all it had to comply with and promote the policies of several government Ministries. We have seen that Rotha stated that 'Officialdom saw it merely as a dull, dreary, non-theatrical picture about food rationing'.[47] However, records of the production mainly deny this assertion. There is every sign from internal memoranda of a high level of commitment to the film in the Films Division of the Ministry of Information. The fact that it was viewed as 'a very important film' was used to justify a longer film than originally envisaged, and extra expenditure on animated diagrams and music.[48] Furthermore, Rotha's stock with the Ministry was high: when he overspent on the Isotypes, Elton wrote to Marshall:

> there is little point in our saying that Rotha must bear the extra expenses himself, because he probably can't afford to do so, and, since he works almost exclusively for us and is a very important part of our production machine, we cannot allow a production company to collapse for this kind of reason.[49]

The main difficulties with the Ministry of Information which concern this chapter focused on the American side of the production. The script had been under discussion for at least two months in New York when, in late August, Sidney Bernstein of British Information Services there wrote to Jack Beddington, head of Films Division at the Ministry of Information:[50]

> is it tactful, or timely to make reference to an unfortunate period in the past when crops were destroyed, and food

ploughed under? The [US] Department of Agriculture assures us 'that such things did not happen' and that there is no film record and although I understand that we can get some shots of the type indicated from the newsreel companies – the Department of Agriculture will not feel very happy about revealing them.

Plate 8.4 Crop destruction in the 1930s. 'The US Department of Agriculture assures us that "such things did not happen"'.
British Film Institute, courtesy Central Office of Information

In support Bernstein enclosed a letter from Duncan Wall, Assistant Director of Information at the Department of Agriculture. Bernstein, clearly nervous about the impact of the film, suggested that the script might be scrapped and the English material turned into a reportage item on Lend–Lease. Beddington told him to have this part of the script rewritten in collaboration with Knight. Rotha argued that the US government was not accused of destroying surpluses; the script merely stated that it had happened, not who was responsible. And, although the final words differ from the script under discussion, the sentiment is no less strong in the released version:

> *East Sider from New York.* We are hungry.
> *Second Announcer.* They are burning coffee by the bushel!
> *Mid-Westerner.* We are tired and thirsty.
> *Second Announcer.* They are ploughing in the wheat crop!
> *Man-in-the-street.* This is tragic! Can't someone *do* something?
> *Second Announcer.* They are throwing back fish into the sea!
> *A Negro* (loudly). Why, in God's name, why?
> *Second Announcer.* (disdainfully). Because *you* haven't got enough money, not enough to make it worth *their* while to feed *you*.[51]

There were several stages at which other Ministries were given the chance to comment. Before commencing the script, Knight was sent to see Howard Marshall, director of public relations at the Ministry of Food, and S. H. Wood at the Board of Education. After receiving Knight's first draft early in February, Marshall sought permission to consult Orr, Russell, Easterbrook and Wilson Jameson, the Senior Medical Officer at the Ministry of Health.[52] After Rotha's delivery of the second draft in late March, copies were sent to the American Division of the Ministry of Information, the Board of Education, and the Ministries of Food, Health and Agriculture.

On 13 June, Robert Westerby at the Ministry of Food wrote a letter whose entire text was: 'This letter is to inform you that the script of the film "Strategy of Food" has been finally checked and approved by the Ministry of Food'. Approvals from all but one of the other Ministries seem to have been equally uncontentious.[53] But the Ministry of Agriculture took a close interest in the script, and its suggestions led to substantial alterations. The differences of opinion between the Ministry of Agriculture and the Ministry of

Information, whilst never exactly rancorous, denote that the alliance I have described had come up against not just the different culture of the Ministry of Agriculture, but also a different set of interests. In the first instance the Ministry's objections centred on the disproportionately small coverage of food production as opposed to distribution. It is worth examining the exchanges in some detail. Early in April, A. Manktelow, Assistant Secretary at the Ministry of Agriculture, contacted Marshall complaining that

> the reference ... to our war-time efforts to increase food production in this country is totally inadequate ... we must at all costs avoid any impression that instead of doing our utmost to increase production from our own soil, we are just sitting-back and relying on supplies sent to us from America under the Lease–Lend arrangements.

Manktelow proposed increasing the coverage, and that the Minister of Agriculture, Robert Hudson, might speak that part of the script. He also complained about 'part three, where it seems to me that undue prominence is given to unofficial speakers on the subject of the future food situation in Europe'.[54] This is most likely to be a reference to Orr, who, as Pearson notes, really becomes the voice of the film in the final section.[55] Once again Manktelow suggested that Hudson might speak at that point instead. Marshall attended a meeting at the Ministry of Agriculture at which Manktelow stated that Hudson 'had been very disappointed at the emphasis on food distribution at the expense of food production'. Given that Manktelow was persuaded that references to food production could not be extended, he asked for them to be expunged. Marshall agreed to reduce them to a minimum. It was agreed that the script would be framed so that Hudson might speak it if he so chose, an option which was subsequently declined. The minutes record that 'Mr Manktelow stated that there was no point of policy in the script ... which was at variance with the policy of the Ministry of Agriculture and he promised every assistance in the preparation of the final script'.[56] On 6 June, Manktelow wrote to Rotha with detailed suggestions for amendments at four points in the script 'to meet the Minister's wish that the references to production should be kept to a minimum that is consistent with the general object of the film'.[57] Rotha responded to Marshall with an equally detailed letter on the losses to the script threatened by the suggested changes: 'if we make the alterations suggested, it will inadequately represent in our opinion the scope of British Agriculture in a film intended as propaganda to the United States'.[58] Negotiations continued for several days.

Most of the proposals were to make the script less specific. Manktelow suggested altering the script on pre-war British agriculture by removing the words 'of home grown foods' from 'Prices of home grown foods fell so low that farming had to be subsidised'. He also asked for the phrase 'Marketing Boards restricted production' to be replaced with 'supplies of some foods were regulated', and wanted to omit the British farmer's speech. Easterbrook's words in the final script are softer than the original, but the farmer is retained. Manktelow suggested that a 164-word speech on increased wartime production, written for Hudson, and based on his own words, should be replaced with a sixteen-word sentence. In the end, Newsreel opened part two with 158 words covering similar ground. Also proposed for omission was a speech given to Hudson about the likely post-war need for Britain, and other countries, to continue a high level of food production. In the final script, this point is made in a more diffuse way by Easterbrook and Newsreel. It could be said that on balance the Ministry of Agriculture got its way.

The degree of attention the Ministry of Agriculture gave the script, compared with other Ministries, is of great interest. It is likely that there was some rivalry between the Ministries of Agriculture and Food. There is also an implication that the Ministry of Agriculture believed that its expertise in agricultural matters was being challenged by an alternative notion of expertise deriving from nutrition science, in the person of John Boyd Orr. Orr's account of Woolton's reported reason for not having set up a panel of experts to monitor food supplies implies such a conflict: 'Lord Woolton then said, "I had it in mind, but it was opposed by the Minister of Agriculture"'.[59] Also, the Ministry of Agriculture's public relations policy was very much targeted inwards towards farmers, not outwards towards the public.[60] The lack of contention in the Ministry of Food indicates that the dominant theme of food distribution in *World of Plenty* served their interests very well.

In April 1943 a series of screenings of the final film was arranged. Once again a comparison between the responses of the Ministries of Food and Agriculture is instructive. The response from the Ministry of Food was very positive. A special showing was organised for staff at Colwyn Bay, and the file contains delighted responses from three officials. Elton reported that Woolton was arranging for his London staff to see the film in relays of 200.[61]

In early May, the Ministry of Agriculture was again in dispute over details of the film, but this time the last few minutes' running time were under discussion. Elton showed the film to Hudson, Sir Donald Vandepeer, the Second Secretary at the Ministry, and the Duke of Norfolk. It was recorded that 'Hudson appeared very impressed by the film and said that it was of the greatest importance, and that, subject to a policy point in the last reel, he would like it shown in this country and everywhere abroad'. This policy point amounted to a request for a page's worth of script to be removed, particularly the use of the example of wheat for the world food plan. In this section Orr also argued that the lessons of war should be applied in the post-war world so that agriculture would be driven by the motor of need rather than by that of profit. The section they wanted cut included Orr's 'revolutionary' speech.[62]

At this stage it was already accepted that the film should be premiered at the Hot Springs conference, which started on 18 May. At the Ministry of Information, Elton adopted the policy of stressing Orr's status; he wrote in a letter to Manktelow: 'On the point of deleting Sir John Orr's statement at the end of the film [the 'revolutionary' speech], Rotha says that Orr collaborated throughout and that any approach to him must be made carefully'.[63] Rotha was sent to discuss matters with Manktelow, but on 12 May Elton reported to Beddington, 'we cannot find a compromise for the end of *World of Plenty* which can satisfy both the technical and propaganda needs of the film, and the desires of the Minister of Agriculture'. They 'agreed to delete everything which appears to be controversial', namely the use of wheat as an example for the world food plan and 'any suggestion that production has been solved, leaving only the distribution problem, or that world trade must, as a matter of course, be based on world food'.[64] The remainder of the discussion focused on Orr's role in summing the film up:

> the Minister said that an important man in the political or economic field should sum up the message of the film ... Lord Woolton differs from Mr. Hudson in that he specifically stated that it was a very good thing that Sir John Orr came in at the end of the film before Wallace, because Sir John Orr is a scientist of world repute and not a politician.

Here is clear evidence of a clash over types of expertise. At this stage

185

the Ministry of Information ceased trying to satisfy the Ministry of Agriculture:

> The film was primarily made for the Ministry of Food, which is apparently well satisfied with it. On matters which affect the Ministry of Agriculture's policy we must of course take their advice, and we have done so in the case of the requested excisions. But on matters of taste and presentation I think we are entitled to follow our own views, supported by the Ministry of Food, even when they do conflict with the Ministry of Agriculture.

This conclusion was expressed in a letter from Elton to Manktelow on 20 May. Vandepeer responded, still seeking further excisions, and he colourfully noted: 'I should like to add, however, that, whatever the Ministry of Food may think about it, my own view is that the film is dangerous, and all the more so because of its undoubted technical excellence'.[65]

CONCLUSION

World of Plenty was made possible by sufficient agreement existing between the participants in its production. But its detailed form was also affected by the interests of separate powerful groups, notably the Ministry of Agriculture, which represented different bodies of expertise. The film also has a place in longer narratives of the establishment of nutrition science. If we were to trace a twenty-year story from 1929, we could show how, as the concerns of John Boyd Orr, one very particular nutritionist, developed from the mineral content of pasture to world feeding, the concerns of documentarists, along with various fellow-travellers, also changed from local to global concerns. This is one way of seeing nutrition – and the process of persuading people of what constituted good nutrition – as part of broader culture. Orr's career in this period, as we have seen, was punctuated by a series of documentary film projects. His continuing commitment to documentary indicates the significance he placed on alliances with film-makers in the achievement of his aims. There is a sense in which the success of both the nutrition and the documentary project were bound up in hopes for the globalisation of scientific planning and participatory citizenship. If *World of Plenty* was typical of those values, it was also close to the acme of their combined influence.

NOTES

I thank Chris Lawrence and David Smith for reading an earlier version of this chapter; the Science Museum for supporting the research; the staff of the National Film Archive for repeated access to their collection; and my family for their forbearance. Thanks go to the Imperial War Museum for Plate 8.1, to BFI Stills, Posters and Designs for the remainder, and to the COI for permission to publish.

1 P. Rotha, 'Interpreting science by film', *Advancement of Science*, 1943, vol. 2, p. 306.
2 Quoted in P. Rotha, *Documentary Film*, London, 1936, p. 43.
3 *Health Education Yearbook*, 1939, pp. 111–44, quotation at p. 111.
4 T. M. Boon, '*The Smoke Menace*: cinema, sponsorship, and the social relations of science in 1937', in M. Shortland (ed.), *Science and Nature. Essays in the History of the Environmental Sciences*, 1993, British Society for the History of Science Monograph No. 8, pp. 57–88.
5 See P. Swann, *The British Documentary Film Movement, 1926–1946*, Cambridge, 1989, and I. Aitken, *Film and Reform. John Grierson and the Documentary Film Movement*, London, 1990.
6 See D. Pearson, 'Speaking for the common man: multi-voice commentary in *World of Plenty* and *Land of Promise*', in P. Marris, *Paul Rotha*, London, 1982, pp. 64–85.
7 'Problems of the screen', *The Times*, 3 June 1943, p. 5.
8 T. Haggith, 'Post-war reconstruction as depicted in official British films of the Second World War', *Imperial War Museum Review*, 1990, vol. 7, pp. 34–45.
9 Second draft script, March 1942, PRO INF 1/214 pt. 1, p. 137. This file has been paginated on the reverse of each document.
10 The script was published as E. Knight and P. Rotha, *World of Plenty. The Book of the Film*, London, 1945. All quotations from the film are taken from here, except where otherwise stated.
11 'Isotypes' were diagrams intended to make statistical information readily comprehensible, using a technique designed by Otto Neurath. See G. Reisch, 'Planning science: Otto Neurath and *The International Encyclopaedia of Unified Science*', *British Journal for the History of Science*, 1994, vol. 27, p. 153.
12 See *Advancement of Science*, 1942, vol. 2, pp. 1–120, especially pp. 26–8; L. G. Crowther, O. J. R. Howarth and D. P. Riley (eds), *Science and World Order*, Harmondsworth, 1942. The conference was filmed by Rotha as *They Met in London* (1942).
13 E. Knight, *Portrait of a Flying Yorkshireman. Letters from Eric Knight in the United States to Paul Rotha in England*, London, 1952, pp. 198–9.
14 See Swann, 1989, op. cit., chap. 7.
15 Rotha, 1943, op. cit., p. 306.
16 Rotha to Elton, 15 October 1941, PRO INF 1/214 pt. 1, p. 32.
17 Marshall to Elton, 14 January 1942, ibid., pp. 30–1.
18 Knight, 1952, op. cit., pp. 198–9.
19 Ibid., p. 178; E. Knight, *This Above All*, London, 1941.
20 Marshall suggested two versions on 2 February 1942, PRO INF 1/214

pt. 1, p. 85. Priority was given to the American version and the idea of a British version was dropped only after the American version was complete.

21 Preserved at PRO INF 1/214 pt. 1, pp. 45–69.

22 Knight to Elton, 28 January 1942, ibid., pp. 43–4.

23 See *The Times*, 22 January, p. 4 and 23 January 1943, p. 6.

24 P. Rotha, *The Film till Now*, London, 1929. See also Rotha's letters quoted in P. Rotha, *Documentary Diary*, London, 1973, pp. 14–15. For Knight's letters see Knight, 1952, op. cit.

25 See Knight to Rotha, 16 August 1941, in Knight, 1952, op. cit., p. 186.

26 Knight to Rotha, 24 August 1939, ibid., pp. 136–7.

27 Knight to Rotha, 6 May 1933, 11 March 1934, ibid., pp. 22, 59.

28 Knight to Rotha, 16 August 1941, ibid., pp. 185–6.

29 Marshall to Elton, 14 January 1942, PRO INF 1/214 pt. 1, p. 31.

30 B. Latour, *Science in Action*, Milton Keynes, 1987.

31 S. Constantine, *Buy and Build. The Advertising Posters of the Empire Marketing Board*, London, 1986, pp. 2–3.

32 H. D. Kay, 'John Boyd Orr, Baron Boyd Orr of Brechin Mearns, 1880–1971', *Biographical Memoirs of Fellows of the Royal Society*, 1972, vol. 18, pp. 43–81, pp. 51, 54. See also 'Walter Elliot', ibid., 1958, vol. 4, pp. 73–80.

33 Elliot was chairman of the film committee in 1927. The pasture film was announced to this body on 23 July 1929. See PRO CO 760/37.

34 Reported at film committee meeting, 30 January 1930. Several draft scripts survive, ibid., and Grierson Archive, Stirling University, G2.2.

35 Anstey to Mellanby, 26 June, 27 July; Mellanby to Anstey, 6 August 1936, PRO FD 1/3427.

36 Notepaper for Films of Fact carries Orr's name at the foot from at least December 1945.

37 J. B. Orr, *As I Recall*, London, 1966, p. 120.

38 D. Smith, 'Nutrition Science and Nutrition Politics during the Second World War', unpublished paper read to the Historians and Nutritionists Seminar, King's College, London, 8 July 1992. See also J. B. Orr, 'The role of food in post-war reconstruction', *International Labour Review*, 1943, vol. xlvii.

39 Rotha to Marshall, 2 February 1942, Marshall to Beddington, 20 March 1942, Duff to Campbell, 8 April 1942, PRO INF 1/214 pt. 1, pp. 100, 169.

40 Rotha to Marshall, 27 October 1942, PRO INF 1/214 pt. 2, pp. 226–8.

41 Knight, 1952, op. cit., pp. 218–19.

42 Rotha to J. Griggs, Ministry of Information, 12 January 1943, PRO INF 1/214 pt. 3, p. 41.

43 Orr, 1966, op. cit., p. 160.

44 For obituaries of Marshall see *The Times*, 22 April 1992, p. 13, and *The Independent*, 23 April 1992, p. 29.

45 See anon., *News for You about the New Book-paper*, London, 1937.

46 A. C. Marshall, *The Innocent Eye*, London, 1963. See also Rotha, 1973, op. cit., pp. 138–40.

47 Knight, 1952, op. cit., pp. 198–9.

48 Elton to Marshall, 29 October 1942; Rotha to Marshall, 24 November 1942, PRO INF 1/214 pt. 2, pp. 229–30, 233.

49 Elton to Marshall, 29 October 1942, INF 1/214 pt. 2, p. 229.

50 A cable from Knight on 2 July 1942 stated that he had 'marked a script noting where I could suggest changes'; PRO INF 1/214 pt. 2, p. 91. Both Beddington and Bernstein were sympathetic to the documentarists; see Swann, 1989, op. cit., p. 154.

51 Rotha also agreed to excise a section of part two featuring the poor physical condition of American army recruits. Bernstein to Beddington, 26 August; Beddington cable to Bernstein, 31 August; Rotha to Beddington, 7 September 1942, PRO INF 1/214 pt. 2, pp. 168–70, 192, 199–200.

52 Marshall to Beddington, 4 February 1942, PRO INF 1/214 pt. 1, p. 85.

53 Westerby to Rotha Productions, 13 June; Rotha to Horder, 27 May 1942, PRO INF 1/214 pt. 2, p. 71.

54 Manktelow to Marshall, 11 April 1942, ibid., p. 130.

55 Pearson, 1982, op. cit., p. 76.

56 Memo of Conference at the Ministry of Agriculture dated 4 May 1943; Manktelow to Rotha, 3 June 1942, PRO INF 1/214 pt. 2, pp. 35, 53.

57 Manktelow to Rotha, 6 June 1942, INF 1/214 pt. 2, p. 64.

58 Rotha to Marshall, 9 June 1942, INF 1/214 pt. 2, p. 65.

59 Orr, 1966, op. cit., p. 120.

60 See file PRO MAF 102/67.

61 S. Smith, Director of Public Relations, Ministry of Food, to Beddington, 7 May; Elton to Beddington, 12 May 1942, PRO INF 1/214 pt. 3, pp. 170, 167, 173.

62 Elton to Mercier, 7 May 1943, INF 1/214 pt. 3, p. 175.

63 Elton to Manktelow, 7 May 1943, ibid., p. 168.

64 The published script follows the excised version but both National Film Archive copies that I have seen retain these sequences.

65 Elton to Beddington, 12 May; Gates to Beddington, 13 May; Vandepeer to Beddington, 24 May 1943, PRO INF 1/214 pt. 3, pp. 172–3, 188.

Note: Subsequent research – which will be reported in a future publication – using the Rotha archive (Special Collections UCLA Library) supports the argument presented here.

9

GOVERNMENT POLICY ON SCHOOL MEALS AND WELFARE FOODS

1939–1970

Charles Webster

Supplementary nutritional benefits constitute one of the less discussed aspects of welfare provision in the post-war welfare state. Nevertheless, the nutritional programme was substantial in scale and cost, and it was highly regarded by recipients. It is not entirely clear what objective importance should be attached to supplementary nutritional benefits with respect to improvements in health since the beginning of the Second World War, but it is likely that the high claims made about the significance of these supplements to generations of mothers, infants and children will not readily be dismissed.

The main nutritional supplements were school meals and school milk administered by local education authorities, and welfare milk and various other supplements made available to mothers and infants by local health authorities. Collectively, these benefits constituted a significant element in welfare expenditure. As indicated below, changes in policy concerning nutritional supplementation were sensitive political issues, which were handled at the highest political level. This topic is more important than might be expected as a contribution to our understanding of social policy.

This short survey examines the supplementary nutritional benefits system at its high-water mark, especially with a view to assessing the record of the wartime coalition and the post-war Labour and Conservative governments. The period between 1945 and 1970 allows for approximately similar lengths of Labour and Conservative government. This exercise is especially useful for assessment of differences in policy between the parties of the left and

190

right during a period which is generally regarded as marking a consensus on fundamental questions of welfare. A second purpose of this chapter is to examine the role played by civil servants in the determination of policy in this field. The discussion will concentrate on the value of the subsidies to the beneficiaries, and the scale of the subsidies provided by the state. These provide an approximate quantitative measure of the importance of the service, and an indication of the scale of redistribution of resources by the state towards mothers and children.

Systematic state provision of nutritional benefits takes its origin from the Education (Provision of Meals) Act 1906.[1] Under this legislation, somewhat inadvertently, the foundations were laid for the principle of providing publicly funded welfare benefits for an entire class of recipient without the imposition of the kind of limitations traditionally imposed under the Poor Law. This led Bentley Gilbert to attach particular importance to the school meals legislation, which he claimed was the 'beginning of the construction of the welfare state'.[2]

The reality was of course less spectacular. Even with the advent during the inter-war period of schemes for providing free or subsidised milk for mothers and infants, or the more systematic provision of school milk from 1935 onwards, state-funded and local-government-organised schemes for nutritional supplementation made an insignificant contribution to the problem of poverty and malnutrition existing before 1939. At the outbreak of war only about 130,000 meals were being served each day; they were reaching about 3 per cent of the school population. By that date, the number taking school milk was more impressive; 50 per cent of children were receiving milk, mostly ⅓ of a pint per day.[3]

The particular significance of the inter-war period lies, not in the scale of nutritional supplementation, but in the growth of a plethora of pressure groups, which were increasingly effective in causing embarrassment to the government over its neglect of nutritional supplementation. The success of these groups was partly attributable to their fruitful partnership of social activists, doctors and scientists, who collectively demonstrated the great scale of the problem of malnutrition, and built up an influential body of support for a programme of remedial action based on the latest thinking in nutritional science.[4]

THE SECOND WORLD WAR

It is generally accepted that the wartime emergency rather than the post-war period marked the fundamental turning point in policy. Indeed, the transformation of attitudes and policies with respect to nutritional supplementation was sufficiently striking to be cited by Richard Titmuss as evidence for his hypothesis that the experience of total war provoked a transformation in attitudes to welfare.

> These developments in the provision of meals and milk at school expressed something very close to a revolution in the attitude of parents, teachers and children to a scheme which, only a few years earlier, had not been regarded with much respect or sympathy. In place of a relief measure, tainted with the poor law, it became a social service, fused into school life, and making its own contribution to the physical nurture of the children and to their social education.[5]

Raising the standards of the nation's health was recognised as an essential prerequisite for maintaining morale. Food policy came to occupy a central part in the government's civil programme. As part of the effort to extend the social services, after some initial administrative failings, the hitherto insignificant nutritional supplement programme was rapidly converted into a national system reaching the majority of those in most severe need. The expansion of the school meals system took place under guidelines provided by the Board of Education circulars issued in 1940 and 1941.[6] By February 1945, more than 1.6 million dinners were being served daily, and these reached 33 per cent of the school population. Of these 14 per cent were free, while the rest were charged at 4d or 5d, the charge being restricted to the cost of the ingredients. The school meals service was supported by a subsidy to local authorities varying from 75 per cent to 90 per cent of the cost of the service. School milk was available to 73 per cent of children by February 1945, and about half the children were receiving ⅔ of a pint.[7] The provision of school meals and milk was imposed as a duty on local education authorities under section 49 of the Education Act 1944.

For the benefit of pregnant women and infants, the National Milk Scheme began in 1940; supplies of liquid and powdered milk were supplemented by orange juice, cod liver oil and vitamin tablets. Milk was almost universally available by 1945; welfare milk accounted for nearly 20 per cent of all milk consumption. Before the war, a large section of the working class knew milk only in the form of condensed milk; fresh milk was unsafe and unaffordable. By the end of the Second World War the drinking of pasteurised milk had become normal for working-class families. This change was symbolic of the revolutionary improvement in nutritional habits brought about as a direct consequence of the food policies adopted during the Second World War.

During the Second World War, many of the supplementary nutritional services, although introduced for the sake of the emergency, rapidly became established to the point where it would have been politically unrealistic for the government to suggest that they should have been eliminated after the war. Whereas civic restaurants were allowed to fade away, and rationing was reduced as the opportunity arose, there was general recognition that nutritional supplements were bringing about great benefits, and there was no call for reversion to the pre-war arrangements. Nutritional supplements therefore became grafted on to the Beveridge package of comprehensive social service reforms. No resistance to this development was offered by the Treasury, partly because of the groundswell of support for the nutritional services, but also because the arrival of these substantial benefits in kind provided an excuse for cutting back the level of the new family allowance. By encouraging the adoption of family allowance set at a low level, supplemented by generous benefits in kind, the Treasury had fortuitously devised a system which was more amenable to curtailment than would have been the case had family allowance been set at a higher level. As subsequent history demonstrated, a reduction in the level of family allowance was politically unacceptable, but piecemeal erosion of the value of nutritional benefits, provided it was done with discretion, could be undertaken without attracting undue attention.

Even before the Beveridge Report, it was appreciated that a new policy was needed. One of the first signs of radical reform emanated from the Board of Education. In June 1941, outlining its plans for reconstruction of education after the war, the board acknowledged:

The rapid development of provision of meals for schoolchildren that has taken place during the war and the expected widespread institution of communal feeding for the general public may produce a marked change in the social habits of the people. It may well be that the provision of a midday meal will become and will remain a normal element in public education. There is much to be said for the view that midday dinners should be regarded as an integral part of full-time education and, as such, provided free.[8]

During debates on the Beveridge Report, Ministers from both sides of the coalition partnership laid emphasis on the provision of benefits available directly to children, in order to reassure the public that the generous provision of benefits in kind would more than compensate for lower rates of cash benefits. John Anderson, the Minister of Reconstruction, who was soon to become the Chancellor of the Exchequer, promised the 'fullest development of the various child welfare services which bring the benefits directly to the children'.[9] Herbert Morrison, the Labour Home Secretary, promised the 'development of the education services, of ... school meals and that sort of thing which it seems to me under this new order of things will have to be on the basis of universal free service'.[10] The White Paper on Social Insurance issued in September 1944 promised that school meals and school milk would be 'free of cost to the parents and will be available for all the children in a family attending school, including the first'.[11] The latter assurance was given on account of the government's decision not to pay family allowance for the first child.

LABOUR, 1945–51

The post-war Labour government was committed to the 'new order of things' promised under the Beveridge scheme for the comprehensive reorganisation of social security, which itself largely coincided with the long-term social aims of organised labour. The Labour government promised high priority for family allowances, school meals and measures to improve the health of families. It was committed to provide school meals for all children, to be provided free when the system was sufficiently developed. In the first instance a compromise was offered whereby the government applied a uniform 100 per cent Exchequer grant to cover the administrative costs of the service, while a uniform charge was maintained at the wartime level of 5d. Generous scales of remission were introduced, permitting those in need to obtain free meals. Universal free school milk was introduced in August 1946, to coincide with the introduction of the family allowance scheme. The system of welfare foods for mothers and infants was continued and extended in scope.

The most expensive part of the nutritional package was the promise of free school meals. On this question the government prevaricated. At first, it was acknowledged that meals should be free of charge, 'but this cannot be until school canteen facilities are sufficient to meet the expected demand. For the present, therefore, parents' payments will continue'.[12] This was a slightly disingenuous excuse, because a universal service was a realistic prospect in 1946; indeed, it was a more realistic proposition than for services such as dentistry in the new health service, where all services were made free and universal from the start of the NHS in 1948. In Cabinet deliberations, Labour decided that it was unrealistic on grounds of expenditure to introduce free meals before 1955 at the earliest.

Rather than introducing free meals, the Labour government increased the school meal charge from 5d to 6d in January 1950, and to 7d in April 1951. These increases were justified on the basis of the increasing cost of raw materials. Accordingly, the Labour government gradually institutionalised the wartime convention for determining the cost of the school meal. Although justified on rational grounds, the increase in the charge for the school meal was part of the general drift towards retrenchment in the social services, made necessary by the high priority given to defence, especially by participation in the Korean War. The first steps towards the introduction of health service charges in 1949, and the imposition of a ceiling on expenditure on the NHS, represented parallel expressions of this policy.

School milk escaped charges, but the original intention to provide ⅔ pint each day was not pursued; children enjoyed their ⅓ pint bottle at the morning break.[13] Provision of welfare foods to mothers and infants, which came under the authority of the Ministry of Health, proceeded according to plan and was not subject to erosion. Welfare milk was charged at 1½d per pint rather than the 1d wanted by the Minister of Health. Access to free welfare milk was rendered more difficult to obtain than during the Second World War because it was made conditional on resort to the National Assistance Board, and therefore carried some of the stigma of the means test and the Poor Law. Labour achieved a reasonable level of compliance with wartime promises and its own policy objectives. However, it was considerably less generous over the provision of nutritional benefits than was originally anticipated when the extent of benefits in kind needed to compensate for the reduction of the cash value of the family allowance and the elimination of the allowance for the first child were originally calculated.

Despite the above limitations, under the Labour government the school meals and milk services continued their expansion. In May 1951 in England and Wales, 49 per cent of the school population took school meals, while 84 per cent drank school milk.[14] The uptake of school meals was slightly lower than the peak of 53 per cent reached in 1949, while the charge was still 5*d*. The government's target of 75 per cent uptake of school meals by 1949 was not reached, and it has in fact never been achieved.[15]

By this stage, the argument for the school meal was largely won, and the energies of its advocates were now devoted to maximising improvements. The school meal was established as an integral part of educational experience and appreciated as a direct asset to the child, to mothers and especially to working mothers, and to the family as a whole. It was also regarded as a positive asset to education and social training. The principle was established that the school meal should be designed as the main meal of the day, and nutritional standards for the meal were laid down on that basis.[16] Obviously, the standards adopted are at variance with current nutritional thinking, but at least they were an attempt to apply the most authoritative level of knowledge available at the time. The attempt to maximise the value of the meal as a social training depended on the degree of professionalism and enthusiasm built up within the individual local education authority or school. As with all services, local authorities varied enormously in their degree of attention to optimising the benefits of the school meal. Penelope Hall rightly noted that 'too often the premises are make-shift and overcrowded, the supervisors harassed, the meal bolted and the children hurried out to make room for a second batch'.[17] Such criticisms echo the damning indictments of school meals before World War II, and they are a reminder that Labour fell short of achieving the idealistic aims of the proponents of nutritional supplementation.

CONSERVATIVES, 1951–64

Faced with strongly entrenched public support for the newly established welfare state, a general lack of dynamism over policy formulation, and a revival of the 'One Nation' philosophy,

Churchill's final term in office, ending in 1955, was characterised by a general disinclination to interfere with the system of social services set in place by Labour. Recovery from the Korean War helped the situation by reducing the demands of armaments; on the other hand the benefit of the peace dividend was not particularly great because Britain was still fighting many colonial wars. The Churchill government limited its activities to clawing back at the fringes of the politically weaker social services such as the National Health Service. Education was more favoured, but at that stage the major constructive energies of the government were directed towards housing.

Supplementary nutritional services were in general protected by the mild paternalistic ethos prevailing within the Cabinet. Old-fashioned Tories tended to regard the working classes as feckless social incompetents, whose shortcomings needed to be addressed by the modern substitutes for soup kitchens. This lenient approach was not shared by Treasury bureaucrats; their primary objective was cutting back the social services on the grounds that the system inherited from Labour was endowed at a level beyond the competence of the economy to sustain. With the change in administration, they set about curtailing expenditure on the weaker services; their destructive criticism was most aimed at services which constituted a historical anachronism, and all supplementary nutritional services fell into that category. The Treasury bureaucracy naturally attempted to co-opt Treasury Ministers as its allies in campaigns of retrenchment. Ministers responded with varying degrees of enthusiasm.

The first attempts by the Treasury to inspire a more parsimonious approach to school meals elicited a Prime Ministerial rebuke to R. A. Butler, the Chancellor of the Exchequer. In response to the modest suggestion from Butler that the price of the school meal should be increased by 1d, Churchill telegrammed from Canada: 'Nothing need be done to reduce the food given to the children or to increase the charges to parents'. Butler was incensed by what he took as a personal slight; he drafted but did not send the following response: 'You need not suspect that we are ogres. We are really quite human and intelligent. I and my forebears for two hundred years have devoted ourselves to children. On school meals we had reached your conclusion by ourselves'.[18] Churchill's sentiment was probably representative of older Tories, but the importance of school meals was appreciated by some of the most able aspiring Ministers. For instance, John Boyd-Carpenter, the Financial Secretary to the Treasury, affirmed his belief that school meals were 'much the most socially valuable of all the Social Services'.[19]

The above vignettes indicate that Treasury bureaucrats were not necessarily greeted by an open door when volunteering supplementary nutritional services for a top place in lists of projected economies in civil expenditure. The only gestures towards economy the Treasury was able to achieve were minor increases in charges for school meals, and these were conceded only after much dissension among Ministers, and maximum obstruction from Florence Horsbrugh and James Stuart, the Ministers responsible for education in England and Wales, and Scotland. The increase in the cost of the school meal was at first postponed in order to avoid its coinciding with a reduction in other food subsidies. The increase from $7d$ to $9d$ was eventually introduced in March 1953.[20] The decision produced much adverse publicity and led to an unwelcome decline in uptake, from 51 per cent to 43 per cent in England and Wales, and from 39 per cent to 32 per cent in Scotland.[21] This trend was embarrassing to the government. It was particularly irritating to James Stuart, the Secretary of State for Scotland, who had argued that the less affluent population which existed in Scotland was being unfairly penalised by the increased level of charges. Scottish officials accepted the argument for increases in charges, but their Ministers disagreed; indeed, James Henderson-Stewart, the Joint Parliamentary Under-Secretary of State with responsibility in this area, threatened resignation if charges were increased.[22]

Higher charges for school meals were to a limited extent compensated for by improvements in quality made possible by updating of advice on nutritional standards, which had been in force since 1941. The new circular issued in 1955 confirmed that the school meal should be 'adequate in quality and quantity to serve as the main meal of the day'.[23]

With the retirement of Churchill in April 1955, Eden became Prime Minister, but after the Suez fiasco in the autumn of 1956 he was replaced by Macmillan, who himself retired in 1963, and was briefly replaced by Alec Douglas-Home, who lasted until the election defeat in October 1964. This period can be discussed as a whole. It was characterised by a more active approach to social policy, including some notable commitments to expansion in the fields of social security, education and health, but they intensified pressure for countervailing economies. Consequently, nutritional services came under much sharper scrutiny, raising the prospect of the complete elimination of subsidy in this field. This was desired by Treasury bureaucrats, and not eagerly resisted by their counterparts in the Ministries of Education and Health. However, hesitation on grounds of conviction or political prudence on the part of Ministers determined that only marginal cuts were implemented.

The antipathy of the bureaucrats to nutritional services was demonstrated in the course of the Five Year Social Service Survey conducted by the Cabinet Social Services Committee in 1956. Both the survey and the committee were a new departure for the Conservative government. The first purpose of this exercise was to assess prospective levels of expenditure in the social services. The subsidiary aim was to check the rate of increase and to ensure that expansion in one area was financed by cuts in another. The supplementary nutrition programme was at that time running at a cost to the Exchequer of about £120 million, compared with the cost of the NHS to public funds of about £550 million. The nutritional services were therefore an attractive target for cuts, and the Treasury concentrated its effort in this field and in cuts or increased charges in the family practitioner services, which were a parallel example of an exposed flank of welfare provision, also offering many different possibilities for cuts and charges. The optimum expectation of the Treasury at the time was the introduction of economic charges for school meals, school milk, welfare orange juice and related supplements, and a major reduction of the subsidy on welfare milk.

The Five Year Social Service Survey possesses historical interest because it looks forward to the method of public expenditure control adopted about five years later under the Public Expenditure Survey Committee (PESC), but as an exercise in control or planning the five-year survey was a failure. The social services Ministers conducting the survey had no particular motivation for making economies; instead they mobilised the committee to argue the case for a larger share of public resources.

With respect to specific targets for immediate savings, the only significant outcome was the decision to increase the prescription charge. Regarding the even more radical proposal to charge an economic cost for school meals, the Treasury was outmanoeuvred by Sir David Eccles. The latter was Minister of Education in succession to Horsbrugh. He was an astute politician, firmly protective of school meals. Eccles warned Butler that 'I believe this is an essential Social Service. More children ought to take the meals, not less'.[24] Eccles deflected the Cabinet in 1955 and the Social Services Committee in 1956 away from proposals for increases in school meal charges on the grounds that a thorough review and a completely new 'coherent policy' would generate even greater economies. At the end of this delaying tactic, Eccles reversed his position and successfully persuaded colleagues that charges should continue to operate on the basis of the cost of ingredients, producing an increase in the price of the school meal by only $1d$ to $10d$ from September 1956.[25] In the context of the Suez emergency, Quintin Hogg, Lord Hailsham (who had just succeeded Eccles), was forced to make a further concession, increasing the cost of the school meal from $10d$ to $1s$ in April 1957, for the first time breaching the principle that the charge should be limited to the cost of raw materials. This compared with the Treasury's objective of the full economic charge for the school meal, which at that date stood at $1s$ $9d$. During 1956, the Treasury tried without success to persuade Ministers to accept a $1d$ charge for school milk. This idea was reintroduced in the context of the Suez crisis, but in view of his concessions over school meals and the danger of controversy Hailsham was able to persuade his colleagues that it was politically unwise to impose a charge for school milk. The Treasury attempted to obtain an increase in the cost of welfare milk at various times in 1955 and 1956, but on each occasion this was rejected by Ministers. They were finally persuaded by the Suez crisis; it was agreed to raise the price of welfare milk from $1\frac{1}{2}d$ to $4d$ from April 1957. It was the first increase since the welfare milk scheme had been introduced in 1946.[26] The alterations in charges introduced in April 1957 represented the first occasion on which substantial reductions in subsidy were introduced in the school and welfare areas, and it was the first occasion on which retrenchment was applied in both areas simultaneously.

Under the administration of Macmillan, the Treasury was given an opportunity to regain the initiative in the context of the campaigns for economy in public expenditure conducted by the new ministerial team at the Treasury, led by Peter Thorneycroft, the Chancellor of the Exchequer, and Enoch Powell, the Financial Secretary, both of whom were committed to a strong line on reduction in public expenditure. The Treasury unearthed all its proposals for social service economies, with the same priorities as before, and these were taken up with avidity by Thorneycroft and Powell. However, the majority of Ministers dragged their heels, the result being the famous confrontation which led to the resignation of the Treasury team in January 1958. This crisis occurred after months of mounting tension between Thorneycroft and his Cabinet colleagues. Neither Macmillan nor other Ministers were willing to contemplate cuts in public expenditure on the level demanded by Thorneycroft. It was not only the scale of the economies, but also their political character that worried Macmillan and his allies. The Treasury Ministers suggested a package involving the removal of the family allowance on the second child, the introduction of a hospital boarding charge, an increase in ophthalmic charges, an increase in the NHS contribution paid in conjunction with National Insurance, and the removal of all subsidies on school meals, school milk, welfare milk and other welfare nutritional supplements.[27] These changes, if implemented in full, would have swept away a good part of the mechanism of family support devised by Beveridge and other wartime planners. Thorneycroft and Powell were therefore using the occasion of minor economic difficulties to force through a major change in social policy, in full recognition that their full package of measures would generate increased unemployment and provoke industrial unrest. This was a consequence unacceptable to Macmillan and the majority of the Cabinet, who were unwilling to launch the nation into an era of social strife, without any real evidence of an economic emergency, and without any certainty that the government's supporters would derive tangible gains in the form of tax concessions, or other economic advantages.[28]

The argument against Thorneycroft is indicated by the following extract from a comment by Iain Macleod, the Minister of Labour and former Minister of Health, which relates specifically to the proposal to reduce the subsidy on welfare milk, but also might apply to the wider programme of Powell and Thorneycroft:

> There would be political difficulties. It would be a retrograde social step and there would be some effect on the nutrition of mothers and young children. Although we know the reason for it, it is obviously wrong that milk should be free over 5 [i.e. to schoolchildren] and charged at 75 per cent to expectant mothers and infants. Again legislation is necessary and

would certainly be extremely difficult. In my field this could not be represented as other than an attack on the family and a blow to the policies of moderation in industrial relations.[29]

The departure of Thorneycroft and Powell permitted the scrapping of plans to cut back the scope of the family allowance, but despite rejection of the Thorneycroft–Powell philosophy by the Cabinet the new Treasury team found it impossible to escape entirely from the retrenchment measures. The most radical economy was the imposition of an increase in the NHS contribution – the second increase within a year. The nutritional services were potentially a second major area for savings. However, in view of the increases in April 1957, it was decided not to increase the price of school meals or welfare milk. The only change in the nutritional services was a reduction in entitlement to subsidised orange juice. The supply of subsidised orange juice was limited to pregnant women and to children below the age of 2, instead of 5. Again this was the first change since the inception of the post-war service. Taking the additional social service charges introduced in the financial year 1957/8 as a whole – the additional NHS charges, the cuts in subsidies on nutritional services, together with the two increases in the NHS contribution – collectively they made a big impact, particularly on low-income families, who were affected disproportionately by these economies.

Notwithstanding the adverse features of the Treasury-inspired erosion of welfare provision, the above economies in social services had relatively little adverse political effect. The government was still able to shelter behind the excuse that Britain was experiencing a residual economic emergency. However, the government also wanted to convey the impression that the nation was enjoying unparalleled prosperity; the Conservatives' success in the 1959 general election suggested that they were successful in communicating an air of well-being.

In the light of its success with the 1957/8 packages of social service economies, Treasury officials redoubled their pressure for further reductions. They hoped to influence the Cabinet Social Services Committee, which was for a second time called into being to consider the financing of the health service. Officials hoped that this new review would establish principles that could be applied widely in the social services. Cuts in subsidies in the nutritional services remained a high priority. The elimination of subsidies in this area was thought to reflect the 'modern social context'. Parents should bear the full cost of feeding their children. Treasury officials ordained that the nation was 'well past the era when there was a risk that a child would be sent to school half-starved and unable to profit from free education'. The Treasury plan was first to establish that school meals and other nutritional benefits should be established without subsidy, then to use this as a precedent for a wide programme of selective charging for other welfare benefits over the whole field of health and education.[30] Treasury officials were therefore by this stage experimenting with radical policies for slashing back the welfare state, far in advance of anything considered by the government of the day, even more stringent than such advanced thinkers as Powell, and more extreme than anything ever again attempted, even by the Thatcher administration.

A fresh opportunity to make progress with economies in the nutritional programme arose in 1960, with the appointment of Enoch Powell as Minister of Health. Powell immediately volunteered to double the prescription charge, increase the NHS contribution and dental and ophthalmic charges, and reduce the subsidy on welfare milk by $2d$ a pint. With respect to the existing subsidy of £24 million on welfare foods, Powell argued that it was 'grotesque and indefensible that we should apply in this way almost as large a sum as we are spending on all hospital capital development'.[31] On the other hand, it might have been pointed out that the cost of the welfare food subsidy was only three times the cost of compensation being paid out for fowl pest, or twice the cost of providing the infrastructure for five bases for intercontinental ballistic missiles.

Powell's proposals were largely a revival of the Thorneycroft–Powell package of economies rejected by the Cabinet in 1958. However, on this occasion, perhaps because the economies were introduced with enthusiasm by the spending Minister himself, the Cabinet went along with the proposals. Despite the big package of cuts offered by Powell, other Ministers were not able to escape completely from making economies. For instance, Eccles was cultivating a large school building programme; he therefore reluctantly considered increasing the school meal charge, and a big rise of $6d$ was offered, $2d$ having been the highest increase previously introduced on any one occasion.

Macmillan and other Cabinet members such as Macleod and Boyd-Carpenter were fearful about the adverse political consequences of such an audacious attack on the welfare system. The economies least welcomed by Ministers were reductions in the subsidies on school meals and welfare milk. The Cabinet first abandoned the idea of increasing school meal charges; next, after considering exemptions for families with four children, then for those with three children, Powell's proposal for an increase in the cost of welfare milk was rejected, on the understanding that it might be introduced at a later stage. Ministers were concerned that a reduction in the welfare milk subsidy 'could easily be represented by the Government's opponents as a direct blow to children and their health'.[32]

This minor palliative proved insufficient to protect the government from accusations of callousness with regard to the least affluent. The entire package of economies was introduced, but only after highly publicised and bruising battles in the House of Commons lasting for three months. This event arguably proved to be the turning point in the fortunes of the Labour opposition, and from then on the Conservative government showed itself increasingly prone to fallibility of judgement. In early 1962, in order to limit the harm and head off further confrontation with the trade unions, Selwyn Lloyd, the Chancellor of the Exchequer, and Macmillan both made statements giving assurances that further cuts in the social services were not envisaged by the government.[33] This capitulation was greeted with ill-concealed anger by Powell, who had not been consulted, and who was relying on the prompt reintroduction of the proposal for the abolition of the subsidy on welfare milk to justify an increase in his community care programme.[34]

After the storm surrounding the social service economies of 1962, it was no longer practicable for the Conservatives to countenance further negative intervention in this field. An increase in the school meal charge of 3d was discussed at length, but it was not pursued, at first, particularly because of opposition in Scotland, on account of the problem of high unemployment; later because of the approach of the general election.[35]

Despite increases in charges and reductions in subsidies under the Conservatives, the demand for nutritional services remained high. The decision in 1961 not to reduce the subsidy on welfare milk meant that the cost to recipients remained at 4d, whereas in 1964 the retail price was 9d. Similarly, the school meal subsidy remained high. In 1953 the school meal charge represented about half the cost of the service, while in 1964 it was only 42 per cent of the total cost. In 1964, the uptake of school meals in England and Wales was 59 per cent, although in Scotland it was only 39 per cent. The uptake of school milk was more than 90 per cent in primary schools, but under 70 per cent in secondary schools. The total cost to the Exchequer of the nutritional services in 1964 amounted to about £110 million.[36] This compared with the cost to public funds of the NHS of about £950 million. Accordingly the nutritional services were still far from negligible in their importance, but their status was declining with respect to related services.

Taken at face value, thirteen years of Conservative government made little difference to the nutritional services. All the services remained in place in 1964, most of them little changed in character since 1951. The nutritional services seem therefore to support the idea of consensus, which dominates interpretations of the social services for the period between 1945 and 1979. However, as I have argued elsewhere with respect to the National Health Service, closer examination indicates that the impression of continuity is somewhat spurious.[37] With respect to the nutritional services, during the Conservative period there was little forward development, and the erosion of subsidies began. The package of cuts in 1958 was particularly stringent in its effects on working-class families. As indicated in the previous narrative, the central bureaucracy, led by the Treasury, conducted a campaign of attrition against the nutritional services, drawing support from some Ministers but not from others. The aim of this campaign was the complete elimination of subsidy for the nutritional services. The fact that it was unsuccessful was due to divisions of opinion among Ministers. Out of conviction, or political calculation, the Ministers were unwilling to countenance more than marginal erosion of the subsidies. The government was still aware of the Beveridge equation, which implied that any reduction of benefits in kind would be compensated for by an increase in the family allowance. Also, at this stage, Conservative susceptibilities were influenced by a general sentiment in favour of services for mothers and children. There was certainly no support from the local party for the attenuation of any of these services. Any step in that direction would be used as political capital by Labour as evidence that the government was embarking on a programme of annihilating the welfare state. This issue was of particular importance politically in less affluent regions such as Scotland. The nutritional issue was also relevant to wage claims, raising the likelihood that cuts in subsidies would lead to disproportionate increases in wages and economic difficulties attributable to wage inflation. Finally, reduction in subsidies on nutritional services was blocked by the 'departmental coalition factor'. In order to achieve a reduction in subsidies, it was necessary to obtain agreement between various Ministers and departments, while strong opposition from a single Minister or department was sufficient to block such action. In the case of nutritional services, the Treasury, the Scottish Office, the Ministries of Health, Education, National Insurance, and Food and Agriculture, and the Colonial Office were all involved. Even a peripheral department such as the Colonial Office was able to mount a rearguard defence of the continuation of the supply of orange juice supplement, not on the grounds of the intrinsic value of the subsidy, but because of possible adverse impact on relations with the West Indies at a delicate period in the decolonisation process. Consequently, for a variety of reasons, many of them not connected with positive commitment to the subsidies, the nutritional services survived tolerably intact during the thirteen years of Conservative administration.

LABOUR, 1964–70

The return of a Labour government created a more protective atmosphere for services connected with family support. Although they were not high policy objectives, Labour was expected to maintain its traditional lines towards the various components within the nutritional programme. The expectation was at least of stabilisation, even if it was impossible to aim at the complete removal of charges, as was promised with respect to the health service. However, the situation was not a stable equilibrium. Since there were many pressures for substantial expansion of expenditure in many of the social services, the question of countervailing economies was inevitably raised, which was exploited by the Treasury to resuscitate its campaign for continuing erosion of the nutritional services. As the economic crisis deepened, the influence of the bureaucrats was strengthened.

At the outset of the Wilson administration, it was announced that the Treasury was 'heavily committed in effect to increasing the school meals charge as much as possible as soon as possible'.[38] Alarming rises in subsidies were forecast. Treasury Ministers were easy converts, and they found themselves in accord with colleagues at the Department of Education and Science and the Ministry of Health; they quickly agreed on proposals for an increase in the school meal charge of 6d and an increase in the charge for welfare milk of 2d a pint.[39] These proposals were taken to the Social Services Committee of the Cabinet in May and December 1965. On both occasions the suggestions received a negative reception. Ministers were especially sensitive to continuing opposition to rises in school meal charges in Scotland, largely on the grounds of unemployment and poverty which had influenced the Conservatives. Accordingly, after 'a lot of fierce argument' the Treasury-inspired proposals were thrown out.[40] The Treasury complained that 'the important thing here is that the Scottish tail should not be allowed to wag the dog'.[41] In the closing months of 1965, the nutritional programme was also debated by the Public Expenditure Survey Committee, by the Cabinet Committee on Public Expenditure, and by the Cabinet. This gave the Treasury fresh opportunities to exercise its casuistry, but to no avail.

The existence of a permanent and active Social Services Committee under the Labour government, dominated by spending Ministers, created an obstacle to Treasury intentions which had not existed under the Conservatives.[42] Ministers were willing to consider an increase in charges in the nutritional services only if they were the outcome of a general review of 'family policy' or 'family endowment', which indeed was one of the objectives of the Social Services Committee. This outcome was disappointing to the Treasury because it was initially hoped that increases in charges on nutritional services could be introduced without compensating increases in other benefits.

The course of events recommended by the Social Services Committee was followed; increased charges were agreed as part of the reorganisation of family endowment.[43] It was agreed with effect from April 1968 to increase the school meal charge from 1s to 1s 6d; this was quickly followed by a further increase to 1s 9d in 1969. This reduced the subsidy for the school meal to 36 per cent.

In April 1968 the supply of milk to children in secondary schools was ended and, finally, the welfare milk charge rose from 4d to 6d a pint. Some relief was provided by exemption from charges for school meals for fourth and subsequent children, and for welfare milk for third and subsequent children as well as expectant mothers. At face value, compensation for these increases was provided by a substantial increase in the family allowance. In 1968, the family allowance for the second child was increased by 7s to 15s, and the level was raised to 17s for later children. This increase was not introduced for the sake of counterbalancing the cuts in nutritional subsidies. It was a response to increasingly effective campaigning by the family poverty lobby, which of course also favoured maintaining the nutritional benefits. Since the family allowance had remained virtually static since 1952, a substantial increase was needed to bring it up to its former purchasing level. In fact the 1968 increase left the family allowance below its 1948 level in constant price terms.[44] Indeed, much of the increase was needed to compensate for the loss of value in the family allowance during the Wilson administration. Also, for wage earners, the greater part of the rise in the family allowance was lost through increases in income tax and the National Insurance contribution. Consequently, the cuts in subsidies in the nutritional programme were entirely at the expense of the living standards of the families involved. Contrary to its original intentions, and to the distress of the family poverty campaigners, Labour had ended up taking the scalpel to the nutritional services, and the cuts over which it presided constituted the biggest package of reductions made by any government since the services were instituted. Paradoxically, the 1960s ended with the same note of disappointment as the 1930s. Although absolute poverty was less, the extent of the disadvantage of the poorest groups was far greater than was acceptable, and campaigners on behalf of family support and the poor were vocal in their complaints about the response of the Labour administration to the problem of poverty. Recriminations over this issue were embarrassing to Labour during the 1970 general election campaign. As far as the nutritional programme was concerned, it is arguable that the actions of the Labour administration in 1968, rather than Thatcher's more notorious snatching of milk from primary schools, marked the beginning of the downward spiral of the nutritional programme.

CONCLUSIONS

Examination of the period from 1939 to 1970 suggests that there were only marginal differences between the two major political parties with respect to the nutritional supplementation. This would seem to add to the evidence concerning consensus over major aspects of social policy. However, examination of the record of the

Labour and Conservative administrations suggests that the two parties may have arrived at a similar position, but they reached it by different routes. Labour's commitment to expand and develop these services was greater than proved feasible in practice, whereas within Conservative administrations there was always a group wanting to eliminate the subsidies in this area, but their influence was limited by a variety of factors discussed above. The Labour Party's self-image of protecting the interests of the working classes, and of consistent promotion of welfare provision, is not particularly assisted by the example of nutritional supplementation. It is also of interest that much of the decline of supplementary nutritional benefits occurred before 1979, the period when welfare rights are supposed to have been protected by broad political consensus. The example of supplementary nutrition indicates the fragility of this political consensus in the face of determined assault from the bureaucrats.

Contrasting with the politicians' weak positive support for the nutritional programme is the consistent negative advocacy within the central bureaucracy, led by the Treasury. After the wartime emergency, the civil servants never accepted the nutritional supplementation programme as more than a ploy to excuse setting the family allowance at the lowest level. Once this objective had been achieved, the Treasury set about reducing the benefits in kind as the occasion presented itself. Within the spending departments, civil servants regarded these services as tangential; they were therefore convenient points of sacrifice, either during rounds of retrenchment, or when sacrifice was needed for the sake of preferred objectives. It was therefore the state bureaucracy which set about destroying this important element in the fabric of the Beveridge system of welfare, and, for reasons of incompetence or lack of conviction, politicians of neither party were able to resist the process of erosion.

Of course it is evident that on some occasions the more radical views circulated only at lower echelons within the Treasury; they attracted little interest from the most senior officials; to the extent that they reached Ministers, it was in a diluted form, and there was no sympathetic response. However, it is revealing that these extreme ideas enjoyed a great deal of currency within the Treasury. Even if not immediately successful, they represented the germs of policies which were eventually ascendant. For instance, ideas which failed to seep up the pyramid of the Treasury hierarchy during the last years of the Conservative administration became an orthodoxy after that date. Wilson's Ministers came under pressure from their most senior advisers, who argued that there was no case for subsidies for school meals and welfare milk, which were attacked as an anachronism, and they called for a 'radical review' or 'radical reform'. This view was accepted by the Chief Secretary, who immediately pressed Kenneth Robinson, the Minister of Health, to accept the case for the 'radical revision' and elimination of such wasteful expenditure. Robinson accepted this proposal on condition that cuts were applied across the board.[45]

It might be argued that the Treasury was essentially correct in its analysis: once the war was over, the nutritional programme was an anachronism, and it was an inefficient way of targeting relief. This question can be raised with virtually any aspect of the welfare state, including most of the expenditure on the health services, which might seem to represent a case invulnerable to criticism on this score. In the period under discussion, it is noticeable that no case against the nutritional programme was developed. Treasury policy was determined *in vacuo*; it was not a considered, scientific argument. It was essentially a layperson's construct, dictated by the social prejudices and the political sympathies of the Treasury class, which was more unsympathetic to this type of social service than either the older type of paternalistic Tory or the new One Nation group. This little case study supports the view that the central bureaucracy was capable of acting as a fifth column, using the cloak of alleged civil service impartiality to push forward political interests which commanded virtually no support at the ballot box.

During the period covered by this study, expert opinion supported the continuation of the nutritional programme and believed that its continuation was essential for keeping up the record of improvement in maternal and child health which was one of the genuine achievements of the wartime period. Continuing support for the nutritional programme emanated from the reports of expert committees such as the *Report of the Joint Sub-committee on Welfare Foods* (1957), the *Report of the Official Committee on Child Nutrition* (1962) and the *Report of the Departmental Working Party on the Nutritional Standard of the School Dinner and the Type of Meal* (1965). Perhaps all of them were guilty of profound misjudgement, and the Treasury was right in wanting to scrap the entire system. On the other hand there was, and still is, a continuing case for active monitoring and positive intervention with respect to the nutrition of mothers and infants, and for a comprehensive nutritional programme in schools.[46] It was of course essential to change the character of these services with the advance in knowledge, but their erosion and neglect will have contributed to depriving the people of the optimal level of health which was one of the fundamental promises of the welfare state.

NOTES

I would like to thank Professor Tim Lang, Professor Philip Payne, Dr Mike Rayner and Dr David Smith for their comments and advice on this chapter. With respect to the files of government departments cited below, files in the Public Record Office are prefixed PRO; otherwise the department is given.

1 For general reviews see F. le Gros Clark, *Social History of the School Meals Service*, London, 1949; J. S. Hurt, 'Feeding the hungry schoolchild in the first half of the twentieth century', in D. J. Oddy and D. S. Miller (eds), *Diet and Health in Modern England*, London, 1985, pp. 204–30.

2 B. Gilbert, *The Evolution of National Insurance in Great Britain*, London, 1966, p. 102.

3 R. Titmuss, *Problems of Social Policy*, London, 1950, p. 510.

4 C. Webster, 'The health of the schoolchild during the Depression', in N. Parry and D. McNair (eds), *The Fitness of the Nation*, Leicester, 1983, pp. 70–85; M. Mayhew, 'The 1930s nutrition controversy', *Journal of Contemporary History*, 1988, vol. 23, pp. 445–64; D. F. Smith and M. Nicolson, 'Nutrition, education, ignorance and income: a twentieth-century debate', in H. Kamminga and A. Cunningham (eds), *The Science and Culture of Nutrition, 1840s–1940s*, Amsterdam, 1994, pp. 288–318.

5 Titmuss, 1950, op. cit., p. 510.

6 Board of Education, Circulars 1520, 22 July 1940, and 1571, 12 November 1941.

7 Titmuss, 1950, op. cit., p. 510.

8 Board of Education, *Education after the War*, London, 1941, pp. 38–9.

9 Anderson, *Parliamentary Debates, Commons*, vol. 126, cols 1664–6, 16 February 1943.

10 Morrison, *Parliamentary Debates, Commons*, vol. 126, col. 2039, 18 February 1943.

11 *Social Insurance*, Cmd. 6550, London, 1944, para. 51.

12 Ministry of Education, Circular 96, 'The Place of the School Milk and Meals Service in the National Policy for Assistance to Families', 28 March 1946. See also Circular 97, 'School Meals and Midday Supervision', 12 April 1946.

13 PRO T 227/1075. Ministry of Education, Circular 119, 'Milk in Schools Scheme', 22 July 1946.

14 PRO T 227/1070.

15 See B. Harris, *The Health of the Schoolchild. A History of the School Medical Service in England and Wales*, Buckingham, 1995, p. 197.

16 Ministry of Education, Provision of Milk and Meals Regulations, 1945.

17 P. Hall, *The Social Services of Modern England*, London, 1952, p. 170.

18 Churchill to Butler, Butler to Churchill, *c.* 15 January 1952, PRO T 227/1071.

19 Boyd-Carpenter minute, 15 December 1952, PRO T 227/1071.

20 CC(52) 105th meeting, 16 December 1952, PRO CAB 128/25.

21 PRO T 227/1072.

22 Treasury minute, *c.* 10 November 1952, PRO T 227/1071.

23 Ministry of Education, Circular 290, 'The Nutritional Standard of School Dinners', 5 August 1955. This superseded Circular 1571 dating from 1941.

24 Eccles to Butler, 18 July 1955, PRO T 227/1072.

25 PRO T 227/1072; PRO CAB 134/1327 (Social Services Committee, 1956); CM (56) 44th meeting, 19 June 1956, PRO CAB 128/30.

26 CC (57) 5th meeting, 31 January 1957, CC (57) 11th meeting, 15 February 1957, PRO CAB 128/31.

27 Thorneycroft, Powell and Sir Robert Hall, draft memorandum for Ministers, *c.* 16 December 1957, PRO T 233/1459; Thorneycroft, 'The 1958/59 Estimates', 19 December 1957, PRO PREM 11/2306.

28 R. Lowe, 'Resignation at the Treasury: the Social Services Committee and the failure to reform the welfare state, 1955–57', *Journal of Social Policy*, 1989, vol. 18, pp. 505–26.

29 Macleod to Macmillan, 5 January 1958, PRO PREM 11/2306.

30 S. H. Wright minute, 31 March 1960, Treasury, SS 133/105/01E; P. M. Rossiter minute, *c.* 20 April 1960, A. J. Collier minute, 22 April 1960, Treasury, 2SS 109/110/05A.

31 Powell to Lloyd, 3 November 1960, Treasury, 2SS 444/01A.

32 CC (61) 2nd meeting, 24 January 1961, PRO CAB 128/35.

33 Lloyd, *Parliamentary Debates, Commons*, vol. 654, col. 1141, 27 February 1962; Macmillan, *The Times*, 6 March 1962.

34 Powell to Brooke, 5 March 1962, Treasury, 2SS 214/324/03A.

35 Treasury, 2SS 1018/110/01.

36 Treasury minute, 15 October 1964, Treasury, 2SS 109/110/05A.

37 C. Webster, 'Conflict and consensus: explaining the British health service', *Twentieth-Century British History*, 1990, vol. 1, pp. 115–51.

38 P. Jay to A. J. Phelps, 24 November 1965, Treasury, 2SS 109/110/05C.

39 Prentice to Diamond, 15 February 1965, Treasury, 2SS 1018/110/01. Reg Prentice was Minister of State at the DES, whose view was supported by Michael Stewart, Secretary of State at the DES; Diamond was Chief Secretary at the Treasury.

40 Treasury minute, 5 May 1965, Treasury, 2SS 109/110/05C.

41 Treasury minute, *c.* 18 May 1965, Treasury, 2SS 1018/110/01. Opposition from the Scottish Office was led by Judith Hart, one of the Joint Under-Secretaries of State. SS (65) 8th meeting, 5 May 1965, SS (65) 19th meeting, 1 December 1965, PRO CAB 134/2535.

42 The Social Services Committee was called into being twice under the

Conservatives, in 1956 and 1960, but for specific purposes, in both cases connected with retrenchment.

43 CC (67) 49th meeting, 19 July 1967, Cabinet Office, CAB 128.

44 R. Hemming, *Poverty and Incentives*, Oxford, 1984, p. 29.

45 Treasury minutes, 7 October 1964 to 4 May 1965, Treasury, 2SS 214/324/03A. Diamond to Robinson, 8 April 1965, Robinson to Diamond, 14 April 1965, Treasury, 2SS 214/324/03A.

46 See, for example, Department of Health, 'Third report of the sub-committee on nutritional surveillance', *Reports on Health and Social Subjects*, 1988, No. 33; Department of Health, 'The diets of British schoolchildren', *Reports on Health and Social Subjects*, 1989, No. 36, and Health Education Authority, *Schoolchildren's Diets*, London, 1994., C. Devine, T. Lang, J. Longfield, O. Maguire and M. Rayner, *An Investigation Into the Nutritional Quality of School Meals in Northern Ireland*, Northern Ireland Chest Heart and Stroke Association, 1995.

10

DOES EARLY NUTRITION AFFECT LATER HEALTH?

Views from the 1930s and 1980s

George Davey Smith and Diana Kuh

Recently there has been a shift in the focus of investigations of the causes of chronic disease from health-related behaviours and risk factors acting during adulthood to experiences occurring during early life: in childhood, infancy and during intra-uterine development. The work of the Medical Research Council (MRC) Environmental Epidemiology Unit in Southampton, under the direction of Professor David Barker, has been largely instrumental in this. The unit's work has occasioned an editorial in the *British Medical Journal* claiming that 'the "early life experience" paradigm is a strong candidate' for the replacement of the 'lifestyle paradigm' of chronic disease aetiology.[1]

The speed with which the findings of this research programme have entered policy discussions is noteworthy. The first publication[2] of the now extensive series[3] from Barker's team appeared only in 1986, but by 1989 the annual report of the Chief Medical Officer was already noting 'the importance of health in childhood as a determinant of subsequent health in adult life',[4] while in 1992 the Department of Health strategy document *The Health of the Nation* made reference to the 'increasing evidence to suggest that there is a relationship between growth and development starting from before birth and during childhood, and risk in later life of CHD' (coronary heart disease).[5]

Barker argues that maternal, foetal and infant nutrition are important early-life influences which affect later adult health.[6] In a review entitled 'Nutrition in early life and later outcome', one of the Southampton researchers comments that 'There have been few studies in humans of the long-term effects of nutrition in early life ... This is not because the possibility of long-term effects of diet has not been considered, but reflects the extreme difficulty in carrying out such studies in humans.'[7] Barker's team have drawn attention to the possible role of early nutrition by studying adults in middle and old age whose early growth and development had been recorded. Those whose early growth had been impaired *in utero* or in early post-natal life experienced an increased risk of a number of adult chronic diseases, most notably cardiovascular disease, diabetes and chronic bronchitis. From this evidence Barker hypothesised that impaired growth during critical periods of early life permanently affects or 'programmes' the structure and physiology of a range of organs and tissues.

The notion that adult health is determined by experiences in early life, in particular by nutrition, was accepted wisdom in pre-Second World War public health – a view which many practitioners considered to be supported by the empirical evidence.[8] The decline in the influence of this view after the war occurred while increased attention was being paid to adult life style in both epidemiological research and public health practice. In this chapter we examine the shifting fortune of ideas linking early nutrition with health in adulthood, relating such shifts to the type of data available during each period, the styles of public health research, the response of the scientific and policy-making communities, and the broader social setting.

Latour has illustrated how scientific controversies and the emergence of scientific 'facts' can be seen as social processes.[9] He argues that the construction of scientific facts is a collective process, the fate of a scientific statement depending on its use and adoption by others. Latour details his 'translation model' of the strategies by which the scientist or research team tries to mobilise allies and to develop networks and alliances advancing their scientific claim to the status of having established a scientific fact. The response of scientists, policy-makers and the general public to research into nutrition and health in the 1930s and 1980s clearly owes much to the assembly of such networks, as we hope to demonstrate.

HEREDITY OR NUTRITION?

The Interdepartmental Committee on Physical Deterioration, set up in 1903 in response to the high proportion of men found to be unfit for military service in the Boer War, highlighted the need to understand the origins of the poor state of health of the British working class.[10] Much of the committee's report was devoted to 'conditions affecting the life of the juvenile population', reflecting the generally held belief that the source of adult health problems lay in childhood. Those giving evidence to the committee recognised the importance of nutrition:

> With the single exception of Mr Edward Rees, whose panacea is fresh air, all the witnesses concurred in claiming the first place for food. 'Food', says Dr Eichholz, 'is the point about which turns the whole problem of degeneracy.' There is, first, the want of food, second the irregularity in the way in which children get their meals, and, thirdly, the non-suitability of the food when they get it; and these three circumstances, want of food, irregularity and unsuitability of food, taken together, are, in his opinion, the determining cause of degeneracy in children.[11]

An editorial in 1904 in the *British Medical Journal* commented that:

> It cannot too often be repeated that a child wisely fed for the first two or three years of its life has every chance of growing up into a strong man or woman; a child rendered rickety and puny by ignorant feeding will in all probability never make up the ground it has lost.[12]

In contrast, social biologists of a hereditarian persuasion, such as Karl Pearson, argued that death in early life had an important role in the process of natural selection, since 'a heavy death-rate does mean the elimination of the weaklings'.[13] This assertion was supported by the demonstration that between 1838 and 1900 infant mortality rates correlated negatively with mortality rates for children aged 1 to 5 years. Improvements in mortality rates for those aged 1 to 5 years were seen to be dependent on rising infant mortality rates, since these were assumed to selectively remove the hereditarily unfit from the population.

For these reasons Pearson viewed the decline in the infant death rate in the early years of the twentieth century, coupled with the low birth rate and differential fertility in favour of the lower classes, as 'nothing short of calamitous'.[14] Since death was seen as a method of removing hereditary inadequacies, to 'check Nature's effective and roughshod methods of race betterment' by adapting the environment to man would be to produce a race of degenerate and feeble stock. Pearson considered that the influence of heredity on health was much greater than the influence of the environment: 'health is a real hereditary characteristic and the health of the parents is far more important than the question of back-to-back houses, one-apartment tenements, the employment of mothers or breast feeding . . .'.[15]

It was fortunate for Pearson's hypothesis that his analysis stopped in 1900, since from the turn of the century infant and childhood mortality rates began to fall in concert; the negative correlation he identified would no longer be evident. Arthur Newsholme, the medical officer to the Local Government Board, and public health activist, directly challenged Pearson's analysis, by demonstrating that those districts with high infant mortality rates were also the districts with the highest rates of child and adolescent mortality.[16] Newsholme and others maintained that environmental conditions underlay the unfavourable health status of the children of the poor, and that improvements in these conditions led to increased survival and better child health. At this time the link between the health of infants and children and later adult health was, apparently, self-evident. George Newman, Chief Medical Officer to the Board of Education, wrote the following in his 1913 report:

> Recent progress has shown a) that the health of the adult is dependent upon the health of the child, that to grow healthy men we must first grow healthy children; that sickness and disease of children lead to disability and disablement among adolescents and adults; and that the State cannot effectually insure itself against physical disease unless it begins with children; b) that the health of the child is dependent upon the health of the infant and mother.[17]

Later eugenicists, such as Dr Frank White came to accept a limited role for environmental influences, including diet, in improving survival. However, he questioned the healthiness of the survivors, and feared they would lower the general health of the population. Writing in 1928, White remarked that

> a careful study of the official volumes relating to the health of our nation leaves one with a feeling of disappointment and oppression . . . a falling death rate may be altogether deceptive as indicative of improvement in inherent healthfulness, since the life of a wretchedly-endowed or even mortality-afflicted infant can be amazingly prolonged by a sedulous system of nursing and dietary.[18]

According to White the survivors were 'for the most part physical and mental defectives who, under a sterner regime, would unquestionably have been eliminated soon after birth by natural selection. And, unhappily, the more of such we save the worse becomes the outlook for the state.'

In the late 1920s and early 1930s, analysis of mortality trends provided evidence to support this emphasis on the early-life origins of health in adulthood. It was suggested by the actuary V. P. A. Derrick that year of birth rather than year of death was the important parameter determining mortality risk: successive cohorts born after the middle of the nineteenth century experienced decreasing mortality risk at all ages.[19] Derrick interpreted this as indicating improved inherited characteristics of succeeding birth cohorts, but others considered that environmental factors acting in early life were important.[20] W. O. Kermack, of the laboratory of the Royal College of Physicians of Edinburgh, published a paper with A. G. McKendrick and P. L. McKinlay which used a different method from that of Derrick to examine the extent to which death rates were a function of year of death and year of birth. They noted that the data behaved as if 'the expectation of life was determined by the conditions which existed during the child's earlier years', and concluded:

> the health of the child is determined by the environmental conditions existing during the years 0–15, and . . . the health of the man is determined preponderantly by the physical constitution which the child has built up.[21]

The exception to the general pattern detected by Kermack and colleagues was mortality under one year of age (infant mortality), which started to decline only after the turn of the century, well after mortality at later ages. They suggested that infant mortality was dependent upon the health of the mother, and thus improvement in infant mortality followed the generational improvement in the vitality of women of childbearing age.

THE ROLE OF NUTRITION

While Kermack and his colleagues discussed 'environmental influences' acting during childhood in general, inter-war developments in nutrition science led to greater recognition of the vital role of nutrition in health and a major shift in definitions of dietary quality. According to Celia Petty, 'Whereas the 1904 Committee on Physical

Deterioration had argued that the diets of the poor were deficient in protein and fat, during the 1920s and 1930s vitamin and mineral deficiencies were widely believed to be the chief nutritional causes of ill health and inferior physique'.[22]

Reports of public health officials such as Newsholme and Newman,[23] and of nutritional surveys carried out under the MRC by D. Noël Paton, Leonard Findlay and Edward Cathcart of Glasgow University, claimed that poor diets were the result of maternal habits and ignorance.[24] However, dietary guidelines issued by the British Medical Association in 1933, as well as earlier recommendations by the Advisory Committee on Nutrition of the Ministry of Health, made it increasingly difficult to justify the view that families on low incomes could secure an adequate diet 'simply by improving budgetary efficiency'.[25] Nutritional surveys carried out by more radical social reformers, such as John Boyd Orr, were influential in establishing the connection between nutrition and health, and relating malnutrition to poverty and low incomes. Orr's survey of over 1,000 family budgets and food expenditure, first published in 1936, showed that at least half the country's children lived in families whose income was too low to secure a diet which met the nutritional standards for optimum health.[26]

New political lobby groups (such as the Children's Minimum Council, the Committee against Malnutrition and the National Unemployed Workers' Movement), social commentators and public health activists were quick to incorporate the new findings from nutritional and epidemiological research into their activities to promote better child nutrition. Dr G. C. M. M'Gonigle, Medical Officer of Health for Stockton-on-Tees, had worked on surveys of child health and nutrition with Kermack's co-author, P. L. McKinlay, a medical officer of the Scottish Department of Health. In *Poverty and Public Health*, published in 1936 by Victor Gollancz, M'Gonigle and the public analyst J. Kirby wrote of the overriding importance of child nutrition:

> Children may, and in fact not infrequently do, grow up healthily in spite of a bad material environment. They may avoid clinical illness due to infections, though exposed to the infections; they may survive, undamaged, illnesses resulting from the invasion of their tissues by pathogenic micro-organisms, but they cannot survive unscathed prolonged deprivations or deficiencies of certain essentials for normal nutrition.[27]

Wal Hannington, leader of the National Unemployed Workers' Movement, utilised the same kinds of evidence in his overtly activist Left Book Club volume *The Problem of the Distressed Areas*, published in 1937. In a chapter headed 'Scientists, diets and realities', Hannington stated that he could 'lay no claim to a sufficient knowledge of medical science to entitle me to embark upon scientific polemics with the wise men of the B.M.A. and the experts of the Ministry of Health', but added that his 'common and everyday experiences of the way the low paid and unemployed workers live' allowed him to judge that 'continuous under-feeding of working-class families through long unemployment and insufficient income has so reduced their stamina that they fall easy victims to physical ailments and disease'.[28]

The under-nourishment of children, Hannington continued, interfered with their education and produced a body of youth prone to illness and in such poor physical condition that work and playing football were beyond the scope of many. He approvingly quoted the Chief Medical Officer of the Board of Education as saying that 'Medical science has proved that disease and incapacity in adolescence and adult life find their source all too often in the seed-time of childhood'. Hannington maintained that 'unemployment has existed for so long in the Distressed Areas that many of the youths who are to-day leaving school were probably handicapped from the moment of their birth as the result of under-nourishment of the mothers during pregnancy'. He agreed with Sir Malcolm Stewart, the Commissioner for the Special Areas of England and Wales, that more medical attention was required for such youth, but thought it 'callous and brutal, to allow conditions to exist in childhood which produce unhealthy youth, and, when the damage is done, to suggest that efforts be made to repair it by medical treatment'.[29]

The ideas regarding the importance of early nutrition to later health influenced an authority with a rather different perspective from those of Hannington and M'Gonigle. H. M. Vernon, investigator for the Industrial Health Research Board, began *Health in Relation to Occupation*, a book published in 1939 which summarised his understanding of the science of public health, with a discussion of the findings of Kermack, McKendrick and McKinlay. Vernon thought that the first of the 'remedial measures that ought to be undertaken to reduce ill health' was the improved distribution of food:

With the provision of adequate nourishment at all stages of human existence, we should find a further diminution of infant mortality, which has already improved so remarkably in recent years, and . . . we should find considerable improvement in the health and physique of the children. Such improvement would certainly lead to a healthier adult life.[30]

When considering the relative importance of different influences on health, Vernon stated that nutrition was

by far the most important of all the factors, broadly classed as environmental, which influence the health of the human organism . . . adequate nutrition is specially important, not only for children but for expectant and nursing mothers, if good physique coupled with good health, is to be attained when the children reach adult life.

For adults other than expectant and nursing mothers, Vernon continued, nutrition was 'not so important . . . as for children', although it should be adequate 'if the maximum degree of health and efficiency is desired'.[31]

In *The Condition of Britain*, published in 1937, G. D. H. Cole and M. Cole commented at length on the increased attention being paid to nutrition:

This question of adequate nutrition has, owing to a combination of circumstances, been forced very much on the public attention during the past few years; and the new importance assigned to it is even now revolutionising popular conceptions of what an efficient public health service needs to be.[32]

The Coles attributed this emphasis on nutrition to four factors. First, there were long-standing concerns about poor national physique as a consequence of the results of medical examinations of recruits for the First World War. Second, there were concerns about the falling birth rate, leading to 'more anxious care about human life as such'. Third, there were advances in knowledge, such that 'we are now far better informed about the kinds of ill health which arise from defects of diet than we have ever been before'. Finally, the Coles noted:

It is, however, doubtful whether the research workers would have been able to direct nearly so much attention to their discoveries had not these been accompanied by a world-wide 'glut' of food, in the sense of a supply larger than the farmers and middlemen have been able to dispose of at a profit. This 'glut' set the statesmen of those countries in which large surpluses of foodstuffs were produced thinking and talking hard about the means of increasing the consumption of food; and the research workers and social reformers promptly seized their chance of putting their scientific conclusions before a public which was readier to listen because a higher food consumption looked like being 'good for trade'.[33]

The threat of war in 1938–9 was a further stimulus to the development of a national nutritional policy based upon advances in scientific knowledge. After the war the Chief Medical Officer of the Ministry of Health felt able to report that 'the national provision of milk and vitamin supplements . . . has done more than any other factor to promote the health of expectant mothers and young children'.[34] However, wartime policies which linked nutrition, poverty and health collapsed in the post-war period. Health policy became dominated by curative medical services; agricultural policy by economic self-interest.[35] Epidemiological research, in its search for the causes of specific chronic disease in later life, shifted its focus to adult life styles.

THE RISE OF 'LIFE STYLES'

As we have seen, during the first four decades of the century there was much public health interest in nutrition in early life as a determinant of susceptibility to disease, interest which dissipated over a relatively short period. One reason was that the central finding upon which it rested – the mortality regularities displayed by Derrick, Kermack and others – ceased to obtain, even while these authors were producing their papers.[36] Examination of age-specific mortality trends in Britain over this period shows why the predictions made by Derrick failed to be confirmed. Over the 1920s and 1930s death rates for adults stopped declining, or increased slightly, as mortality from cardiovascular causes and cancers replaced death from infectious diseases. The increase in cancer mortality could be attributed to a rise in lung cancer.[37] Regarding cardiovascular disease mortality there was much speculation, a suggestion by Morris being the prevailing view: 'the principal factor in [the] recent, very unsatisfactory, trend of mortality in middle-aged men [is] . . . an increase in ischaemic heart disease'.[38]

In the 1930s some commentators suggested that increases in lung cancer followed from increases in cigarette smoking.[39] During the 1950s evidence from studies of lung cancer cases and controls was complemented by the use of more formal cohort analysis techniques, which implicated smoking as the aetiological agent responsible for the dramatic rise in lung cancer mortality.[40] The concentration on nurture in early life as a determinant of susceptibility to illness in general gave way to a focus on environmental factors in adult life which increased the risk of particular causes of death, in particular death from lung cancer and CHD. Epidemiological research proceeded through ecological comparisons and through prospective studies. The former related the 'life styles' of adults – dietary habits, smoking, and physical activity, plus factors seen to be related to life style, such as blood pressure and serum cholesterol – to the large international differences in CHD rates.[41] In 1948 the first major prospective study was initiated, in Framingham, Massachusetts.[42] Middle-aged men were recruited and followed to see how those who died from heart disease differed from the survivors. The aetiological factors studied were generally the same as those examined in the ecological studies.

The pre-war pronouncements regarding the importance of childhood environment and adult health had usually been primarily concerned with health in general, and with all-cause mortality as a particular indicator of this, rather than with specific illnesses. The post-war shift towards adult environment, on the other hand, was concerned with particular health problems. Official pronouncements reflected a preoccupation with the apparent increase in CHD. Thus the Registrar General wrote in 1954:

> we must try to determine the factors responsible for the occurrence of the disease at the present time – among which diet, mental stress and lack of physical exercise have come under suspicion – and judge whether the varying influence of the causative factors can have produced a rising incidence of disease.[43]

From the mid-1950s Thomas McKeown began to attribute the dramatic fall in mortality since the mid-nineteeth century mainly to better nutrition, which he argued had improved host resistance to infectious disease,[44] a view which has only recently been challenged.[45] In contrast, when considering mortality rates from non-infective conditions such as cardiovascular disease, which had yet to show signs of decline, McKeown argued, as did other epidemiologists, that 'personal behaviour' was a more important influence than 'food deficiency'.[46]

THE REDISCOVERY OF CHILDHOOD

In the tradition of post-war epidemiology, the major concern with regard to the nutrition of infants and children usually related to the possible effects of over-nutrition. Thus, when it was suggested that 'adult coronary disease is really a major paediatric problem', this referred to the need for

> cardiovascular health promotion and the encouragement of healthy lifestyles in childhood. Diet, exercise, and the prevention of unhealthy lifestyles and behaviours, e.g. cigarette smoking, consumption of alcohol and harmful drugs, are the main areas for intervention.[47]

A few researchers and practitioners, generally coming from outside of the field of epidemiology or public health, took a different view of the relationship between nutrition in early life and the risk of coronary disease. The starting point for the investigations of Osborn in the 1960s was the state of the coronary arteries of decedents who came to autopsy. He noted that normal coronary arteries were often found among elderly people who, according to relatives, took little exercise, ate high-fat diets and smoked. Furthermore, fit young men with exemplary life styles were being killed by their extensive coronary atherosclerosis. Osborn turned to infant feeding for a possible explanation. He interviewed the mothers of 109 people who died under 20 and found that coronary atherosclerosis was worse among those who had been bottle-fed, rather than breast-fed, as infants. The questions distressed the mothers of the decedents, however, which made Osborn suspend his enquiries, with the observation that in '20 or more years a satisfactory answer to this question could be obtained if the mothers of e.g. entrants into the armed services were questioned; this enquiry would be similar to that of the doctors and their smoking habits'. Osborn noted that 'the high incidence of coronary diseases in the most civilised countries is commonly ascribed to this or that dietetic habit in its cultivated citizens' but asked:

Is it not more likely to be due to the fact that as civilisation advances breast feeding becomes increasingly inconvenient and so declines? Unfortunately this is a subject which is apt to arouse unscientific emotions even in medical men; the subject is too important to pay any attention to these ... The greatest problem facing us must be how to raise our children so that they do not eventually share our great liability to untimely death from coronary disease.[48]

While a couple of studies were carried out to examine Osborn's hypothesis,[49] with equivocal results, and the occasional claim was made that 'breast is best for coronary protection',[50] this line of research was not taken further. However, theories of the aetiology of CHD were developed which rejected the overriding importance of unhealthy adult life styles, in part in response to the observation that the major risk factors – high-fat diet, high blood pressure, smoking and elevated blood cholesterol – failed to account for the social, geographical and temporal variations in CHD rates. Thus an ecological study carried out by A. Forsdahl in Norway demonstrated geographical correlations between past infant mortality rates and current adult mortality rates.[51] This was considered to provide evidence of the persistent effects of conditions in childhood. Children born in areas with high infant mortality rates were taken to have experienced greater levels of deprivation than those born in areas with lower infant mortality rates. Forsdahl considered that nutritional deficit in childhood, followed by relative affluence, could increase the risk of CHD in adult life.[52]

In Britain Barker and his colleagues entered the debate regarding the validity of the 1984 recommendations produced by the Committee on Medical Aspects of Food Policy (COMA).[53] Reducing fat and increasing fibre consumption were advocated by COMA as ways of reducing population CHD rates. Favourable trends in CHD during the war had been widely taken to be evidence in favour of the COMA recommendations, since wartime food policy produced dietary changes in the advised direction. A re-analysis of the data by Barker's team suggested that no such favourable CHD trends actually occurred, and hence that there was no support for 'the view that compliance with the COMA recommendations on fat, fibre, and sugar consumption will lead, by itself, to an appreciable fall in coronary heart disease mortality in middle aged men'.[54]

The alternative notion, that development in early life underlay the risk of coronary heart disease, was put forward in the paper 'Infant mortality, childhood nutrition, and ischaemic heart disease in England and Wales', published in 1986.[55] Essentially, this paper reported on an extended analysis of British data along the lines of Forsdahl's study in Norway. Using 212 local authority areas as the unit of analysis, Barker and Osmond found that adult mortality from stroke was most strongly correlated with neonatal mortality, adult mortality from CHD was strongly correlated with both neonatal and post-neonatal mortality, and adult mortality from chronic bronchitis was associated with post-neonatal mortality only. They suggested that 'the geographical distribution of ischaemic heart disease in England and Wales reflects variations in nutrition in early life, which are expressed pathologically on exposure to later dietary influences'. A second study using the same methods showed that adult mortality from stroke was strongly correlated with maternal mortality, which Barker and Osmond argued reflected the dominant influence of maternal physique and health.[56] Similar conclusions were drawn from a study comparing the current mortality rates in three neighbouring northern English towns. Disparities between the towns, in mortality from CHD, stroke and bronchitis, appeared to be more closely related to differences which existed when the elderly (and now dying) residents were children than to present-day differences.[57] Factors such as maternal health and physique, infant feeding, housing and overcrowding were advanced as possible determinants of current variations in adult mortality.

This line of investigation was developed through studies of reconstructed cohorts of individuals born earlier this century. The detailed records kept by midwives and health visitors in east Hertfordshire between 1911 and 1930 allowed the examination of the association of birth weight, growth in the first year of life, and mode of infant feeding, with CHD risk in later life. Babies who were born with a low birth weight and male infants who grew poorly during the first year of life were at increased risk of dying of a heart attack as adults.[58] By studying survivors from this cohort, and from similar 'catch-up' studies, Barker and his colleagues showed that different patterns of impaired foetal growth ('characterised by low birthweight, or low birthweight relative to placental weight, or thinness at birth, or shortness at birth with subsequent failure of infant growth') were associated with different adult risk factors for cardiovascular disease.[59] These included blood pressure, glucose tolerance, cholesterol and apolipoprotein B, fibrinogen and factor

VII. This evidence, it was argued, suggested that differences in the timing of under-nutrition in pregnancy had different effects on organs and tissues according to their stage of development.[60] Their interpretation of the findings was guided by earlier animal studies of programming, in particular those that examined the effect of nutritional deficiencies before birth, or immediately preceding birth, on subsequent growth and development.[61]

While the proposal that forces acting during infancy and childhood influenced later health was considered largely uncontroversial during the decades before the Second World War,[62] the later championing of this view with respect to the aetiology of CHD, stroke and diabetes has initiated much debate. The conventional wisdom, against which these hypotheses were pitted, was that overnutrition was one of the root causes of such chronic diseases. Thus the suggestion that their origin lay in malnutrition – albeit malnutrition occurring during early development – ran directly counter to the bulk of both cardiovascular research and health policy. The stream of publications from the Southampton group continued, and the ideas were supported by the MRC,[63] by editorials in the *British Medical Journal*,[64] and by the findings of other research teams.[65] In contrast, those with a long-term investment in cardiovascular epidemiology have tended to criticise[66] or, more usually, to ignore Barker's research.

The critical responses to Barker's studies have focused on the difficulties involved in interpreting the observed associations between early-life experiences and health in adulthood when nothing was known about the period in between.[67] It has been argued that it is likely that children born into poor socio-economic circumstances will, on average, tend to experience retarded growth, compared with those born into a more favourable environment. Indeed, studies carried out in the 1930s had demonstrated this:

> The rate of growth of infants is found to depend to some extent on the economic resources of the family. When a group of working-class families at Birmingham was divided into three, according to wages per head, it was found that there was no characteristic difference in the weight of the infants for the first three weeks, but after thirteen weeks a distinction was quite evident and it persisted throughout the first year. Observations made at Glasgow showed this

divergence from the age of 2 till the age of 10 years, and at Stuttgart it has been noted up to the age of 19 years.[68]

Isabella Leitch, who in the mid-1930s had been centrally involved in planning the Carnegie nutrition and health survey with Boyd Orr, considered, in 1951, whether good nutrition and growth in early life influenced later health. She cautioned that:

> Since all the social circumstances, housing, sanitation, spacing of population and hence exposure to infection, as well as education and, on the whole, facilities for prompt medical attention, improve with, and at about the same rate as, growth, it is difficult to judge whether inhibition of growth itself has any effect on morbidity.[69]

These comments suggested that there was a need to examine whether it was possible that aspects of later childhood, adolescence and adulthood could account for the association of early growth with adult disease. In epidemiological parlance, the issue is that of confounding.[70] Catch-up studies such as those conducted by Barker's team have not had the prospective data needed to examine how poor nutrition, overcrowding, and other forms of social disadvantage in childhood may affect the relationship between early growth and cardiovascular disease. They argue that the specific nature of the relationship between early growth and cardiovascular disease, the strong and graded dose response, and the continued importance of the associations after adjusting for adult social class, smoking and body weight are indicative of causal relationships. However, many commentators consider that further research involving long-term prospective data throughout the life course is needed, if this issue is to be resolved.[71]

EARLY NUTRITION AND LATER HEALTH: THE CONTEXTS OF THE 1930s AND THE 1980s

In the first four decades of the century, childhood nutrition was firmly established as a factor underlying health in adulthood, a position which was undermined as poor child health lost importance as a social problem. Over the last decade, the resurgence of interest in the early-life origins of adult disease has also been concerned with childhood nutrition, but as the theories have developed, greater emphasis has been placed on nutrition during foetal and infant development than on nutrition during later childhood. This reflects the different strengths of the various networks which worked to keep childhood nutrition an important issue. In the 1930s the suggestion that the action of crucial forces during childhood determined later health was quickly translated into a consideration of nutrition. To develop the explanation of Cole and Cole: the combination of the activities of food producers and distributors, nutritional experts armed with 'newer knowledge', public health doctors increasingly freed from the burden of infectious disease control, political activists, and the state functionaries charged with restraining such activism ensured that nutrition remained a key social problem of the period.

Throughout the 1930s infant mortality rates in Britain fell,[72] although some economically depressed regions proved to be exceptions to the rule.[73] Similarly, the evidence of any sharp decline in nutritional status or health during the Depression is lacking.[74] The Ministry of Health claimed that 'the evil effects had been so small as to be barely noticeable'.[75] This was rejected by the Coles, M'Gonigle, Hannington and other contemporary observers. The Coles considered that it was fully possible for 'a rapid fall in infant deaths to occur, even while the health of the survivors is getting worse'.[76] The vital role of good nutrition in guaranteeing the health of the future generation was a part of accepted wisdom that was not dependent on verified statistics.

An illustration of the resilience of the notion that poor early nutrition impairs later health is provided by the manner in which a classic experiment in animal nutrition was reported in 1935. C. M. McCay and colleagues carried out a four-year study in which food restriction was applied after weaning to one group of rats while others were allowed to feed as desired.[77] The result of this study, which has been replicated many times since, was that the longevity of male rats was greater if their feeding was restricted. This finding would, on the face of it, run counter to the expectations of researchers such as Kermack and his colleagues, who saw poor material circumstances in early life as a cause of increased mortality risk in adulthood.[78] Nevertheless, the work of Kermack *et al.* was quoted by McCay *et al.* in a way which suggested that the two sets of findings were complementary.

The nutrition of children was one of the major social problems of the years leading up to the Second World War. Such was not the case in the mid-1980s, the time when the Southampton group were publishing their first papers on the topic. The attitude to the optimal nutrition of children had greatly changed. In *The Schoolboy: A Study of his Nutrition, Physical Development and Health*, published in 1935, Dr G. E. Friend, Medical Officer of Christ's Hospital, was much concerned with adequate calorie intake and considered that '25–30 per cent of the total daily calories should be derived from fat and as much of this as possible should be derived from certain animal fats'.[79] Similarly, M'Gonigle and Kirby thought that there was 'no limit to the proportions of animal proteins and fat which the human can eat over prolonged periods without physical injury'.[80] Their table of 'highly protective foods' featured milk, eggs, cheese and butter; wholemeal bread, root vegetables and margarine were consigned to the 'less protective and non-protective foods'. By the 1980s, on the other hand, recommendations regarding the diet of children were pointing in almost exactly the opposite direction. The prevention of obesity through limiting calorie intake and the avoidance of foods high in fat – and high in animal fat in particular – had become the target. Rather than screening children for health problems caused by under-nutrition, screening is now advocated for elevated blood cholesterol levels which, in part, are taken to reflect dietary excess. In keeping with these changed circumstances, childhood under-nutrition featured only briefly as a key component of the current interest in early-life experiences and later health.

Several research networks have been involved in the development and maintenance of the recent early-life origins model of adult disease. Prominent research groups investigating the role of mechanisms of disease production which are not automatically associated with the adult environment, such as processes of blood clotting,[81] and impaired glucose metabolism,[82] have engaged in collaborative projects with the Southampton team, and have thereby come to have a shared interest in this model. Funding agencies such as the MRC, the Wellcome Trust and the British Heart Foundation have been keen to support research into the early-life origins of disease, seeing them as an exciting area of research with which they want to be associated. Other funding agencies which have supported the work, for example the Milk Marketing Board,[83] have their own particular interest in moving the focus of aetiological research from adult life styles to early development.

Barker's theories of the origins of cardiovascular disease have attracted considerable television coverage and positive feedback from the 'quality' press. Groups such as the Maternity Alliance, whose interests straddle the academic and policy debates, have shown interest in the relevance of these emerging scientific facts for questions of policy. Their own study in 1988 showed that an adequate diet in pregnancy is beyond the means of women on low incomes,[84] and a recent study of low-income families by National Children's Home showed that 10 per cent of children under 5 had gone without food at some time during the previous month because of insufficient household income.[85] However, alliances between Barker's team and children's organisations are unlikely to be as strong as those that developed between researchers and children's organisations in the 1930s. This is because Barker argues that, in order to ensure appropriate levels of foetal and infant nutrition, preventive strategies should focus on improving the health and nutrition of girls and young women, and mothers during pregnancy and lactation, even at the expense of improvements in the nutrition of children.[86] Furthermore, rising public concern about the state of the nation's children today does not focus so much on nutrition but rather on what is seen as the sorry state of contemporary family life and the unprecedented strains under which families live.[87]

The context in which the recent studies of the late effects of early development have occurred is one in which considerations regarding genetic influences on health are again coming to the fore. The subject of genetic influences on health and behaviour has been a strongly contested one.[88] Although genetic explanations could be advanced for the reported associations between patterns of foetal and infant development and later health outcomes, the Southampton group have emphasised environmental factors – in particular maternal nutrition during pregnancy – as being key. Furthermore, a co-worker with the Southampton group has suggested that their findings present a serious challenge to the validity of the twin studies which are used to investigate the genetic influences on health,[89] a claim which has been strongly contested by advocates of a major genetic component in disease aetiology.[90]

In 1927, at a time when the relative importance of natural selection and environment was being actively debated, Derrick interpreted the evidence that mortality risk was determined early in life as indicating the predominantly hereditary character of generational robustness. This interpretation was rejected by most of the authorities who developed these ideas through a period when childhood nutrition was a central concern of public health and social policy. Whether the interests of researchers now investigating the early-life origins of adult disease and the interests of those involved in the rapidly developing genetics programme in medical research will continue to be opposed, or will become integrated in a mutually supportive network, remains to be seen.

NOTES

Thanks are due to Mel Bartley, two anonymous referees and David Smith for useful comments and suggestions on this chapter.

1 R. J. Robinson, 'Is the child father of the man?', *British Medical Journal*, 1992, vol. 304, pp. 789–90.

2 D. J. P. Barker and C. Osmond, 'Infant mortality, childhood nutrition, and ischaemic heart disease in England and Wales', *The Lancet*, 1986, vol. i, pp. 1077–81.

3 D. J. P. Barker, *Fetal and Infant Origins of Adult Disease*, London, 1992.

4 Department of Health, 'On the State of Public Health for the Year 1989', London, 1990, p. 7.

5 Department of Health, *The Health of the Nation. A Strategy for Health in England*, London, 1992.

6 D. J. P. Barker, P. D. Gluckman, K. M. Godfrey, J. E. Harding, J. A. Owens and J. S. Robinson, 'Fetal nutrition and cardiovascular disease in adult life', *The Lancet*, 1993, vol. 341, pp. 938–41; C. Osmond, D. J. P. Barker, P. D. Winter, C. H. D. Fall and S. J. Simmonds, 'Early growth and death from cardiovascular disease in women', *British Medical Journal*, 1993, vol. 307, pp. 1519–24.

7 C. Fall, 'Nutrition in early life and later outcome', *European Journal of Clinical Nutrition*, 1992, vol. 46, Supplement 4, pp. S57–S63.

8 D. Kuh and G. Davey Smith, 'When is mortality risk determined? Historical insights into a current debate', *Social History of Medicine*, 1993, vol. 6, pp. 101–23.

9 B. Latour, *Science in Action*, Milton Keynes, 1987.

10 For an account of the origins of the Interdepartmental Committee see B. Harris, *The Health of the Schoolchild. A History of the School Medical Service in England and Wales*, Buckingham, 1995, pp. 18–20.

11 *Parliamentary Papers*, 1904, vol. xxxii, 'Report of the Interdepartmental Committee on Physical Deterioration', vol. 1, pp. 56–7.

12 Quoted in D. Dwork, *War is Good for Babies and Other Young Children. A History of the Infant and Child Welfare Movement in England 1898–1918*, London, 1987, p. 20.

13 K. Pearson, 'The intensity of natural selection in man', *Proceedings of the Royal Society of London*, 1912, series B, vol. 85, pp. 469–76.

14 Quoted in B. Semmel, 'Karl Pearson: socialist and Darwinist', *British Journal of Sociology*, 1958, vol. 9, pp. 111–25.

15 K. Pearson, *Eugenics and Public Health. Questions of the Day and of the Fray No. VI*, London, 1912, pp. 32–3.

16 A. Newsholme, *Report on Infant and Child Mortality. Supplement to the Thirty-ninth Annual Report of the Medical Officer of the Local Government Board*, London, 1910.

17 Board of Education, *Annual Report for 1913 of the Chief Medical Officer of the Board of Education*, London, 1914, pp. 16–17.

18 F. W. White, 'Natural and social selection: a "blue-book" analysis', *Eugenics Review*, 1928, vol. 20, pp. 98–104.

19 V. P. A. Derrick, 'Observations on (1) errors on age on the population statistics of England and Wales and (2) the changes in mortality indicated by the national records', *Journal of the Institute of Actuaries*, 1927, vol. 58, pp. 117–59.

20 D. Heron, 'Discussion', *Journal of the Institute of Actuaries*, 1927, vol. 58, pp. 151–3.

21 W. O. Kermack, A. G. McKendrick and P. L. McKinlay, 'Death rates in Great Britain and Sweden: some general regularities and their significance', *The Lancet*, 1934, vol. 226, pp. 698–703.

22 C. Petty, 'Primary research and public health: the prioritization of nutrition research in inter-war Britain', in J. Austoker and L. Bryder (eds), *Historical Perspectives on the Role of the Medical Research Council*, Oxford, 1989, pp. 83–4.

23 Newsholme, 1910, op. cit.; G. Newman, *Infant Mortality. A Social Problem*, London, 1906; Board of Education, *Annual Report for 1913 of the Chief Medical Officer of the Board of Education*, London, 1914.

24 D. N. Paton and L. Findlay, 'Child life investigations: poverty, nutrition and growth. Studies of child life in cities and rural districts in Scotland', *Medical Research Council Special Report Series*, 1926, No. 101; E. P. Cathcart and A. M. T. Murray, 'A study in nutrition: 154 St Andrews families', *Medical Research Council Special Report Series*, 1931, No. 151.

25 Petty, 1989, op. cit., p 97.

26 J. Boyd Orr, *Food, Health and Income*, London, 1936.

27 G. C. M. M'Gonigle and J. Kirby, *Poverty and Public Health*, London, 1936, p. 148.

28 W. Hannington, *The Problem of the Distressed Areas*, London, 1937, pp. 58, 62.

29 Ibid., pp. 78–81.

30 H. M. Vernon, *Health in Relation to Occupation*, London, 1939, p. 9.

31 Ibid., p. 97.

32 G. D. H. Cole and M. I. Cole, *The Condition of Britain*, London, 1937, p. 88.

33 Ibid.

34 Ministry of Health, *On the State of the Public Health during Six Years of War. Report of the Chief Medical Officer of the Ministry of Health 1939–45*, London, 1946, p. 93.

35 A. M. Thomson, 'Problems and politics in nutritional surveillance. Fourth Boyd Orr Memorial Lecture', *Proceedings of the Nutrition Society*, 1978, vol. 37, pp. 317–33.

36 Kuh and Davey Smith, 1993, op. cit.

37 R. A. M. Case, 'Cohort analysis and cancer mortality in England and Wales, 1911–1954, by site and sex', *British Journal of Preventative and Social Medicine*, 1956, vol. 10, pp. 172–99.

38 J. N. Morris, 'Epidemiology and cardiovascular disease of middle age' 1, *Modern Concepts of Cardiovascular Disease*, 1960, vol. 29, pp. 625–32.

39 F. Lickint, 'Der Bronchialkrebs der Raucher', *Münchener Medizinische Wochenschrift*, 1935, vol. 82, pp. 1232–4. See also G. Davey Smith, S. Ströbele and M. Egger, 'Smoking and health promotion in Nazi Germany', *Journal of Epidemiology and Community Health*, 1994, vol. 48, pp. 220–3.

40 J. Clemmesen (ed.), 'Symposium: cancer of the lung epidemiology', *Acta Union Int. contra Cancer*, 1953, vol. 9, pp. 426–635; W. Haenszel and M. B. Shimkin, 'Smoking patterns and epidemiology of lung cancer in the United States: are they compatible?', *Journal of the National Cancer Institute*, 1956, vol. 16, pp. 1417–41. The major early case-control studies were E. Schairer and E. Schöniger, 'Lungenkrebs und Tabakverbrauch', *Zeitschrift für Krebsforschung*, 1943, vol. 54, pp. 261–9; E. L. Wynder and E. A. Graham, 'Tobacco smoking as a possible etiologic factor in bronchiogenic carcinoma', *Journal of the American Medical Association*, 1950, vol. 143, pp. 329–36; R. Doll and A. B. Hill, 'Smoking and carcinoma of the lung', *British Medical Journal*, 1950, vol. ii, pp. 739–48.

41 See, for example, A. Keys, 'Prediction and possible prevention of coronary disease', *American Journal of Public Health*, 1953, vol. 43, pp. 1399–407.

42 T. R. Dawber, G. F. Meadors and F. J. Moore, 'Epidemiological approaches to heart disease: the Framingham study', *American Journal of Public Health*, 1951, vol. 41, pp. 279–86.

43 Quoted in: M. Bartley, 'Coronary heart disease and the public health 1850–1983', *Sociology of Health and Illness*, 1985, vol. 7, pp. 289–313.

44 The most complete statement of T. McKeown's views is to be found in his *The Modern Rise of Population*, London, 1976.

45 S. Szreter, 'The importance of social intervention in Britain's mortality decline, 1850–1914: a reintegration of the role of public health', *Social History of Medicine*, 1988, vol. 1, pp. 1–37.

46 T. McKeown, *The Role of Medicine. Dream, Mirage or Nemesis?*, Oxford, 1979.

47 G. S. Berenson, S. R. Srinivasan, D. S. Freedman, B. Radhakrish-namurthy and E. R. Dalferes, Jr, 'Atherosclerosis and its evolution in childhood', *American Journal of Medical Science*, 1987, vol. 294, pp. 429–40.

48 G. R. Osborn, 'Stages in development of coronary disease observed from 1,500 young subjects: relationship of hypotension and infant feeding to aetiology', *Colloques Internationaux du Centre National de la Recherche Scientifique*, 1967, vol. 169, pp. 93–139.

49 D. D. Cowen, 'Myocardial infarction and infant feeding', *Practitioner*, 1973, vol. 210, pp. 661–3; M. L. Burr, W. H. Beasley and C. B. Fisher, 'Breast feeding, maternal smoking and early atheroma', *European Heart Journal*, 1984, vol. 5, pp. 588–91.

50 R. W. D. Turner, 'Breast is best for coronary protection', *The Lancet*, 1976, vol. ii, pp. 693–4.

51 A. Forsdahl, 'Are poor living conditions in childhood and adolescence

an important risk factor for arteriosclerotic heart disease?', *British Journal of Preventative and Social Medicine*, 1977, vol. 31, pp. 91–5.

52 A. Forsdahl, 'Living conditions in childhood and subsequent development of risk factors for arteriosclerotic heart disease: the cardiovascular survey in Finnmark 1974–75', *Journal of Epidemiology and Community Health*, 1978, vol. 32, pp. 34–7.

53 Department of Health and Social Security, *Diet and Cardiovascular Disease*, Report on Health and Social Subjects No. 28, London, 1984.

54 D. J. P. Barker and C. Osmond, 'Diet and coronary heart disease in England and Wales during and after the Second World War', *Journal of Epidemiology and Community Health*, 1986, vol. 40, pp. 37–44.

55 D. J. P. Barker and C. Osmond, 'Infant mortality, childhood nutrition, and ischaemic heart disease in England and Wales', *The Lancet*, 1986, vol. i, pp. 1077–81.

56 D. J. P. Barker and C. Osmond, 'Death rates from stroke in England and Wales predicted from past maternal mortality', *British Medical Journal*, 1987, vol. 295, pp. 83–6.

57 D. J. P. Barker and C. Osmond, 'Inequalities in health in Britain: specific explanations in three Lancashire towns', *British Medical Journal*, 1987, vol. 294, pp. 749–52.

58 D. J. P. Barker, P. D. Winter, C. Osmond, B. Margetts and S. J. Simmonds, 'Weight in infancy and death from ischaemic heart disease', *The Lancet*, 1989, vol. ii, pp. 577–80.

59 Barker, Gluckman *et al.*, 1993, op. cit.

60 D. J. P. Barker, *Mothers, Babies, and Disease in Later Life*, London, 1994.

61 R. A. McCance and E. M. Widdowson, 'Nutrition and growth', *Proceedings of the Royal Society of London*, 1962, series B, vol. 156, pp. 326–37; R. A. McCance and E. M. Widdowson, 'The determinants of growth and form', *Proceedings of the Royal Society of London*, 1974, series B, vol. 185, pp. 1–17.

62 Kuh and Davey Smith, 1993, op. cit.

63 Medical Research Council, *Medical Research Council Corporate Plan*, London, 1992.

64 Robinson, 1992, op. cit.

65 As discussed in Barker, 1992, op. cit., and D. J. P. Barker, 'Fetal origins of coronary heart disease', *British Medical Journal*, 1995, vol. 311, pp. 171–4.

66 J. Elford, P. Whincup and A. G. Shaper, 'Early life experience and adult cardiovascular disease: longitudinal and case control studies', *International Journal of Epidemiology*, 1991, vol. 20, pp. 833–44; J. Elford, A. G. Shaper and P. Whincup, 'Early life experiences and adult cardiovascular disease: ecological studies', *Journal of Epidemiology and Community Health*, 1992, vol. 46, pp. 1–11.

67 Y. Ben-Shlomo and G. Davey Smith, 'Deprivation in infancy or adult life: which is more important for mortality risk?', *The Lancet*, 1991, vol. 337, pp. 530–4; D. Baker, R. Illsley and D. Vagero, 'Today or in the past? The origins of ischaemic heart disease', *Journal of Public Health Medicine*, 1993, vol. 15, pp. 243–8; J. Elford *et al.*, 1991, op. cit.; J. Elford

et al., 1992, op. cit.; N. Paneth and M. Susser, 'Early origins of coronary heart disease', *British Medical Journal*, 1995, vol. 310, pp. 411–12.

68 Vernon, 1939, op. cit., p. 129.

69 I. Leitch, 'Growth and health', *British Journal of Nutrition*, 1951, vol. 5, pp. 142–51.

70 G. Davey Smith and A. N. Phillips, 'Confounding in epidemiological studies: why "independent" effects may not be all they seem', *British Medical Journal*, 1992, vol. 305, pp. 757–9.

71 Paneth and Susser, 1995, op. cit.; M. Bartley, C. Power, D. Blane, G. Davey Smith and M. J. Shipley, 'Birthweight and later socio-economic disadvantage: evidence from the 1958 British cohort study', *British Medical Journal*, 1994, vol. 309, pp. 1475–8; D. J. P. Barker, 'The fetal and infant origins of adult disease', *British Medical Journal*, 1990, vol. 301, p. 1111.

72 J. M. Winter, 'Unemployment, nutrition and infant mortality in Britain 1920–1950', in J. M. Winter (ed.), *The Working Class in Modern British History*, Cambridge, 1984.

73 C. Webster, 'Healthy or hungry thirties?', *History Workshop Journal*, 1982, vol. 13, pp. 110–29.

74 Winter, 1984, op. cit.

75 Cole and Cole, 1937, op. cit., p. 99.

76 Ibid., p. 100.

77 C. M. McCay, M. F. Crowell and L. A. Maynard, 'The effect of retarded growth upon the length of life span and upon the ultimate body size', *Journal of Nutrition*, 1935, vol. 10, pp. 63–79.

78 Kermack *et al.*, 1934, op. cit.

79 G. E. Friend, *The Schoolboy. A Study of his Nutrition, Physical Development and Health*, Cambridge, 1935, p. 4:

80 M'Gonigle and Kirby, 1936, op. cit., p. 150.

81 D. J. P. Barker, T. W. Meade, C. H. D. Fall, A. Lee, C. Osmond, K. Phipps and Y. Stirling, 'Relation of fetal and infant growth to plasma fibrinogen and factor VII concentrations in adult life', *British Medical Journal*, 1992, vol. 304, pp. 148–52.

82 C. N. Hales, D. J. P. Barker, P. M. S. Clark, L. J. Cox, C. Fall, C. Osmond and P. D. Winter, 'Fetal and infant growth and impaired glucose tolerance at age 64', *British Medical Journal*, 1991, vol. 303, pp. 1019–22.

83 Barker *et al.*, 1989, op. cit.

84 L. Durward, *Poverty in Pregnancy. The Cost of an Adequate Diet for Expectant Mothers*, London, 1988.

85 National Children's Home, *Poverty and Nutrition Survey*, London, 1992.

86 Barker, 1994, op. cit.

87 National Children's Bureau, *Investing in the Future. Child Health Ten Years after the Court Report*. Policy and Practice Review Group, London, 1987; G. A. Cornia, 'Child poverty and deprivation in industrialised countries: recent trends and policy options', *Innocents Occasional Papers*, No. 2, Florence, 1990; V. R. Fuchs and D. M. Reklis, 'America's children: economic perspectives and policy options', *Science*, 1992, vol. 255, pp. 41–6; B. Spock, *Baby and Child Care*, sixth edition, London, 1992.

88 S. Rose, L. J. Kamin and R. C. Lewontin, *Not in our Genes. Biology, Ideology and Human Nature*, Harmondsworth, 1984.

89 D. I. W. Phillips, 'Twin studies in medical research: can they tell us whether diseases are genetically determined?', *The Lancet*, 1993, vol. 341, pp. 1008–9.

90 R. D. G. Leslie and D. A. Pyke, 'Twin studies in medical research', *The Lancet*, 1993, vol. 341, p. 1418; D. L. Duffy, 'Twin studies in medical research', ibid., pp. 1418–19.

11

GOING PUBLIC

Food campaigns during the 1980s and early 1990s

Tim Lang

In the 1980s, food policy became the subject of some political sensitivity for the first time since the winding down of the wartime system of food controls in the early 1950s. It is argued here that over the last ten to fifteen years a new generation of activists and non-governmental organisations (NGOs) helped to create a new context for food policy decision-making, by taking food issues to the public. The full history of this period should, of course, feature many more people than can be mentioned here; the focus in this chapter is on the NGOs and people of the new food movement rather than on the industry, government and academic experts involved in food policy.

The new generation of activists and organisations injected new understandings into the discourse of food policy through its focus, themes, politics, language and methods of working, but it also represented, in areas such as food adulteration, poverty and school meals, the rebirth of older concerns. In the 1980s NGOs became a significant force in food policy, owing partly to the dominance of Thatcherism and disarray in the political opposition, partly to a reaction to great changes in the food system since the Second World War, and partly because of the fissure in state food policy between production, run from the Ministry of Agriculture, Fisheries and Food (MAFF), and health, run by the Department of Health and Social Security, later the Department of Health. The NGOs could analyse and exploit this, taking the rhetoric of the market at face value, and placing more emphasis on the public than on politicians.

This chapter argues that food policy can best be seen as contested space, a battleground of competing interests and ideologies, rather than as a consensus topic. Food always has the capacity to bring out emotions. It is, after all, a daily need and intake.[1] A Whig interpretation of history is inappropriate, as there are many competing versions of the study of the food system, the purposes of food policy, and the shape of food culture.[2] Food NGOs became a key element in the moulding of mass consciousness, much as environmental NGOs did in the same period. In this respect alone, the new movement constitutes a rich vein for historical exploration of how culture and politics are shaped in the global age. Already, in the writings about modern food culture, there are some writers who recognise the role of NGOs,[3] but others who do not.[4]

THE NEW FOOD MOVEMENT

In the 1980s, food suddenly came out of the consumer and women's pages and hit the headlines. In two extraordinary periods, at either end of the decade, a series of scandals grabbed public and political attention. There were other occasions when consumption made headlines, such as the campaign over pesticide residues waged by Friends of the Earth (FOE),[5] but these two periods appear to have been of a different order.

The first period in 1983–4 was sparked off by sections of the food industry, particularly the sugar industry, filibustering over a report by the National Advisory Committee on Nutrition Education (NACNE) on diet and heart disease.[6] NACNE was set up in 1979 by the government with representatives from the Department of Health, MAFF, the Health Education Council and its Scottish equivalent, and the food industry-funded British Nutrition Foundation (BNF). A succinct account of the events behind this *cause célèbre* has been given by Caroline Walker, the Secretary of NACNE, and Geoffrey Cannon, her collaborator and later husband.[7] This row brought to a head unease within epidemiological and nutrition circles about evidence on the impact of diet on health. Following the pioneering work of Ancel Keys and co-workers in the Seven Countries study,[8] and of Dennis Burkitt and others on fibre,[9] evidence had grown that the modern diet was implicated in the so-called diseases of affluence, a wide range of illness including heart disease, tooth decay, irritable bowel and food-related cancers. Surgeon Captain Cleave called this constellation of illness *The Saccharine Disease*.[10] A new era of public interest in food had been born.

With the growth of public and professional interest in the

consequences of modern eating, sensitivity in the food industry was considerable, and there was a furious reaction by sections of industry to NACNE's proposed message. In fact, NACNE was adopting a 'soft' approach, calling for public education, better labelling, and so on, in line with recommendations from the Department of Health's Committee on Medical Aspects of Food Policy.[11] This public education approach was sorely tested in a series of tussles between the Health Education Council (HEC) and government. The HEC was semi-independent, but at least two of its directors-general (Alistair Mackie and David Player) fell in the 1980s after confronting the tobacco, food and drink industries. In 1987, the HEC was replaced by the Health Education Authority, firmly under government control.

The health education approach of NACNE was a half-way house between a regulatory approach and non-intervention and reflected the contemporary reality that intervention was unacceptable to a government committed to winding back the 'nanny state'. The clash over NACNE rapidly educated many in the nutrition world and engendered a sceptical view of the food industry. As the NACNE story filtered out – first exposed by Cannon in the *Sunday Times*[12] – the world of health promotion changed. The need to campaign and not just negotiate with civil servants or companies, already clear to some,[13] became clear to many. Professor Philip James, vice-chair of the NACNE (and main author of the report), was first chair and ultimately president of the National Food Alliance (NFA), the voluntary sector umbrella, set up in 1985 by the National Council for Voluntary Organisations. There was considerable indignation that corporate self-interest could come before the public health. And far from evidence on the diet–disease connection being inconclusive, as some food industry-friendly academics argued, evidence strengthened as the decade progressed.[14] With the publication of *The Health of the Nation* in 1992, the Department of Health accepted that a new strategy was needed.[15] A Nutrition Taskforce was set up, drawn from government, industry, academia and the voluntary sector. By 1994, twelve working parties on subjects as diverse as school meals, low income, catering education and product promotion were established. This represented the voluntary sector coming in from the cold Thatcher years.[16]

In 1983, as the NACNE row unfolded, the NGOs, notably the Coronary Prevention Group (CPG), and sympathetic academics, assumed new roles, feeding journalists with information and brief-

240

ing politicians. They broke out of the medical–academic model of change into a campaign mode. The CPG had been founded in 1979 after a British Heart Foundation annual general meeting at which Keith Ball, a physician, and Caroline Walker, a nutritionist, asked why so little work was going into prevention. The CPG's appeals to the food industry for assistance proved unsuccessful. Campaigns, not co-operation, seemed to be needed.[17]

Caroline Walker became secretary of the CPG in 1980,[18] and was later a founding member of the board of the London Food Commission (LFC). Others for whom CPG offered an early home included Geoffrey Cannon, a journalist turned food researcher, Jack Winkler, an academic and later freelance researcher, Maggie Sanderson, a nutritionist, Michael Crawford, a biochemist and author of an early critique of modern food,[19] and Aubrey Sheiham, a professor of community dentistry, co-author of a report on sugar for the Health Education Council.[20] Sugar was an especially important theme in 1980s campaigns. Sugars were added to a vast number of foods and drinks and strong vested interests had to be confronted.

If the first wave of scandals was over food's impact on health, the second, in 1988–90, was about adulteration and contamination, and whether consumers were informed enough to protect themselves. It began with the eggs and salmonella issue in late 1988, which forced the resignation of the junior Health Minister, Edwina Currie, for having over-stated the case that eggs were contaminated. A seemingly endless series of new exposés followed: listeria in soft cheese and cook–chill meals, residues of Alar in apple juice, baby food contamination, bovine spongiform encephalopathy (mad cow disease), botulism in yoghurt, lead in milk, and inadequacy of microwave ovens.[21]

It is hard, in retrospect, to grasp this process. At the time, I was Director of the LFC, an NGO set up in 1984. The LFC had helped break the story about food poisoning, with a report by Julie Sheppard published as part of a book on food adulteration in July 1988.[22] Publicity on the book introduced the Leeds University microbiologist Professor Richard Lacey to journalists and the public. Julie Sheppard and I had met Lacey in 1987 when the LFC was asked to conduct a study of Wakefield Hospital's cook–chill plant. It was carried out by Sheppard and Richard North, an independent environmental health officer. Lacey's advice on the dangers of its plant had been ignored, despite some deaths of inpatients from food poisoning. The LFC book received considerable media coverage, and helped engender two television programmes on food poisoning, which set the scene for the Edwina Currie saga. A key argument at the time, developed by the LFC, was that consumers were being blamed for poor standards of hygiene further up the food chain.

The Commons Agriculture Committee held an enquiry into salmonella and the government's handling of the affair. This included some draconian action, such as the slaughtering of flocks and closure of plant, vehemently questioned by free-marketers to this day.[23] A routine updating of food legislation was turned into a major new Act, the Food Safety Act 1990. The Ministry of Agriculture, Fisheries and Food (MAFF) was restructured, with a new food safety division. Two sets of regular meetings between Ministers and consumers groups were set up. British food scandals became international news.

CONTESTED SPACE

How had these two periods of scandal come about? In both cases, the role of NGOs and activists as mediators of opinion, argument and facts stands out. NGOs became commentators and actors simultaneously. It would be wrong to argue, however, that NGOs made events happen, as some beleaguered right-wing politicians tried to. Nor did these two periods of scandal emerge from the blue. Years of work and build-up preceded them. A critique of the post-war food system took time to develop. This critique came from many quarters: agricultural, nutritional, technological, feminist and consumer.[24] If NACNE brought nutrition politics to the fore, the adulteration scandals carried an implicit criticism of excessive concentration upon nutrition. Nutrition, narrowly or technocratically defined, could not explain the nature of diet; it was too mechanistic. What was exposed was a clash of position on food policy, the role of the state, the balance of forces within the food system, and the rhetoric about consumer sovereignty. If consumers were under- or ill-informed, how could they be said to be sovereign?[25] In neither period of scandal would there have been an outcry if the public was not already uneasy.

Broadly, we may distinguish between three competing positions. First, there was an interventionist perspective, developed during the Second World War, which argued for regulation of the food system through a system of committees of experts drawn from

MAFF, industry and academia. If there were to be regulations and policy objectives, let them be agreed.[26] The second position was anti-interventionist, and blossomed under Thatcherism. The less government the better; the state should withdraw from both subsidising and 'nannying'. This position was developed through the patient work of a group of right-wing think-tanks critical of corporatism, and espousing a then unfashionable 'leave it to the market' approach; it also turned distinctly anti-European, pillorying the Common Agricultural Policy in particular.[27] The third was developed by the NGOs from the 1970s. This argued that food policy could not be left to the free market, and that post-war affluence had apparently resolved some food problems only to create new ones. New priorities were needed. Production should be extensified, rather than intensified, to stop the public and environmental health costs of current production; consumers were not receiving proper support to enable them to make informed choices; and the state should prevent food industry excesses.

THE BSSRS AND RADICAL FOOD SCIENCE

A significant source of ideas and people was the British Society for Social Responsibility in Science (BSSRS), founded in 1968, which had a considerable effect in nurturing the radical scientists and perspectives which came to prominence in the 1980s. During the 1970s BSSRS was based at 9 Poland Street, a Rowntree-funded hive of radical NGOs near London's Oxford Street. Although BSSRS itself has ceased to exist, some of its products still do, such as *Hazards Bulletin*, which is now published from Sheffield.[28] The BSSRS approach was influenced by arguments about the labour process of science and the view that science could not be judged purely from a 'use–abuse' framework. It asked who and what sets the questions that science addresses. Charlie Clutterbuck was also a key person in organising and motivating the emerging food movement's arguments. He founded the BSSRS Agricapital Group after calling a public meeting on food, as part of a BSSRS series on science and technology in 1975–6. Clutterbuck was a soil scientist whose Ph.D. had been on pesticides, the value of which he increasingly questioned.[29] He moved ultimately into trade union education but retained an interest in food.

The Agricapital Group saw early on that the debate about food needed to be wider than it had been in the 1950s or 1960s.

Technical fixes like pesticides and the Green Revolution were inadequate, indeed socially unjust. The food revolution was being driven by corporations and a willing state, which provided infra-structure and research. This modern food system needed to be studied better, and more critically. Although critical of the role of experts, BSSRS tacitly argued that 'alternative' experts were needed to take issues to workers, the poor, or people with health problems.

I remember meeting Clutterbuck, BSSRS's first full-time worker, at a conference on technology in 1976, hosted by David Elliott of the Open University, another long-time BSSRS activist. We found our mutual interest was food and he asked me to join the fledgling Agricapital Group. Our first work was to produce a special issue of *Science for People*, BSSRS's magazine, in 1976.[30] Agricapital groups were developed in the south and north of Britain. The southern group was ultimately more productive, publishing *Our Daily Bread*, a report on bread quality and production, produced with help from bakery workers.[31] This almost led to BSSRS being sued by one of the three big companies then dominating bread production. The northern group failed to finish a report on potatoes, but was larger, and did better in experimenting with local food campaigning, with a week-long campaign on food in Sheffield in 1978. This was of doubtful impact, but great fun. Both groups met regularly. A social life was emerging in this middle-class, educated circle.

The Agricapital Group was an important grounding for socially aware young scientists and others who were questioning the shape of the modern food economy. The membership included Sandra Hunt and Joyce Treuhertz, who were both nutritionists, Erik Millstone, a physicist and philosopher,[32] Geoff Tansey, editor of *Food Policy*, Carole Smith, who is now a naturopath, and Lizzie Vann, who now owns an organic baby food company. Others included Colin Hines, an environmentalist who now works for Greenpeace,[33] people working on development such as Dave Bull, now head of Amnesty UK, and John Clarke, who is now at the World Bank, as well as Clutterbuck, and myself, a social psychologist. Bull and Clarke worked in Oxford, close to Uhuru, a bookshop, café and education centre, and then at Oxfam.[34] They produced a cartoon version of the Agricapital bread report, which taught the impor-tance of producing accessible information, not just worthy tomes or work for lawyers! Some of these people are still in touch and collaborating in the world of food policy, but others, inevitably, moved away.[35]

The Agricapital Group tended to focus on production, but another BSSRS group, the Politics of Health Group (POHG) Food Group, worked more on diet and nutrition. Both were active in the late 1970s and early 1980s, making BSSRS a focus for critics of food policy. In 1979, POHG produced *Food and Profit: It Makes You Sick*, a critique of health policy. POHG Food Group included Tim Lobstein, a psychophysiologist, now of the Food Commission (UK) (FCUK); Aubrey Sheiham, now at University College London; Helena Sheiham, now at the London School of Economics; Michael Joffe, a public health physician; Liz Dowler, a nutritionist, now at the Centre for Human Nutrition in London, and Sandy Hunt. In fora such as POHG or Agricapital, a wide range of disciplines were drawn on to argue out a perspective which was neither corporatist, nor 'top down' planning-oriented, nor free market, but pro the public health, workers, the 'people'. Another BSSRS-related group, the Radical Statistics Group, survived BSSRS, and continues to produce statistical and epidemiological critiques. People such as Mel Bartley, George Davey Smith and others played a vital role in food policy debates in the 1980s from this perspective.

A common perspective to much BSSRS work was the argument that the nature of technology both reflects a set of social relations and reinforces them. This perspective could be found in the work of Millstone and Miller on additives, Sheppard on cook–chill technology, and Brunner on bovine somatotropin, which highlighted the imminence of the biotechnology revolution.[36] A campaign on food irradiation was run for the LFC by Tony Webb. Webb had formerly been involved in the Labour Party-oriented Socialist Environment and Resources Association, which, like BSSRS, had been based at 9 Poland Street, and the London Hazards Centre, another GLC-funded and BSSRS-inspired advice centre.[37]

BSSRS developed radical left-of-centre perspectives which were often critical of both traditional left/right positions. There was a genuine desire to understand what was happening in the developing countries, while focusing on the developed world where we lived. This perspective was then unfashionable. The dominant position was that 'capitalism has resolved the problems of agriculture and food for rich countries like ours, but not for developing countries'. This logic was disputed by both POHG and Agricapital. Many radical and traditional food scientists, industry and policy specialists alike, were bemused. Food adulteration and contamination, they argued, are the stuff of history. Any claims to the contrary are either unscientifically based or politics masquerading as science.[38] Science has resolved the old bugbears of contamination, and engendered undreamed-of choice, said the traditionalists.[39]

A decade on, the new food movement's perspective appeared to be more in touch with public sentiment while supporters of the *status quo* became increasingly defensive, resorting to *ad hominem* attacks. In a much-quoted phrase John Gummer, MP, Minister of Agriculture in the late 1980s and early 1990s, referred to the need to counteract 'food fascism'. His junior Parliamentary Secretary at MAFF in 1992 referred to 'food terrorists', a phrase first thrown at one of my colleagues at the LFC in 1986.[40] The director of the right-wing Social Affairs Unit talked of 'food Leninism'. These kinds of gibes were constantly thrown at the food movement, but became less frequent as the implications of the food scandals sank in.[41]

In the 1980s, on foundations laid by BSSRS, a remarkable coalition of people, groups and interests came together. The coalition bridged academic and voluntary sectors. The collapse of the formal left opposition, and the triumph of the New Right, opened the way for newer analyses. By the 1990s, this coalition had, in my opinion, become a classic alliance, in the tradition of alliances like the anti-adulteration movement of the mid-nineteenth century. Modern food policy had been transformed. The WHO's 1990 report on preventable diseases, for instance, included concern about new adulterations and contamination from additives and pesticides, and recognition that the production process had to be understood, even if diseases such as CHD and cancer were the primary focus.[42] Equally, NGOs like FOE could now argue that coronary heart disease was part of an environmental food strategy which otherwise focused on the land, or issues like packaging. Food became a rallying point.

THE LONDON FOOD COMMISSION

No review of 1980s campaigning could be complete without acknowledging the role of the LFC. It picked up many of BSSRS's themes, and coupled them with the medical–epidemiological thinking about food policy represented by the CPG, and later by the National Forum for Coronary Heart Disease Prevention. The LFC was unusual in a number of respects. It was not just supported by, but was set up by, a local authority, the Greater London Council

(GLC) and the support came in the form of a five-year, one-off grant of just over £1 million in March 1985. A trust was set up to administer the funds and to ensure that they were spent by 31 March 1990. The LFC was less a service provider than a hybrid of think-tank, strategic campaigner and public education point. It also had a very large board of directors, the council, of fifty people chaired by Mike Joffe, representing four 'chambers' of interest: local authority, workers/ trade unions, professionals and consumers.

Formally, the LFC ran for six years, 1984–90, and then became the Food Commission (UK). It was the brainchild of Robin Jenkins, a former community development project worker and researcher into development aid. Jenkins and Sandra Hunt began to work for the GLC in 1982/3 under the Economic Development Unit, where they drew up a number of reports on food, nutrition and the case for radical change.[43] Jenkins held talks around London, and suggested that an independent public group should be set up to pursue the issues. The LFC was steered through the GLC decision-making process with help from Tim Lobstein in the summer of 1984. Appointments were made in autumn 1984. Four people started work in November 1984, and by 1986 fifteen were employed. With volunteers and students on placement, the office at times held twenty people.

The LFC's workers included two nutritionists, two psychologists, a biochemist, a food technologist–economist, an environmental scientist, a biologist, a philosophy graduate turned journalist, a science campaigner, and ultimately five administrative staff supervised by Sue Dibb, now co-director with Lobstein of the FCUK. Dibb brought vital experience from her work with Des Wilson at CLEAR, the campaign to remove lead from petrol, and the Campaign for Freedom of Information. The LFC had a steady stream of visitors and placement students, and had good relations with a few academic departments. Diane McCrea, now head of food at the Consumers' Association, came on a year's sabbatical from Middlesex Polytechnic to write a report on water in food.[44]

Internally, the LFC was a relatively 'flat' pyramid; the director was generally responsible, but project officers researched subjects, wrote reports, and prepared and presented the public education and information to follow. Its brief, laid down in the trust documents, was to provide information and education to alleviate food-related ill health. It was clear that part of the goal was to confront the role of the BNF in representing the public interest; the BNF's role and near-total dependence on food industry funds had been exposed in the NACNE debacle. The LFC was run on a project basis, broadly covering the following areas: nutrition, social aspects, technological impact, general food policy, consultancies, and education and training. Some projects were picked up by the media; other work was not, such as the reports on labelling, and Brunner's early report on catering education.[45] But a corporate *oeuvre* and style were emerging, and media contacts and credibility were built. By any standards the LFC was productive – forty or so reports, five books, and numerous courses, speeches, campaigns and meetings, which generated box files of press coverage, helped usher in a Food Safety Act, educated the public, and built a cross-party consensus in the media.

The LFC also set up and serviced a number of co-ordinating committees such as the global Food Irradiation Network and a more informal one on BST. Such international work was necessitated by UK domestic politics. The government's belief in the market meant devolving responsibility for food policy to the commercial sector: supporting business took priority. NGOs increasingly turned to Europe to win state support. The LFC was no exception, and cultivated good relations with civil servants and politicians in Brussels.

Following the LFC's packed launch at the Festival Hall in spring 1985, questions were asked about why the GLC was wasting its money on this body. When it handed over to the smaller FCUK in 1990, questions had turned round: the food scandals of 1988–90 meant that the public was asking the government what *it* was doing. The legacy continues through the *Food Magazine*, set up to disseminate information in a more accessible way than the weighty reports. *Food Magazine* has became the mainstay of the FCUK's finances.

SWIMMING WITH OR AGAINST THE TIDE?

It is hard to measure the effectiveness of NGOs. By conventional 'business' measures such as output, the CPG and the LFC were highly productive. Much of their campaigning left a mark on public culture. Irradiation, for example, was legalised by the UK government in the 1990s, but was made almost unusable, such was consumer hostility. The campaigns made the market work by providing information to the public which otherwise would have been given only half the story. The LFC, for example, was central in shifting thinking on BST, food poverty, children's food and adulteration. It could claim considerable credit for leading the campaign on food safety, which culminated in the Food Safety Act 1990.

High-profile activities were only a portion of LFC work. For example, Sara Hill and Issy Cole-Hamilton, LFC dietitians, organised a conference on 'Food for Black and Ethnic Minorities' which drew over 200 people, and led to a huge report.[46] Another example was the project on food poverty which Cole-Hamilton ran; this is still part of the FCUK's work and was greatly enhanced by Suzi Leather, the National Consumer Council's nominee to the MAFF consumer panel in the 1990s.[47]

The food poverty work was one of my deepest commitments. I had come to London in 1984. At Manchester Polytechnic, we had set up a small food policy unit in 1982 and had begun three projects, including a large pilot survey on poverty.[48] This was set up with encouragement and help from Sandra Hunt and Caroline Walker. Walker had worked with the Child Poverty Action Group on benefit levels for her M.Sc. thesis.[49] One of the attractions of the LFC job was the chance to start up a comprehensive programme of work, with pride of place for poverty. The LFC produced a paper against the 1985 Social Security Bill proposals, and conducted some terse correspondence with the junior Minister, John Major. Major assured us that there was no set cost of a diet included in welfare payments 'as each claimant is free to decide how to budget their income according to their individual requirements'.[50] The correspondence continued with the Chief Medical Officer at the Department of Health, who wrote in response to our report *Tightening Belts* of 1986, 'A healthy diet is not necessarily a more expensive one'.[51] The LFC calculation that it was 35 per cent higher upset the implicit health education message that diet was a matter of choice. The retailers desperately tried to show that shopping in their giant superstores meant parity, but the evidence was strong on our side, too.[52] The LFC had added weight to the argument that modern poverty takes new forms.[53]

The work on school meals was another aspect of the anti-poverty work, which became sorely needed in the 1980s as structural unemployment built up. The Education Act 1980 removed obligations on local education authorities (LEAs) to provide school meals to standards set by government.[54] School meal take-up fell from around two-thirds of the population in 1979 to just over 40 per cent in 1990, yet poverty rose. In 1980 there had been the first of three attempts to counteract this removal of a nutritional safety net. It was regional, rather than national, for example in Edinburgh, Lincolnshire, Lancashire. The second was national, with a private member's Bill in 1986 introduced by Tony Lloyd MP with LFC and CPG backing, and a set of guidelines produced by CPG. The third, much larger and with a broader range of backers, was the 1992 School Meals Campaign, launched with support from fifty-four national NGOs, including the British Medical Association, the National Association of Head Teachers and the National Federation of Women's Institutes. By 1992 the government had been embarrassed enough to set up a working party on school meal guidelines as part of the Nutrition Taskforce. This was not the reintroduction of modern nutrition standards that campaigners wanted, but moving in the right direction compared with the 1980 Act, and the result of increasingly well co-ordinated lobbying and evidence.

The LFC's style was collaboratory. Almost always it set up a working party. In this respect it developed the BSSRS critique of experts and tried to build a radical consensus about the problems and challenge of food policy. In the process, alternative experts were made, but information which otherwise would have been withheld was given to the public.

Although well funded, and by the end of the 1980s quite high-profile, the LFC was not alone in this style of work. Partly owing to financial pressure and partly on account of their effectiveness, coalitions were more common by the 1990s than they had been earlier. Baby Milk Action, for instance, had been constituted in 1979 as part of an international network to promote breast-feeding and to campaign against companies selling breast-milk substitutes.[55] Another campaign, the Hyperactive Children's Support Group, was also founded in the 1970s. A coalition active in the 1980s was Action and Information on Sugars (AIS), set up by dentists such as Aubrey Sheiham with doctors and health promotion specialists. This was more professionally based but also represented an understanding that campaigning was necessary. AIS ran an effective campaign to 'Chuck Sweets off the Checkout', targeting supermarkets profiting from children's 'pester power' when queuing at the till. In the 1980s, many groups for whom food was not a primary focus were drawn into the new movement, and became part of the National Food Alliance. The Maternity Alliance, an umbrella group for NGOs working for mothers, conducted one of the first pieces of research and campaigned on modern food poverty, with Lyn Durward's report on the cost of a maternity diet.[56]

Because it was well staffed with committed, articulate professional people, the LFC was well placed to build bridges with NGOs, and across sectors. Different projects brought in different organisations and 'constituencies'. Close links were set up with organisations working in fields as diverse as animal welfare,[57] poverty, the environment, medicine and trade unions. Steve Pryle and Donna Covey for the General Municipal and Boilermakers' Union, and Nigel Bryson for the Bakers', members of the LFC Council, were particularly active and helpful.

CORONARY PREVENTION GROUP

If the NGO world was run like business it would be dominated by competition for funds, attention and prestige. Sometimes there was competition and jealousy, but the new food movement was and is remarkably co-operative. The organisation most obviously close to LFC interests was the CPG. CPG's first director was Christopher Robbins, an academic in the 1970s, a writer and campaigner in the 1980s, and a herbalist in the 1990s; then Ann Dillon, who later became head of corporate relations at the National Farmers' Union; then Michael O'Connor, a former civil servant responsible for tobacco at the Department of Health. It was under O'Connor that the closest links between the CPG and the LFC/FCUK developed, but CPG's profile, staff and output declined within eighteen months of his departure in 1993.

The CPG and LFC worked by a *de facto* division of labour. CPG was more medically driven and 'inside track' in that it tried to influence Department of Health circles, whereas the LFC was more radical and 'outside track'. Both groups worked closely over school meals, but there were differences of emphasis. The CPG was more 'realistic', calling for the introduction of guidelines,[58] whereas the LFC was for the reintroduction of standards. Both strategies had ground to nothing by the early 1990s, but the two traditions came together most effectively when O'Connor offered office space to Parents for Safe Food (PSF) in 1991, and then to the FCUK in 1992, leading to the formation of the School Meals Campaign. The activities of the campaign resulted in the *Health of the Nation* promise to develop 'healthy schools'.[59]

PARENTS FOR SAFE FOOD

When the LFC formally closed and the FCUK was established, I went to work as director of a pesticide-based campaign that the LFC had helped to set up over a year earlier. PSF continued to operate until 1994. Its original members were a group of celebrities from the world of the media and entertainment, and it was founded and energised by Pamela Stephenson, who with her husband, Billy Connolly, and concerned friends such as Olivia and George Harrison, Jenny Seagrove, Patricia Hodge and Gay Exton, turned PSF into a very unusual NGO. The NGO world is famous for low pay, hard work, long hours, worthiness and unconventional career structures. In the 1980s, the environment movement had built bridges with entirely different kinds of people from business, the media and entertainment. FOE, under Jonathon Porritt, for example, had set up The Arts for the Earth (TAFE) which became both a major fund-raiser and a source of street credibility. Pamela Stephenson's vision was to build a parents' organisation which would front with stars and act as a campaign vehicle to improve food quality.

The stimulus to PSF's creation was the US-induced scare about a plant growth regulator, marketed under the brand name Alar. Pamela Stephenson quickly built up contacts in the NGO world, drawing considerably on the *Guardian* consumer correspondent James Erlichman and myself. She pulled together about seventy celebrities, including the surviving Beatles and their wives, Dame Judi Dench and Jeremy Irons, to back the organisation's launch calling for the withdrawal of Alar pending an enquiry. The idea was based on a US initiative, Mothers and Others for Safe Food, set up at arm's length by the Natural Resource Defense Council (NRDC), whose report sparked off the Alar cause in early 1989.[60] In the scientific literature, Alar had long been a 'grey area' pesticide, with some studies suggesting there were health problems, others disagreeing.[61] Within months of PSF's launch the maker withdrew the product, still professing its clean bill of health. All the NGO pesticide specialists consulted by the embryonic PSF recommended caution, on the grounds that the evidence was equivocal. Pamela Stephenson and colleagues agreed to argue that the public, not the producer, deserved the benefit of the doubt. At the year's end a special 'Alar-lujah' concert was held at the Albert Hall to celebrate the withdrawal. The approach of appealing direct to the public had worked and had left government and the Pesticide Advisory Committee floundering.

This experience of working with celebrities was a big change for food NGOs; a number of useful collaborative projects were set up, such as joint residue testing with FOE's countryside campaigner, Andrew Lees, who died in December 1994 on a project in Madagascar. After Alar, one of the most inconclusive but fruitful things PSF did was to host a number of alliance-building meetings at the Stephenson–Connolly house at Windsor Great Park in 1990 and 1991. For two years or so, 1989–91, the food movement had a rare showbiz edge to it, but the victory over Alar paradoxically took the wind out of PSF's sails; the Stephenson–Connolly household, always the driving force, moved to Hollywood. PSF subsequently moved into more strategic areas such as work on the international harmonisation of food standards, running the School Meals Campaign, and conducting a project on cooking skills for the NFA, funded by the Department of Health and backed by the *BBC Good Food Magazine*.[62]

CORE THEMES IN THE EMERGENCE OF MODERN FOOD ALLIANCES

It could be argued that what is described in this chapter as a food movement is no more than a collection of campaigns on single issues, such as breast-feeding, animal welfare, new food technologies, pesticides, or food advertising targeted at children.[63] This would be wrong, for three reasons. First, from the early days of the 1970s, a cross-over of members and participants bonded these single-issue campaigns through friendship, debate and social intercourse. Second, in the 1980s, considerable energy went into increasing co-ordination by setting up umbrella groups. These include the NFA, run by Jeanette Longfield, the National Forum for CHD Prevention, run by Imogen Sharpe, the Public Health Alliance, run by Maggie Winters, which was formed under the aegis of David Player in the dying days of the HEC, and, in the 1990s, the Sustainable Agriculture Food and Environment (SAFE) Alliance, run by Hugh Raven, a former Labour agriculture researcher. SAFE was supported by the Goldsmith brothers, Teddy, founder of *The Ecologist*, and Sir James, a former food entrepreneur, who is now deeply critical of the food industry.[64] Other alliances with food interests included the Maternity Alliance and the Green Alliance.

Third, the NGOs and campaigns possessed a shared vision of

what was wrong with the modern food system, and of what it ought to be. This vision had a number of common themes. One was that the nature of food and food production had changed, a theme clearly articulated by the Agricapital Group in the 1970s. The emergence of contemporary environmental and consumer concerns, such as food additives or pesticide residues, reflected profound changes in the nature of food production, on the farm and in the factory.[65] The second core theme was that, even as the modern food system appeared to have resolved old problems such as scarcity or malnutrition, it had created new problems. Notably these were environmental problems such as pollution, and health problems, ranging from heart disease to food poisoning and allergies.[66] This latter theme was the *raison d'être* of groups such as the POHG Food Group, and the CPG. The third theme was that decision-making about food left much to be desired, with too much power and influence being accorded to unaccountable corporate and industrial interests, a theme common to both BSSRS and the consumer-oriented NGOs. In the eggs and salmonella affair of 1988–9, the free-market-oriented Health and Welfare Unit of the Institute of Economic Affairs (IEA) argued that there was no point in interfering in the working of the market. In their report for the IEA, Richard North, an environmental health officer who earlier had worked with the LFC on cook–chill, and Teresa Gorman, a right-wing Conservative MP, spoke of 'health and safety fascism' at work.[67] Their enemy was the state. The new food movement, in contrast, appealed to the public to force the state to help protect them. Contesting the relationship between state, industry and the public was central to the new food policy debate.

Historically, food policy has inevitably been focused upon the state as agent, either in and out of war-led food planning, or to meet social policy goals. Less attention, however, has been paid to modern movements which try to articulate public, rather than sectional, pressure on food policy. One classic study by Self and Storing of British farmers after the Second World War highlighted their transition from a disparate group to an effective lobby of legendary proportions.[68] The 1980s brought some interest in NGOs, but often as subjects, or manipulators, of the media. Following the food scandals of 1988–90, there was a flurry of studies by business and academics.[69] Business was concerned because of profits, but soon saw opportunities for new markets in areas such as biotechnology and functional foods – deemed technical fixes by the NGOs. Consumers and NGOs could be 'managed' through risk assessment techniques and better use of public relations.

CONCLUSION

This chapter has argued that the role of NGOs is best understood as that of a social movement arguing a case in a contested space. The modern food movement focused the attention of the public upon changes it was already aware of in the products which it consumed daily. The movement offered new interpretations of what these changes entailed. In this role, the NGOs could be said to have taken on some aspects that E. P. Thompson attributed to the crowd. Thompson explored how people fought food price rises and sought to articulate their resistance to the transition to market forces from a more feudal and paternal culture.[70] This study, like another classic, *Captain Swing* by Hobsbawm and Rudé,[71] described widespread dissent. Such protest has almost become the archetype of social movements concerned with food.[72]

Romantic though such a model could be, it would not fit the modern food world. More appropriate is that given in Paulus's depiction of the British anti-adulteration movement of the mid-nineteenth century.[73] Paulus suggests that the success of the nineteenth-century movement was in part due to the alliance that made it: middle classes, gentleman scientists, enlightened aristocrats, politicians, popular agitators, and so on. Such alliances are entirely familiar to observers of the modern environmental movement,[74] and may be appropriate to the food movement, too.

It should be stressed that the eruption of interest in food policy in the 1980s built upon the long-term thinking and work of many pioneers. A full account should include some earlier voices. Derek Cooper, a former journalist with *World in Action*, and later presenter of the BBC Radio 4 *Food Programme*, wrote *The Bad Food Guide* in 1965.[75] As editor of the *Good Food Guide*, founded by the socialist Raymond Postgate after some articles in the magazine *Lilliput*, Christopher Driver also wielded considerable influence. In the 1960s, too, Elspeth Huxley wrote articles for *Punch*, systematically analysing the impact of changed food production techniques.[76] The *Guardian* played an important role in articulating the growing awareness and gave strong coverage to the 1980s movement through James Erlichman, an American historian turned consumer correspondent.[77] Colin Spencer, an artist turned novelist and playwright and then food writer and vegetarian cook, was another influential writer.[78] The revulsion expressed by restaurant critics and food writers like Jane Grigson throughout the food scandals of 1988–90 was important in reinforcing the NGOs' message.

Articulate though these voices were, it was only with the development of the NGOs in the late 1970s that they became organised. Another feature of the new food movement was that it moved the policy debate beyond the purely medical health framework. The problem was not just saturated fats, but saturated markets. The post-war food revolution meant that industry was highly concentrated, internationalising, and keen on increasing market share.[79] An estimated 10,000 new products and processes came on to the European market each year. Consumers were inevitably guinea pigs in this process, and NGOs argued that they knew it.

The lessons of this food revolution and the changes it brought to the relationship between public, state and commerce are still unfolding.[80] The food movement of the 1980s and 1990s argued that, if government will not regulate, a new system of market forces will emerge, with a more volatile, opinionated and sceptical consumer.[81] NGOs helped set a cultural tone for the 1990s, arguing for eternal vigilance by the public and providing a stream of insights, arguments and spokespeople. The arrival of a strong, independent voluntary sector, working to high standards, and watching what those with the financial muscle to mould our diet were doing, introduced a new actor in mass food culture. Ironically, the NGOs thereby became part of the food system's dynamic. They had become change agents, observers, critics and participants.

NOTES

The chapter draws heavily upon my experience of working with voluntary sector organisations, in particular the LFC, NFA and PSF in the period 1984–94. My thanks to colleagues and friends with whom these issues have been discussed, and in particular to Keith Ball, Jeanette Longfield, Erik Millstone, Aubrey Sheiham, Sue Dibb, Eric Brunner, Martin Caraher and Charlie Clutterbuck for comments on drafts. I also thank Mike Rayner for his comments, as discussant, at the conference at which a spoken form of this chapter was first presented.

1 M. Visser, *Much Depends on Dinner*, Harmondsworth, 1989; J. MacClancy, *Consuming Culture*, London, 1992.
2 G. Tansey and T. Worsley, *The Food System*, London, 1995, p. 2.

3 M. Mills, *The Politics of Dietary Change*, Aldershot, 1992; D. Maurer and J. Sobal (eds), *Eating Agendas. Food and Nutrition as Social Problems*, New York, 1995.

4 S. Mennell, A. Murcott and A. H. van Otterloo, *The Sociology of Food*, London, 1992.

5 A. Lees and K. McVeigh, *An Investigation of Pesticide Pollution in Drinking Water*, London, 1988.

6 National Advisory Committee on Nutrition Education, *A Discussion Paper on Proposals for Nutritional Guidelines for Health Education in Britain*, London, 1983.

7 C. Walker and G. Cannon, *The Food Scandal*, London, 1984, pp. ix–xvi.

8 A. Keys (ed.), 'Coronary heart disease in seven countries', *Circulation*, 1970, vol. 41, pp. 1–211.

9 D. Burkitt, 'Some diseases characteristic of modern Western civilisation', *British Medical Journal*, 1973, vol. 1, pp. 274–8.

10 T. Cleave, *The Saccharine Disease*, Bristol, 1974.

11 Department of Health and Social Security, *Diet and Coronary Heart Disease. Report of the Advisory Panel of the Committee on Medical Aspects of Food Policy*, London, 1974.

12 *Sunday Times*, 3 July 1983.

13 R. Turner and K. Ball, 'Prevention of coronary heart-disease: a counterblast to present inactivity', *The Lancet*, 1973, vol. 2, pp. 1137–40.

14 W. P. T. James, A. Ferro-Luzzi, B. Isaksson and W. B. Szostak, *Health Nutrition. Preventing Nutrition-related Diseases in Europe*, Copenhagen, 1988; G. Cannon, *Food and Health. The Experts Agree*, London, 1992.

15 Department of Health, *The Health of the Nation*, London, 1992.

16 The NFA co-ordinated briefings and pooled intelligence for NGOs and representatives on the working parties throughout the period 1993–5.

17 See announcement in *The Lancet*, 1979, vol. 2, p. 1253; K. Ball, personal communication, August 1995.

18 G. Cannon, *Fight the Good Fight. The Life and Work of Caroline Walker*, London, 1989, pp. 89–90.

19 M. Crawford and S. Crawford, *What We Eat Today*, London, 1972.

20 A. Quick, H. Sheilham and A. Sheiham, *Sweet Nothings*, London, 1980.

21 AGB Market Intelligence, *Food Scares. An Assessment of the Effect in the Marketplace*, London, 1989; R. Lacey, *Unfit for Human Consumption*, London, 1991; J. Taylor and D. Taylor (eds), *Safe Food Handbook*, London, 1990.

22 J. Sheppard, 'Food poisoning: the chicken comes home to roost', in London Food Commission, *Food Adulteration and How to Beat It*, London, 1988, pp. 234–70.

23 House of Commons Agriculture Committee, *Salmonella in Eggs*, London, 1989; Q. Seddon, *Spoiled for Choice. Food Scares Unscrambled*, Finchingfield, 1990; R. North and T. Gorman, *Chickengate. An Independent Analysis of the Salmonella in Eggs Affair*, London, 1990.

24 C. Robbins, *National Food Policy in the UK*, Reading, 1979; C. Clutterbuck and T. Lang, *More than We Can Chew*, London, 1982; S. Orbach, *Fat is a Feminist Issue*, London, 1978; M. Hanssen, *E is for Additives*, Wellingborough, 1984.

25 T. Lang, 'The contradictions of UK labelling policy', *Information Design Journal*, 1995, vol. 8, pp. 3–16; Y. Gabriel and T. Lang, *The Unmanageable Consumer*, London, 1995.

26 M. Millstone and J. Abraham, 'Food additive controls: some international comparisons', *Food Policy*, 1989, vol. 14, pp. 43–57; M. Millstone, 'Food additive regulation in the UK', ibid., 1985, vol. 10, pp. 237–52.

27 R. Body, *Agriculture. The Triumph and the Shame*, London, 1982; R. Cottrell, *The Sacred Cow. The Folly of Europe's Food Mountains*, London, 1987; R. Cockett, *Thinking the Unthinkable. Think-tanks and the Economic Counter-revolution, 1931–1983*, London, 1994.

28 No history of BSSRS exists, but see D. Albury and J. Schwartz, *Partial Progress. The Politics of Science and Technology*, London, 1982, for an account of the kind of politics it espoused.

29 T. Lang and C. Clutterbuck, *P is for Pesticides*, London, 1991.

30 *Science for People* No. 34, *Food, Farming, Finance*, winter 1976–7.

31 Agricapital Group, *Our Daily Bread. Who Makes the Dough?*, London, 1978.

32 Millstone became a policy researcher specialising in food additives and regulation. He co-founded the Food Additives Campaign Team (FACT) with Melanie Miller, a former student of the BSSRS stalwart Fred Stewart of Aston University, Julie Sheppard, a philosopher turned journalist, Felicity Lawrence, of the *Daily Telegraph* magazine, Walker, Cannon and myself.

33 Hines co-authored a study of agribusiness in Africa. See C. Hines and B. Dinham, *Agribusiness in Africa*, London, 1983. With David Baldock, who is now at the Institute of European Environmental Policy, he wrote a guide to food co-operatives for FOE. See C. Hines, *Food Co-ops. How to Save Money by Getting Together and Buying in Bulk*, London, 1976.

34 Bull wrote a study of pesticides for Oxfam. See D. Bull, *A Growing Problem*, Oxford, 1982.

35 Such people included Tony Gordon, now at Aberystwyth, Jonathan Jones, now joint head of the Sainsbury Laboratory at Norwich, Mike Knee, a researcher at East Malling Research Station, and David Smith, editor of this volume.

36 M. Miller, *Danger! Additives at Work. A Report on Food Additives, their Control and Use*, London, 1985; J. Sheppard, *The Big Chill. A Report on the Implications of Cook–Chill Catering for the Public Services*, London, 1987; E. Brunner, *Bovine Somatotropin. A Product in Search of a Market*, London, 1988.

37 T. Webb and A. Henderson, *Food Irradiation. Who Wants It?*, London, 1986; T. Webb and T. Lang, *Food Irradiation. The Facts*, London, 1987.

38 A persistent source of such pronouncements was David Conning, Director General of the BNF; see, for example, comments in the *Sunday Times*, 20 October 1985.

39 M. Pyke, *Food and Society*, London, 1968; N. W. Pirie, *Food Resources: Conventional and Novel*, Harmondsworth, 1969, 1976.

40 Interview with Nicholas Soames, MP, in T. Forrest, 'Food Minister: an appetising job', *SuperMarketing*, 4 December 1992; T. Sanders, interview

for BBC TV *London Plus* programme, 4 March 1986, quoted in G. Cannon, *The Politics of Food*, London, 1988, p. 4.

41 Many such comments appeared in *Farming News*. See, for example, A. Rosen, 'We can't ignore this conspiracy', *Farming News*, 16 August 1989.

42 World Health Organization, *Diet, Nutrition and the Prevention of Chronic Disease*, Technical Series No. 797, Geneva, 1990.

43 R. Jenkins, *Food for a Great City*, London, 1983.

44 D. McCrea, *Opening the Floodgates. A Report on the Excessive Use of Water in Food*, London, 1987.

45 A. Luba and I. Cole-Hamilton, *Food Labelling. A Critique of the Government's Proposed Fat Content Labelling Regulations and Nutritional Labelling Guidelines*, London, 1986; E. Brunner, *Catering for All?*, London, 1985.

46 S. Hill, *More than Rice and Peas*, London, 1991.

47 T. Lobstein and S. Leather, *Food and Low Income. A Pack*, London, 1994.

48 T. Lang, E. Hannon, H. Andrews, C. Bedale and J. Hulme, *Jam Tomorrow?*, Manchester, 1984.

49 C. Walker and M. Church, 'Poverty by administration: a review of supplementary benefits, nutrition and scale rates', *Journal of Human Nutrition*, 1978, vol. 32, pp. 5–18.

50 J. Major to T. Lang, 17 January 1986.

51 D. Acheson to T. Lang, 24 June 1987.

52 I. Cole-Hamilton and T. Lang, *Tightening Belts*, London, 1987. Many local studies backed our argument, for example C. Mooney, *Cost, Availability and Choice in Some Camden Supermarkets*, London, 1987.

53 J. Mack and S. Lansley, *Poor Britain*, London, 1984; P. Townsend, P. Corrigan and U. Kowarzik, *Poverty and Labour in London*, London, 1987.

54 N. Berger, *The School Meals Service*, Plymouth, 1990, pp. 101–6.

55 Baby Milk Action, *1939–1992 . . . Fifty-three Years of Infant Feeding Action*, Cambridge, 1992; A. Allain, 'Breastfeeding is politics: a personal view of the International Baby Milk Campaign', *The Ecologist*, 1991, vol. 21, No. 5, pp. 206–13.

56 L. Durward, *Poverty in Pregnancy*, London, 1984.

57 Compassion in World Farming joined the NFA. The BST work created contacts with animal welfare activists such as Mark Gold, Joyce d'Silva and Peter Stevenson. They pushed the arguments about the nature of production, as argued in M. Gold, *Assault and Battery. What Factory Farming Means for Humans and Animals*, London, 1983.

58 Coronary Prevention Group and Assistant Masters' and Mistresses' Association, *Diet or Disease. The Case for School Meals Guidelines*, London, 1987.

59 School Meals Campaign, *School Meals. Take Action!*, London, 1992.

60 K. Motte *et al.*, *Unacceptable Risk*, Washington, DC, 1989.

61 See P. Hurst, A. Hay and N. Dudley, *The Pesticide Handbook*, London, 1991, pp. 123–4.

62 N. Avery, M. Drake and T. Lang, *Cracking the Codex*, London, 1993; National Food Alliance, *Get Cooking!*, London, 1993.

63 G. Palmer, *The Politics of Breastfeeding*, London, 1988; P. Snell, *Pesticide Residues and Food. The Case for Real Control*, London, 1986; S. Dibb, *Children. Advertisers' Dream, Nutrition Nightmare?*, London, 1993.

64 J. Goldsmith, 'Intensive Farming, the CAP and GATT', Caroline Walker Lecture given at the Royal Society, 16 October 1991.
65 See the discussion in London Food Commission, 1988, op. cit., pp. 1–20.
66 House of Commons Agriculture Committee, *The Effects of Pesticides on Human Health*, vol. 1, London, 1987; E. Millstone, *Food Additives. Taking the Lid off What We Really Eat*, Harmondsworth, 1986; R. Mackarness, *Chemical Victims*, London, 1980.
67 North and Gorman, 1990, op. cit.
68 P. Self and H. Storing, *The State and the Farmer*, London, 1962.
69 See AGB Market Intelligence, 1989, op. cit.; D. Miller and J. Reilly, 'Making an issue of food safety: the media, pressure groups, and the public sphere', in Maurer and Sobal, 1995, op. cit.; W. Grant, 'Food policy formation: the role of pressure groups', in S. Henson and S. Gregory (eds), *The Politics of Food*, Reading, 1994, pp. 21–6.
70 E. P. Thompson, *The Moral Economy of the English Crowd in the Eighteenth Century*, 1971, in Thompson, *Customs in Common*, Harmondsworth, 1993.
71 E. J. Hobsbawm and G. Rudé, *Captain Swing*, London, 1969.
72 See, for example, the clarion calls against the bread tax in *The Hungry Forties. Life under the Bread Tax*, with an introduction by Mrs Cobden Unwin, London, 1904.
73 I. Paulus, *The Search for Pure Food*, Oxford, 1974.
74 F. Pearce, *Green Warriors. The People and the Politics behind the Green Revolution*, London, 1991.
75 D. Cooper, *The Bad Food Guide*, London, 1966.
76 E. Huxley, *Brave New Victuals*, London, 1965.
77 J. Erlichman, *Gluttons for Punishment*, Harmondsworth, 1986.
78 See the collection of articles from *The Guardian*, 1979–83: C. Spencer, *Good and Healthy*, London, 1983.
79 T. Lang et al., *This Food Business*, London, 1989; H. Raven, T. Lang and C. Dumonteil, *Off our Trolleys? Food Retailing and the Hypermarket Economy*, London, 1995.
80 T. Lang, 'Local Sustainability in a Sea of Globalisation? The Case of Food Policy', paper presented at a conference on 'Planning Sustainability', Political Economy Research Centre, Sheffield, 8–10 September, 1995.
81 Gabriel and Lang, 1995, op. cit.

INDEX